Y0-EPN-527

Vincennes University Library

Fashioning Teenagers

September 1944 *Seventeen*, photographer Elliot Clarke

Dedicated to Helen Valentine and Estelle Ellis,
two extraordinary women who inspired generations,
this author included. May their story
continue to inspire generations more.

Fashioning Teenagers

A CULTURAL HISTORY OF *SEVENTEEN* MAGAZINE

Kelley Massoni

Vincennes University
Shake Learning Resources Center
Vincennes, In 47591-9986

Left Coast Press Inc.

WALNUT CREEK, CALIFORNIA

302.23
M421f
2010

LEFT COAST PRESS
1630 North Main Street, #400
Walnut Creek, CA 94596
http://www.LCoastPress.com

Copyright © 2010 by Left Coast Press, Inc.

All rights reserved. No part of this publication may be reproduced, stored in a retrieval system, or transmitted in any form or by any means, electronic, mechanical, photocopying, recording, or otherwise, without the prior permission of the publisher.

ISBN 978-1-59874-503-0 hardcover
ISBN 978-1-59874-504-7 paperback

Library of Congress Cataloguing-in-Publication Data
Massoni, Kelley.
Fashioning teenagers : a cultural history of Seventeen magazine / Kelley Massoni.
p. cm.
Includes bibliographical references and index.
ISBN 978-1-59874-503-0 (hardcover : alk. paper) -- ISBN 978-1-59874-504-7 (pbk. : alk. paper)
1. Mass media and teenagers. 2. Seventeen--History. 3. Periodicals--Publishing. 4. Teenage girls--United States--Attitudes. 5. United States--Civilization--20th century. I. Title.
HQ799.2.M35M372 2010
302.23'2408352097309045--dc22
2010006396

Printed in the United States of America

The paper used in this publication meets the minimum requirements of American National Standard for Information Sciences—Permanence of Paper for Printed Library Materials, ANSI/NISO Z39.48–1992.

CONTENTS

LIST OF FIGURES AND TABLES

FIGURES

TABLES

PREFACE

In the 1940s, two contemporary themes appeared in the American media and the American consciousness: the teenager and the teen magazine. These themes crystallized in the creation of *Seventeen,* the first teen magazine. The story of *Seventeen*'s origins is a fascinating one, with the twists and turns of a novel. It features powerful personalities engaged in professional alliances, personal disputes, and private betrayals. It also provides a genealogy for understanding our modern version of youth culture and the teen girl ideal.

Seventeen originated in the mind of its founding editor-in-chief, Helen Valentine—who referred to the magazine as her "baby." Valentine envisioned a service and fashion magazine for high school girls, an idea that she sold to publisher Walter Annenberg in 1944. As the first teen magazine, *Seventeen* developed and modeled the emerging teen girl ideal in its editorial pages, promotional materials, and advertisements. In the earliest issues, *Seventeen*'s editorial staff crafted a magazine that balanced fashion and beauty with articles on work and citizenship, writing for a teen readership that Valentine described as "whole human beings." But *Seventeen* also marketed teen girls—as consumers—to business, often through their prototype, "Teena." Advertisers responded by selling to *Seventeen*'s readership not just products but a consumer role and a feminine ideal.

Seventeen's representation of the teen girl ideal shifted dramatically between the magazine's birth and fifth birthday. Over time, consumerist content increased as *Seventeen* moved away from Valentine's progressive model of service and citizenship and toward the more traditional model of fashion, romance, and homemaking. The Teena ideal of the editorial pages—"editorial Teena"—became more reflective of "promotional Teena"—the Teena being sold in the magazine's promotional materials and by its advertisers.

In this book, I explore the social and cultural forces that exerted pressure on Valentine and *Seventeen* from the beginning, including the end of the war; the economic structure of the magazine industry; reader preferences; and power relations at the magazine. By *Seventeen*'s sixth birthday, Valentine was no longer editor-in-chief, and the magazine and its teen girl ideal had departed from their wartime citizen-oriented roots and entered a domesticated (and highly gendered) consumer future.

Researching *Seventeen* Magazine

I used an extended case study design to investigate *Seventeen*'s birth and early development as a teen magazine. Drawing on archival materials, historical sources, oral histories, interviews, and the magazine's text, images, and advertisements, I examined *Seventeen* as a magazine, a business, a workplace, and a cultural phenomenon during its first six years, paying particular attention to two periods: September 1944 to September 1945 (the World War II period) and September 1949 to September 1950 (the postwar period).

I chose this periodization for several reasons: it parallels the magazine's own milestone commemorative dates ("birthdays"); it encompasses the tenure of first editor-in-chief Helen Valentine and the aftermath of her dismissal; archival documents are available for these years at *Seventeen*; and it spans a short but significant historical period. This case study approach includes historical research (using both primary and secondary sources), biographical interviews with former *Seventeen* staffers and their family members, and textual analysis of the magazine issues from cover to cover.

I drew on relevant historical documents, including newspapers, magazines, industry publications such as *The Writer's Market,* and government publications such as the *Magazine War Guide.* I also drew on secondary sources, such as academic monographs and books about the historical periods covered and the magazine industry in the twentieth and twenty-first centuries.

I gathered information on Helen Valentine from a variety of sources, including her oral history, taken by the American Jewish Committee in 1982; my interviews with her daughter, Barbara Valentine Hertz, and granddaughter, Valentine Hertz Kass; and personal correspondence made available to me by the Valentine family. For information on Walter Annenberg, I used two biographies written about him, one by John Cooney and the other by Christopher

Ogden, the latter having been allowed access to Annenberg and his papers, as well as news media reports about Annenberg's life (and death).

I also drew on the experiences of former *Seventeen* staffers, including Estelle Ellis, the magazine's first promotion director, who knew and worked with Helen Valentine and Walter Annenberg. I conducted four interviews and had other personal correspondence with Ellis, and also used her published oral history, taken by the American Jewish Committee in 1990. I conducted telephone interviews with two former *Seventeen* editorial assistants, Alberta Eiseman and Ingrid Loewenstein Sladkus. Although Alice Thompson, who played an important role in Helen Valentine's life and career, died in 1985, I tried to gather as much information as I could about her, drawing on newspaper and magazine accounts of her career and interviews with colleagues. For my textual analysis of the magazine's content, I closely read every page of each sampled issue of *Seventeen*, including the front cover and all copy, editorial and advertising, words and pictures, gathering both quantitative and qualitative data through detailed note-taking.[1]

The Chapters

The Introduction, "Mirror, Mirror, On the Wall: Women's Magazines and the Modern Beauty Mandate," considers the place of beauty and consumption in women's lives from the 1940s until today, and the role of women's magazines in defining and modeling the modern beauty ideal. The emergence of the teen magazine and teen girl ideal is set within the context of this women's beauty ideal.

Chapter 1, "The Birth of the Teen Magazine," explores *Seventeen*'s September 1944 debut, focusing on its creators. I highlight the personal and family histories of Helen Valentine and Walter Annenberg, whose unique life experiences, work backgrounds, and personal agendas shaped the magazine in its formative years.

Chapter 2, "*Seventeen* Magazine at War," examines the magazine's war-period editorial content during its inaugural year, from its birth in September 1944 through its first birthday in September 1945. Because a table of contents represents a magazine's own mapping of its content, I began by noting how *Seventeen* categorized its articles in its table of contents. Originally, articles were organized under the topical categories—from top to bottom—"What You Wear," "How You Feel and Look," "Getting Along in the World," "Your Mind," and "Having Fun." In January 1945, the magazine added "Fiction" to these categories, followed by "Food and Home Doings" in November 1946.[2]

I read every article under these topical headings, taking notes on each article's main themes, as well as quotes from the articles that exemplified the themes. I identified the dominant themes as: consuming (shopping, buying, products); body (hygiene, health, grooming, clothes, appearance); school (high school, college); work (paid employment, either now or later); home (entertaining, decorating, domestic activities); relationships (boys, family, friends); citizenship (democracy, war/postwar, community, U.S., world); otherness (nondominant race, ethnicity, religion, nations); celebrities; and fun (recreation, entertainment, fiction).

I measured the dimensions of every article, calculating the space that *Seventeen* devoted to each topic area ("What You Wear," and so on) and assessed the value that *Seventeen* put on each of these topical areas by comparing the magazine's allotment of page space to articles under each of the table of contents categories. I supplemented these quantitative measurements with a qualitative analysis of text and pictures inspired by the semiological strategies of Erving Goffman and Roland Barthes.[3]

Chapter 3, "Teena Goes to Market," details *Seventeen*'s innovative promotional campaign and the woman who crafted it, Estelle Ellis. Ellis fashioned a publicity campaign around the embodiment/personification of the ideal teen girl, whom she christened "Teena, the prototypical teen-age girl." This chapter closely examines *Seventeen*'s early promotional documents, drawing on the materials from the Estelle Ellis Collection, an archival collection of *Seventeen* memorabilia housed at the National Museum of American History in Washington, D.C. This collection includes market research reports, correspondence, survey data, advertisements, and promotional literature for *Seventeen* magazine from 1944 to 1950.

Chapter 4, "Teena Means Business," describes *Seventeen*'s advertising during its first and sixth years. As major contributors to the magazine's overall discourse, advertisers joined the editorial and promotional staff in constructing the feminine teen ideal. I compared *Seventeen*'s advertisements during the two thirteen-month sample periods (September 1944 to September 1945; September 1949 to September 1950), which represented the wartime and postwar periods. I began by reading and taking notes on every advertisement, both text and pictures; I also measured each ad for spatial coverage and noted where it appeared in the magazine. Finally, I organized the different kinds of advertised products into seven categories, which I identified as: body wear (clothing, undergarments, shoes, accessories, jewelry); body care (cosmetics, hair care, perfume, feminine hygiene, deodorant, medicine); entertainment (movies and records); education/employment (home correspondence courses, vocational schools, colleges); snacks (sodas and candy); domestic (linens, cookbooks, hope chests, sterling silver); and miscellaneous (pens, paper, wallets). I calculated the percentage of advertising space devoted to each category of advertisements. Using these quantitative data as a guide, I explored the narratives of both typical and atypical advertisements.

Chapter 5, "*Seventeen* Magazine at Peace," analyzes the magazine's editorial content during its sixth year, from September 1949 through 1950. Using the same strategy as with Chapter 2, I began at the magazine's table of contents, which offered a map of *Seventeen*'s elaboration of the ideal teen girl's world. The most obvious change between first and fifth birthdays occurred with *Seventeen*'s introduction of a new contents category, "Food and Home Doings," in November 1946. Creating a new category had a dramatic effect on the editorial proportions among the existing categories.

As with Chapter 2, I read every article under these topical headings, taking careful notes on each article's main theme, as well as quotes from the articles that exemplified the themes of consuming, body, school, work, home, relationships, citizenship, otherness, celebrities, and fun. I measured the dimensions of each article and calculated the space that *Seventeen* devoted to each topic area. I assessed the value that *Seventeen* put on each of these topical areas by comparing the magazine's allotment of page space to articles under each of the table of contents categories. I supplemented these quantitative measurements with a qualitative analysis of text and pictures.

Chapter 6, "Divorce in the Family," details the events that shattered the stability of *Seventeen*'s workplace and brought an end to Helen Valentine's editorship. I analyze the framing of the magazine's editorial ideology within the cultural contexts of gender, social class, and power in the late 1940s and early 1950s. I also explore the magazine's competing origin narratives. To understand how *Seventeen* remembered its origins, I examined the magazine's Birthday/Anniversary issues: September 1954, September 1964, September 1969, September 1974, September 1984, October 1994, and September 2004, looking for instances where the magazine's history was mentioned or documented.

The Epilogue, "*Seventeen* Magazine and Teena in the Twenty-First Century," investigates how *Seventeen,* the teen magazine genre, Teena (the teen girl ideal), and the teen consumer market are faring in the twenty-first century. The Epilogue draws on a wide range of sources, including *Seventeen*'s sixty-fifth-birthday issue (September 2009), *Seventeen*'s various websites, mainstream media reports (such as the *New York Times*), magazine and advertising industry sources (such as *Folio, Advertising Age,* and the Audit Bureau of Circulation), market research reports, interviews with Estelle Ellis, and personal documents belonging to Helen Valentine's family.

I begin by following *Seventeen* from the 1950s through 2009, tracking changes in the magazine's editors and publishers. Next, I explore the cultural landscape of the new millennium, paying particular attention to the place of *Seventeen,* teen magazines, teenagers, and the youth market within it. Finally, I ask the question, What would *Seventeen*'s creators think about their creation today?

On Memories and Voices

Like all historical research, this study is filtered through memories. One of my first lessons in memory came via Helen Valentine's oral history, in which she described having found her inspiration for *Seventeen* in a picture of a crowd of teenagers entering the United Nations building in New York City. Imagine my surprise when I recalled that the UN didn't officially exist until October 24, 1945—well after *Seventeen* began publication. From my perspective, this was an interesting incongruity; as oral history scholar Alessandro Portelli notes: "Subjectivity is as much the business of history as the more visible 'facts.' What the informant believes is indeed a historical *fact* (that is, the *fact* that he or she believes it) just as much as what 'really' happened."[4]

Equally important is what each individual leaves out of his or her narrative.[5] For example, years after their first meeting, Valentine didn't report that she spoke to Annenberg of the consumer potential of young women. Annenberg, in turn, remembered his insistence that the magazine be wholesome, but nothing about Valentine's service mandate. Their omissions seem to indicate that each wanted their legacy to be that of creating a service magazine for teens, and not for the magazine's service to business. These protagonists were not just telling stories and promoting origin myths but also doing the work of identity construction.

Origin myths are not only individual but also collective. I recognized early in my research that there were two entrenched "camps" proposing two different narratives about *Seventeen's* origins. For the Valentine camp, whose surviving members include Estelle Ellis, Barbara Valentine Hertz, Valentine Hertz Kass, and Barbara Hertz Burr, the story told is bittersweet—one in which Helen Valentine created an iconic American magazine, only to have her role in it undermined and eventually minimized through the betrayals of two very important people in her life, *Seventeen*'s owner, Walter Annenberg, and her best friend and mentee, Alice Dickey Thompson Beaton. Estelle Ellis goes so far as to describe it as "tragic."[6]

For the Annenberg camp, whose version is told through biographies and media accounts, *Seventeen* is an American success story, one that portrays *Seventeen* as the product of Walter Annenberg's business genius and one of his many enduring legacies. Indeed, in Annenberg's biographies, Helen Valentine plays little more than a bit role in the story of *Seventeen*, portrayed as a former employee worthy of no more than a couple of pages in a several-hundred-page examination of his life. Even public critiques of Annenberg, like those of *Slate*'s Jack Shafer, do not necessarily restore Valentine to the narrative.[7]

One of my purposes in this project is to give voice to the many previously unheard voices in the narrative of *Seventeen*'s origins; this was made possible by interviewing those who are still living, such as Estelle Ellis. The major protagonists—Helen Valentine, Walter Annenberg, and Alice Thompson—are all dead. Being able to interview Helen Valentine's living relatives, and having access to her oral history, was invaluable.

Although I had to rely on Walter Annenberg's biographies for his side of the story, I am less disturbed by the exclusion of Annenberg's testimony than I am of Alice Thompson's, since Annenberg's story has been told often. I regret the omission of the words and perspective of Alice Thompson Beaton, whose voice (beyond the articles she wrote) is lacking from this story. I tried to find her children and/or other relatives, but her rather common professional name (Thompson) and exit from the world of magazine publishing made this difficult, ultimately impossible; however, I did discover that she died in the Virgin Islands in 1985.

My interviews with *Seventeen* editorial assistants Ingrid Loewenstein Sladkus and Alberta Eiseman illuminate a vantage point from the lower end of the magazine hierarchy, offering a counterpoint to that of the owner and editorial staff. Sladkus's and Eiseman's observations, in conjunction with contemporary media reports on the events at *Seventeen*, supported my own perception of the injustice meted out to Helen Valentine by Walter Annenberg. Valentine would take her genius (as well as many in her editorial staff) to *Charm* magazine, which she would revamp as *Charm: The Magazine for Women Who Work.* Following *Charm,* she wrote a monthly advice column for young wives for *Good Housekeeping* magazine. In 1989, the Publishing Hall of Fame posthumously inducted her into the ranks of the most influential publishing luminaries, including William Randolph Hearst and Richard Leo Simon and Max Lincoln Schuster, founders of Simon & Schuster, Inc.[8] In that way, she herself represented an American success story. However, after years of "reading, sifting, weighing, comparing and analyzing the evidence in order to tell the story,"[9] the story that I tell of Helen Valentine's role in the creation of *Seventeen*—and the eventual editing of her role from the public accounts of its origins—is indeed bittersweet.

Acknowledgments

Much like the relationship between Helen Valentine and *Seventeen,* this book began as my conceptual creation and became my "baby." And as with Helen and *Seventeen,* it took a village to raise this baby, and I am grateful and indebted to the people who assisted in this process.

This book started as my dissertation project, so I'll begin by thanking my dissertation committee members. Joey Sprague, my advisor, dissertation chair and editor extraordinaire, helped me distill and analyze a sometimes overwhelming amount of data. As with the very best labor coaches, she knew when to cajole, to push, to soothe—and when to just leave me be. Bob Antonio's faith in this project never flagged, and he offered me wise guidance along the way, talking me off the occasional ledge and encouraging me to labor on. The graduate seminars of Bill Staples and Carol Warren shaped me as a scholar and, in doing so, shaped this project. Sherrie Tucker shared her American Studies expertise, but also the inspiration of her own life's journey. Although journalism school professor and former magazine editor Carol Holstead did not serve on my committee, she was always available to answer my questions about the magazine business. In addition, she encouraged me to contact Estelle Ellis, a step that proved pivotal to my project.

Among the most fulfilling aspects of researching and writing this book was the opportunity to get to know some of the special people who knew Helen Valentine. I am infinitely indebted to Estelle Ellis, former *Seventeen* promotion director and Helen Valentine's lifelong friend. Estelle continues to emphatically and articulately promote Helen Valentine's *Seventeen* to anyone who will listen. Having listened, I can only say that I am a believer! Estelle's wit, intellect, and zest for life forever changed my vision of aging. So, too, did two other former *Seventeen* staffers, Alberta Eiseman and Ingrid Loewenstein Sladkus, both of whom shared with me their memories of *Seventeen* as a workplace more than 60 years ago. I feel so fortunate to have met these extraordinary women, and for their willingness to help me bring my own baby to life.

I am extremely grateful to Helen Valentine's family for their support of this project. Susan Valentine-Cooper, Helen's granddaughter, was my first family contact, and she enthusiastically encouraged my exploration of *Seventeen*'s origins. Barbara Valentine Hertz, Helen's daughter, graciously spoke to me about her memories of her mother and about her mother's experiences at *Seventeen*. I am particularly indebted to Barbara's daughters and Helen's granddaughters, Barbara Hertz Burr and Valentine Hertz Kass, who shared with me their memories, as well as invaluable documents from Helen's life, including correspondence and pictures. These materials serve as the factual bones of my narrative; without them, the story would not be as convincing or as powerful.

I am grateful for the financial aid that I received to pursue my research. The University of Kansas funded a year of my work through a Dissertation Fellowship, and the Midwest Sociological Society provided the funding for one of my trips to the National Museum of American History at the Smithsonian Institution through a Professional Development Grant. At the Smithsonian, I received patient assistance from the archivists in charge of the Estelle Ellis collection, particularly Mimi Minnick and Reuben Jackson, who answered my questions and offered direction for copying such precious and often fragile documents. Later, Kay Peterson helped me navigate the permissions process at the Smithsonian. I also thank the *Journal of American Culture* for permitting me to reprint a version of my article, "Teena Goes to Market: *Seventeen* Magazine and the Early Construction of the Teen Girl (as) Consumer," which appears as Chapter 3 in this book.

I am especially thankful for the people who gave me a context in which to write my text: my friends and family. No scholarly endeavor can substitute for the loving support of real people. The special friendships of Jason Capps, Anne Dotter, Ann Marie Hickey Wood, and Shelley Koch kept me sane during the sometimes arduous journey of graduate school and book writing. My children, Vanessa, Justin, Josh, and Marissa, and my granddaughter Cora made me laugh along the way, reminding me of what is really important in life and helping me to put this "baby" in its place.

Finally, several people made significant contributions and deserve considerable credit for this book's existence. Carol Warren, upon reading my dissertation, promptly wrapped it up and mailed it off to publisher Mitch Allen of Left Coast Press. Even more, she agreed to serve as my editor for no pay other than my unending gratitude. Mitch Allen surrounded me with a team of talented professionals, including Katie Peña, Rachel Fudge, Lisa Devenish, and Anne Brown. These people made the final stages of labor an enjoyable experience.

I save my final and most heartfelt thanks for my husband, Steven. No other person paid the same kind of price that he did in my pursuit of this undertaking. Steven married a *Seventeen* reader and ended up with a *Seventeen* researcher—a transition not always easy. Nevertheless, he remained my staunchest supporter, calming me when I panicked, feeding me marinara when I hungered, and giving me practical advice (by the list-full). I am thankful and delighted to have you as my companion.

Kelley Massoni

Mirror, Mirror, on the Wall

Women's Magazines and the Modern Beauty Mandate

> January is traditionally the month of new and soon-to-be-broken resolutions—of sharp self-criticism and honest appraisal. Along with blithely promising ourselves to do our homework and make our beds promptly, we take a long look in the mirror, analyze our defects and our virtues and make plans to change ourselves into a Perfect Beauty. It's a natural female desire—for all of us would like to be prettier than we are at the moment, both to please ourselves and the men (eventually the man) in our lives. ["Who's a Dummy?" *Seventeen*, January 1950, 51]

Contemporary Western citizens are surrounded by media, immersed in media, dependent on media, influenced by media . . . we have become, quite literally, a media culture.[1] We spend our everyday lives reading newspapers, perusing magazines, watching television, playing video games, surfing the internet, and listening to music, without thinking about what we are doing—or what the media are doing. Media have become "like the air we breathe, ever present yet rarely considered."[2]

Media, with their images of utopian lifestyles and bodily perfection, are a key site for the construction of identity in contemporary Western society.[3] The relationship between media and identity is particularly significant for women and girls, since the media direct cultural attention on female beauty. Although ideals of feminine beauty have existed throughout history—represented in art, literature, and religion—the intensity of the American media focus on the feminine ideal is a product of contemporary culture.[4]

Today, mainstream media typically represent beauty as a commodity that can be bought, and women as its primary purchasing agents.[5] Women's magazines and their advertisers, in particular, barrage women with messages about the transformative possibilities of buying and using certain products.[6]

According to historian Lizbeth Cohen, this gendered trend began at the end of World War II, when the concept of the "good citizen" became dichotomized into men as producers and women as consumers.[7] Fast-forward to today, and we find that educated women spend more time shopping than any other segment of society.[8] Because advertisers seek to shape consumption patterns as early as possible, they are now targeting tweens and teens—boys, to some extent, but mainly girls, following the logic of this gender dichotomy.[9]

The societal mandates of feminine beauty and endless consumption have become intertwined, with the ideal woman represented in culture as a beautiful—or beautifying—consumer. Well-socialized women pursue the beauty ideal as the means to self-fulfillment and social acceptance, which inevitably requires them to purchase products or services.[10] Matters get more urgent as a woman ages. Contemporary media celebrate youth, their images revealing (and reveling in) the superiority of youthful beauty and sexuality.[11] But aging is a different matter for men and women. For men, whose value is measured by power and wealth, maturity may actually increase their social worth. For women, however, aging strikes at the heart of their value, for the more a woman's body ages the less it is able to achieve and display the youthful ideals of sexuality, beauty, physical fitness—and, of course, slenderness.[12]

For women and girls, and to a lesser extent men and boys, the media promote many routes to bodily perfection, from plastic surgery to diet programs, from fashion to cosmetics. Grooming is a particularly important daily discipline that many women engage in, using purchased brushes, pencils, wands, and other tools of the trade. To groom properly, a woman must partition her body, keeping each individual section trained, tidied, and toned[13]—a process so time-consuming that upkeep becomes an ongoing, never-ending "body project."[14] Skin must be kept soft and smooth, with leg, underarm, facial, and pubic hair bleached or removed.[15] Head hair, on the other hand, must be conditioned, gelled, moussed, dyed, streaked, permed, curled, cut, straightened, coiffed, and/or adorned.[16] The face framed by hair is not satisfactory "as-is"; in order to be presentable, one has to "put one's face on," through the application of makeup, including foundation, blusher, eye shadow, eye liner, and mascara.[17] Of course, this necessitates having to "take one's face off" at nighttime, which involves the application of cleansers, astringents, eye creams, and face lotions.

Women's value, as presented by the media, lies in their bodies, not their minds. But this does not mean that only less-educated women pursue the beauty ideal. To the contrary, female beautifiers are often high achievers who, upon identifying the cultural bar for body as well as mind, labor intensively to measure up.[18] They do this consciously and rationally, because they recognize that society rewards beautiful women with overwhelming approval and economic remuneration in all venues, including courtship and the workplace.[19] Although the pursuit of beauty offers women the opportunity to achieve relationship and workplace success, they risk becoming ensnared in a never-ending cycle of assessment, body dissatisfaction, and consumption. Even more, they are engaged in a pursuit that will inevitably lead to failure once the signs of aging become uncontrollable.

Magazines for Women and Teens: Helpful Hints on Ideal Femininity

For those women in pursuit of the feminine ideal, assistance comes neatly packaged in the glossy pages of women's magazines. Produced "just for her," women's magazines constitute a significant element of women's culture. Invited into millions of homes, they are also found in public places from doctors' offices to supermarket checkout stands.[20] Through words and images, editorial content and advertisements, these magazines instruct women on how to look, dress, and behave. Pictures model bodily ideals (including this society's ideal skin color through the dominance of white models) and articles advise on their achievement. Although there are some magazines specifically for women of color, most of the content of women's and girls' magazines is aimed at white women.[21]

What elements constitute a magazine? In subsequent chapters, I will explore those elements that are relevant to the reader: the cover, the table of contents, editorial (everything but advertising) and advertising content, words, and images. There are also elements of relevance to the magazine's staffers: the masthead, which lays out the hierarchy of workers who contribute to the magazine; bylines and credits, the presence or absence of which either recognize or obscure the individual contributions of writers, photographers, or models; and the frontispiece, a picture and/or essay that precedes or introduces the main editorial section of a magazine.

Magazines generally structure editorial and advertising copy using "wells," which are blocks or sections of content. In a "monowell" system, a large uninterrupted block of editorial material in the middle of the magazine is flanked on either side by wells made up of a mix of some editorial content but mostly advertising.[22] Advertisements are the work of advertisers, and are the economic *raison d'être* of a magazine. But they do not stand alone. Rather, advertisers and editors work together to ensure that the magazine's editorial content is consistent with the advertisers' purposes. At times, advertisers can and do dictate to editors what words and images can appear in editorial sections surrounding their ads.[23]

Through much of their history, women's magazines conveyed two kinds of female ideals: the domestic homemaker of "service" magazines and the stylish beauty of "fashion" magazines.[24] The best-known service magazines, referred to as the "Seven Sisters" by industry insiders, are *Good Housekeeping, Family Circle, Women's Day, Redbook, McCalls, Ladies' Home Journal,* and *Better Homes and Gardens.* Major contemporary fashion magazines include *Vogue, Harper's Bazaar, Elle, InStyle, Cosmopolitan, Glamour, Allure,* and *Marie Claire.*

At the beginning of the twentieth century, these two magazine genres were clearly demarcated. *Better Homes and Gardens* founder E. T. Meredith described the service magazine in contrast to the fashion magazine: service magazines like his have "no fiction, no fashion, no piffle, no passion."[25] Today, the main mission of service magazines is to give female readers advice and direction in navigating the (usually domestic) challenges of life, while the main mission of fashion magazines is to represent the feminine beauty ideal and to assist women in its achievement. But over time, the line between the two began to blur, with service magazines including more fashion and beauty coverage. New magazines meshing service and fashion, such as *Real Simple* and *O, The Oprah Magazine,* entered the market to a welcoming readership, as measured by high circulation and subscription rates.

The increasing prevalence of beauty and fashion sections in magazines once dedicated to domesticity indicates the growing significance of the body in the late twentieth and early twenty-first centuries.[26] Today, women's bodies hold center stage in both service and fashion magazines, advised about and agonized over in articles and advertisements. Actresses and models, as the reigning representatives of the female body ideal, primp and preen in fashion spreads and cosmetic advertisements. (*Roget's Thesaurus* offers "model" as a synonym for "ideal.")[27] These contemporary body goddesses are thin beyond the attainability of the average (size 12) American woman,[28] and often—due to the computerized tweaking of images—unrealistically so.[29] Not coincidentally, most of these bodies are white; if nonwhite they have Caucasian features.

Arguably, women of all ages learn about and internalize the feminine ideal via media, including magazines, but some may be more impressionable than others. For many young girls, adolescence often marks a period of intensive gender study,[30] and there is evidence from interview data that they use teen magazines—the "little sisters" of women's magazines—as primary textbooks.[31]

Unlike women's magazines, which have parallel men's magazines such as *GQ* and *Esquire,* teen magazines are produced for young women only. While teenage boys may read magazines such as *Sports Illustrated* and *Maxim,* these magazines are not written for and marketed to them as "teens." Thus, girls are targeted by the magazine industry for more gender messages than are boys. And, unlike adult women who have attained a certain amount of self-understanding and may read women's magazines critically,[32] female adolescents are on a mission of self-discovery that makes them more susceptible to magazines' messages.[33]

The messages in teen magazines rarely conflict with those of their "older sisters" or even with each other.[34] Teen magazines reflect a younger parallel universe, depicting a world inhabited by thin, beautiful white women[35] who spend their time pursuing beauty, clothing, and heterosexual relationships.[36] These gender primers offer young women explicit instruction toward achieving these goals through consumption[37] and sexual allure.[38]

The overall message of women's and teen magazines is that heterosexual romance requires that the reader be beautiful and sexy, both of which take products and body work to achieve. Overt sexual messages, such as those in *Cosmopolitan,* are often considered out of place in teen magazines. Instead, teen magazines walk a narrow (and sometimes confusing) line, in which they often discourage sexual activity for teenagers while encouraging sexiness in dress, cosmetics, and body image.[39] These different messages are in part a function of the contradictory goals of advertising and editorial copy; advertisers cajole young women to buy products that signal sexiness while editors encourage controlling sexuality while being sexy.[40] Despite their flirtation with transgression through sex talk and imagery, teen magazines resolve possible contradictions by falling back on sexual dichotomies in which women are sexy objects and men are sexual pursuers.[41]

Illustrating the maxim that "the more things change, the more they stay the same," the influx of young women into higher education and the workplace hasn't found much representation in the pages of teen magazines. Although twentieth-century *Seventeen* purported to cover "fashion, beauty, health, fitness, food, cars, *college, careers,* talent, entertainment, fiction, plus crucial personal and global issues,"[42] researchers have discovered surprisingly little emphasis on education and occupations between its covers. When Kate Peirce studied work and occupations in the fiction stories of *Seventeen* and *Teen,* she found people assigned to jobs in gender-stereotypical ways.[43] My own exploration of the representation of work and careers in the articles and columns of 1990s-era *Seventeen* found a similarly gendered occupational world, one in which men held not just the majority of the jobs but also the most powerful and prestigious occupations.[44] Women, on the other hand, were most often relegated to work roles such as assistants and secretaries. The *real* work of women, as represented in *Seventeen* and other teen magazines, is *body* work, and the most prestigious career path ends at fashion modeling.[45]

Texts Within Context

How do we explain the dominance of such limited and limiting gendered messages in magazines that market themselves as guides for the improvement of women's and girls' lives? Understanding how and why media messages develop as they do requires placing media texts within a larger system that consists of media creators, readers/consumers, and the larger culture. For example, cultural inequalities based in gender, class, race, sexuality, and body characteristics shape and influence the composition and organization of the media creators as well as media consumers.

If we research the people who run media organizations at the highest corporate level, we find board rooms and prestigious corner offices populated by white men of high socioeconomic status.[46] This top echelon of executives and owners may be the least researched dimension of media, due in part to the relative inaccessibility of the corporate suite and its powerful residents. More research exists on the less elite middle-echelon managers and production staff in media industries, demonstrating that women and people of color remain underrepresented in the media workforce as a whole.[47] As sociologist Dorothy Smith points out, restricting culture making to just one group of people (in this case, affluent white men) results in a single-standpoint media system that excludes the viewpoints of the majority of the population.[48]

Both women's and teen magazines employ a higher percentage of female editors and writers than other media.[49] Although women may be running the magazine workplace, their work is overseen and controlled by the corporate executives and owners, most of whom are elite men. A historical study of the "Seven Sisters" magazines explored these patterns of ownership and control and their consequences. Examining the ratio of female editors in relation to the magazines' traditionally gendered content over a twenty-year period (1965–1985), the authors found no reduction in gender-stereotypical messages even as the number of female editors increased.[50]

In the mid-1990s, researcher Melissa Milkie received rare access to the editorial offices of two major teen magazines.[51] Her interviews with ten editors (nine women and one man, all white) offer insight into the decisions that these mostly female editors make in choosing images and content for a teen magazine and its readership. Milkie asked the editors to respond to what she termed the "real girl" critique, in which young female readers ask to see more authentic "real girls" as models in the magazine. Some of the editors' responses referred to constraints that prevent them from using this authentic real girl: the art world (including photographer preferences), advertiser influence, and the broader culture. Others argued that the authentic real girl critique was misguided, asserting that nobody *really* wanted to see pictures of normal girls with freckles, braces, or ample bodies, since fashion is fantasy and not meant to be authentic. The editors also claimed that, overall, the magazine's content was empowering to girls.

Teen magazines that attempt to promote the authentic real girl tend not to fare well. One example is *Sassy*, a magazine marketed to teen girls from 1988 to 1996. *Sassy* set out to be different from its teen magazine counterparts.[52] To this end, it railed against gender stereotypes, questioned gender norms, and explored social issues rather than celebrities. Ultimately, however, *Sassy* couldn't compete in the teen magazine field, in part because advertisers were not comfortable with the magazine's "subversive" content.[53] Upon its demise, *Sassy* was supplanted by several new teen magazines, including *Teen Vogue, Elle Girl, Teen People,* and *CosmoGirl!,* all true "little sisters" of mainstream women's magazines.

Contenders for the hearts and dollars of the teen girl reader have come and gone in the competitive teen magazine field, but none have ever been able to knock the original "queen of the teens" from her throne. First published in 1944, *Seventeen* magazine has remained unchallenged as the top-selling teen magazine. In October 2004 (one month beyond its actual September anniversary), this grande dame of teen magazines celebrated its sixtieth birthday, featuring actress Katie Holmes as cover girl. Directly under the hot pink *Seventeen* logo skimming Holmes's flawless forehead, a large, bright yellow caption invites the reader to "celebrate!" The birthday announcement—in a tiny green oval on the upper-right side of the page—is overshadowed by the larger white caption directly beneath "celebrate!" that reads "Your Personal Style"—making this the actual object of celebration. Bright yellow star bullets mark hot pink captions that list the facets of "your personal style"—the parameters of the feminine beauty ideal:

- Hair
- Makeup
- Clothes
- Body

Another hot pink italicized caption, this time in the bottom right corner of the cover, highlights the goal of all that body work: love. The cover communicates an equation of sorts, in which beauty through grooming and consumption will lead to love. *Seventeen,* on the occasion of its sixtieth anniversary, directed its readers to celebrate ideal femininity by pursuing their own "body projects" with the ultimate human need—love—as the end goal. As we shall see in the Epilogue, these messages continue well into the first decade of the twenty-first century in *Seventeen* and other teen magazines.

The 2004 cover, so ordinary by the standards of contemporary teen magazines, is actually ironic in light of *Seventeen*'s origins. *Seventeen* began publication in the midst of World War II, the brainchild of founding editor-in-chief Helen Valentine, a working mother and grandmother who imagined and created a novel medium: a magazine devoted to the education, edification, and entertainment of young women of high school age. Valentine affectionately referred to *Seventeen* as her "baby"—appropriately so, as she did, quite literally, deliver a new genre to the magazine industry—the teen magazine.

Valentine's creation, however, was quite different from its later iterations. Valentine envisioned a magazine that balanced fashion with service, addressing teen girls as "whole human beings" and "future American leaders," and she and her staffers (nearly all women) brought that vision to life in the first issues of their magazine. Together, they filled *Seventeen* with messages of gender and racial equality, religious freedom and tolerance, world citizenship, and community volunteerism. Fashion spreads, grooming features, and fiction stories were counterbalanced with articles about art and science, government and politics, geography and social studies, education and employment, and service to community, nation, and world. Helen Valentine's *Seventeen* paid serious attention to a young woman's "life of the mind," something that Betty Friedan found lacking in women's magazines of a later era.[54]

My comparison of magazines and magazine issues then and now leaves me with questions: How did this happen? Under what conditions did *Seventeen* enter the world and how (and why) was it transformed from a magazine that defined women as "whole human beings" to just another in a genre critiqued for objectifying and trivializing young women as shopping bodies in search of romance? I believe that we can answer these questions, to some degree, by examining the socioeconomic, historical, and biographical context of the development of *Seventeen,* the "queen of the teens."

CHAPTER 1

The Birth of the Teen Magazine:

Delivering *Seventeen* Magazine to the U.S. Marketplace

> Out of this complex social maze has come a new classification of human beings—the teen-ager. As problems have multiplied in number and severity, contemporary Americans, reaching an age which fifty years ago would have represented adulthood, are not prepared to assume the responsibilities of an adult in the modern world. A longer period of preparation—an apprenticeship to maturity—is necessary. ["Too Young to Marry?" *Seventeen*, November 1949, 142]

Teenager. Today, the word immediately elicits images and stereotypes. Raging hormones and bare midriffs. Tattoos and body piercings. Acne and cosmetics. Valley girls and mall rats. As an integral part of contemporary Western culture, teens inhabit our environs, our media, our psyches. Teens, it seems, are everywhere!

But teens have not always been everywhere; in fact, they are actually a recent cultural construction. G. Stanley Hall is most often credited with introducing the idea of adolescence as a specific (and troublesome) state of life through his widely read 1904 psychology text, *Adolescence*.[1] Historians report that the word itself, in its first incarnation as the hyphenated "teen-ager," didn't become a part of the popular lexicon until the late 1930s and early 1940s.[2] The *New York Times*, for example, first used "teen-ager" on October 18, 1942, in an article that documented the sale of war stamps to high school girls at Saks, the New York City department store.[3]

It is quite apropos that this first editorial reference mentions "teen-age" girls in relation to a consumer event at a department store, since retailers and advertisers signaled their awareness of this age group long before other media. In fact, advertisements for department store "teen shops" and teen-specific department store areas began appearing in newspapers and magazines nearly a decade before any editorial mention of teen-agers. The first teen-targeted advertisement in the *New York Times* ran on October 4, 1934, in an announcement for the opening of New York City department store Lord & Taylor's "new shop for girls of 12, 14, 16."[4] The ad heralded the teen shop as a unique "solution" to a teen apparel "problem":

> "Here you will find clothes that reach a happy compromise between 'mother's little girl' and the 'I'm grown up' idea. We have designed suitable things for this difficult in between age [. . .] and we're calling it the in-be-teen shop."[5]

Clothing manufacturers first introduced special teen-size attire in the 1930s. Prior to the 1920s, women who did not sew their own clothes could buy ready-made clothing for their daughters and themselves in either children's or women's sizes. In the next two decades, however, retailers and clothing manufacturers became increasingly aware of the sales potential for women of college and high school age. They began to manufacture and market clothing for these two age groups, first with "junior" sizes for older teens and young adult women, and later with "teen" sizes for their younger sisters. Although women's and juniors' clothes employed different size ranges (8–20 and 7–15, respectively), they were both cut for a woman's fuller figure; "teen" wear (sizes 10–16), on the other hand, was produced to fit the leaner, less developed figure of a "budding" woman.[6]

It was not a coincidence that the decade of the 1940s saw the birth of *Seventeen*—the first fashion and service magazine targeted to high school age girls—today known as a "teen magazine." Indeed, the logic of the market explains *Seventeen*'s conception during the same period that the concept of the American "teen-ager" was emerging. By the early 1940s, retailers had identified a new consumer group in girl teen agers and a corresponding market in teen age girl clothing; *Seventeen* emerged as a vehicle to bring the two together. Upon its entry into American life, *Seventeen* became one of the major sources of teen girl culture.

Teen Publications and *Seventeen* Magazine

The first issue of *Seventeen* was published in New York City and distributed across the United States in September 1944. While other magazines targeting adolescent girls existed at that time, each differed in significant ways from *Seventeen*. For instance, *Calling All Girls*, first published by *Parents* magazine in July 1941, was geared toward a slightly younger readership—girls referred to today as "preteens" or "tweens."[7] In the 1943–44 edition of *The Writer's Market*, a biannual publication for freelance writers that listed editorial descriptions of magazines, *Calling All Girls* reported that it published material that "appeal[ed] to girls of 9 to 14," including "some 'how-to-do' articles, personality sketches or just informational."[8] *Calling All Girls* also included comics, fiction stories, and advertisements for clothing, grooming aids, and snacks.

Another competitor in the girls' magazine market of the early 1940s was *The American Girl*. Published by the Girl Scouts of America from 1917 through 1979, *The American Girl* featured short stories and articles deemed "suitable" for teen-aged girls.[9] This "suitable" territory covered the lives of people in other countries, grooming advice, and Girl Scout history and current events. *The American Girl* included advertisements for grooming, medical, and hygienic products; auto and appliance companies; and Girl Scout–affiliated merchandise. Other "girl" magazines of the period were religiously affiliated: *The Catholic Girl* and *Catholic Miss* were published for young Catholic women, while *Queens' Gardens* marketed itself as appropriate for Christian girls.[10]

The magazine closest in spirit and strategy to *Seventeen* was *Mademoiselle*. *Mademoiselle* debuted in February 1935 as an alternative for young women ages 18 through 34 who were interested in fashion specifically geared to their (as opposed to their mothers') age and spending range.[11] Subtitled *The Magazine for Smart Young Women*—"smart" meaning both "intelligent" and "fashionable"—*Mademoiselle* strove to integrate smartness into the magazine's mission. Editor-in-chief Betsy Talbot Blackwell's concern for her readership as "whole persons" was expressed through quality art and fiction.[12] Although *Mademoiselle* ceased publication in 2001, it left behind a legacy of publishing fiction by important writers, including John Cheever, William Faulkner, Carson McCullers, Sylvia Plath, and Truman Capote.

Despite the fact that it was marketed to a slightly older constituency, *Mademoiselle* could be regarded as *Seventeen*'s foremother. A 1946 *Business Week* article listed *Mademoiselle* as among the "antecedents of the teen-age exploitation" of the '40s.[13] Blackwell, *Mademoiselle*'s editor from 1937 to 1971, recognized the economic value in identifying a specific audience as a demographic consumer market niche. With the help of Helen Valentine, her promotion director from 1939 to 1944, Blackwell made *Mademoiselle* successful with both readers and advertisers by targeting upper- and middle-class college-age women—a group with the financial potential to become influential consumers.[14] *Seventeen* entered the magazine market in 1944 as a bridge between existing girls' magazines (*Calling All Girls* and *American Girl*) and young adult women's magazines (*Mademoiselle*).

World War II

Seventeen magazine debuted during World War II, a context that shaped both its production and content. During the war, the U.S. government worked with advertisers and media to craft a propaganda campaign directed at women.[15] By the time *Seventeen* began production, the Office of War Information (OWI) and the War Advertising Council were in full swing, urging women to support the war effort through their labor and with their pocketbooks. In order to ensure that women received the "right" messages on a regular basis, the OWI distributed several publications to magazine editors, foremost among them the *Magazine War Guide* (*MWG*), which offered monthly suggestions for "war information suitable for use in magazines."[16] Another OWI publication, *War Jobs for Women*, was distributed to both editors and the public, and listed the many employment opportunities open to women during the war—opportunities that they were encouraged to pursue.[17] "It's a woman's war right now," the brochure proclaimed, "and women should be thinking in terms of going to full-time work and carrying along many of their volunteer activities as side lines."[18]

Records kept by the OWI indicate that American magazine editors followed the *MWG*'s directives when choosing material for publication during this period.[19] American women also took their marching orders seriously, securing employment outside the home, volunteering for community war efforts, and spending their money frugally and patriotically.[20] Women in the workforce were given access to jobs in male-dominated industries that had previously been beyond their reach, earning "man-size" wages that brought more money into their households.[21] In turn, many working mothers (both paid and volunteer) transferred their home duties to their teen age daughters, giving their daughters a practical lesson in overseeing a family's consumer needs and economic resources.[22]

Although many World War II historians focus on women's increased employment rates during the war, others note that consumer spending also surged during this period.[23] As durable goods became less available, manufacturers and advertisers put their efforts into making and marketing nondurable goods such as clothing. At the same time, teen girls were becoming more and more responsible for spending—both their own earnings and the household income. Thus, the war gave teen age girls a newfound economic power, both individually and as family managers. A 1946 *Business Week* article marveled at the deep and wide teen consumer market that developed during the war period, measuring it via four indicators: (1) increased spending of teen girls; (2) clothing lines developed just for teen girls; (3) "teen-shops" in which to buy them; and (4) the introduction of the teen magazine genre.[24]

The war and its aftermath influenced the development of *Seventeen* magazine, out so too did its creators. The backgrounds and agendas of *Seventeen*'s first editor-in-chief, Helen Valentine, and publisher, Walter Annenberg, shaped the magazine in its formative years.

Meet Helen Valentine

Helen Rose Lachman was the only child of German Jewish immigrants, Gustave Lachman and Bertha (Kahn) Lachman. Born in New York City on June 25, 1893, Helen spent her childhood—and most of her adult life—in the borough of Manhattan. Her mother was a homemaker, while her father supported the family as an accountant and businessman. Although the family was upper middle class, Helen later alluded to periods of financial instability: "In spite of the fact that we went through many physical changes, financial changes [*laugh*], quite a bit of drama on the outside, the inside was always calm."[25] When asked about whether her mother did the family cooking, Helen answered, "No. Well, she did sometimes and sometimes we had help. We went through . . . various [*laugh*] life stages."[26]

Whatever form these life stages took, Helen's parents were able to send her to a private high school, followed by Barnard College, a prestigious and expensive all-women's college affiliated with Columbia University in New York City. In reflecting on her early life in her secular Jewish family, Helen says: "I had a very happy, relaxed childhood, a very happy education. I was delighted. I went to the Ethical Culture School, where I was very happy. I went to Barnard, where I was very happy, and I didn't feel the need to do anything outside at that time at all."[27]

Helen graduated from Barnard in 1915 with a degree in English, and in 1920 she married Herbert Irwin Valentine—known to friends and family as "Big Val." Although Helen reported that she never planned on working outside the home, she engaged in paid employment most of her adult life. As she describes it, after several years of spending her time at home caring for both Big Val and her father (who lived with the newlyweds after her mother's death), she developed an "itch" that demanded to be scratched: "I began to get a little itchy, wanted to do something, and that's how I decided that probably the best thing I could do would be to use what little writing ability I had and, in trying to decide which field to go into, I picked a very natural one, which was advertising. It was logical.[28]"

Helen began her career in 1922 as a copywriter for the Lord & Thomas Advertising Agency in New York City, staying there until 1930, when she was among twenty-six people who lost their jobs due to Depression-related cutbacks.[29] Despite industry-wide layoffs, Helen was not interested in returning to homemaking. After being laid off:

> I went home and thought about it and I said, "Well, the agency business is dead right now, but there must be some other way to use whatever little talent you have," and I decided that maybe it would be a good idea to see if I could promote something that I knew something about and that I was interested in, and by some strange coincidence, the mail brought me a piece of promotion from *Vogue* and it was one of the snootiest pieces of writing that you ever could have read, and I thought, "I've got it!" I called up and I asked for the name of the promotion director, which happened to be Mr. Keep, O. D. Keep, of blessed memory, an absolutely darling man, and I called Mr. Keep and I asked him if I could come in and talk to him, and he said, "What about?" and I said, "Well, I'm interested in *Vogue* and I just would love to come in and talk to you, and nothing may come of it, but I would be enormously grateful if you would give me a few minutes." So he said, "Okay, come in."[30]

Helen impressed Keep with her promotional ideas, and he arranged a meeting for her with Condé Nast, *Vogue* publisher and head of Condé Nast Publications. Publisher Nast's reputation was that of a powerful man who controlled the destinies of his workers during a time when jobs were scarce. But Nast's reputation did not intimidate Helen, as evidenced by her description of their first meeting:

> And when I got there ... on his desk . . . there were a couple of proofs from *Vogue* and one of them was a picture of a . . . double spread of a backgammon board with a hand moving a tile. That was the day when backgammon was it. And I suppose Mr. Nast, being gracious and wanting to break the ice, said, after the first how-do-you-do's, "Do you play backgammon, Mrs. Valentine?" and I said, "No, Mr. Nast, nor bridge nor golf," [*laugh*] whereupon he threw back his head and roared, you know, instead of just looking at me blandly, which he might have. He just thought that was so funny. So we had this long,

long, long, long talk and he said, "You know, you're so critical of what we're doing, would you do something for me? Would you take a piece of our copy and would you rewrite it as you think it should be?" "Oh," I said, "I'd love to," so that's how I left. Well, when I got outside, Mr. Keep was standing way down around the corner in the hall with his eyes glued to his wristwatch and he said, "You were in there forty-five minutes!" [*laugh*] in this roaring voice in disbelief [*laugh*]. And so that's how I was hired at Condé Nast.[31]

Helen spent the next seven years (1930–1937) at Condé Nast Publications, refining her skills in the promotions department at *Vogue,* and later as the editor of the *Vogue Pattern Book.* She received an invaluable education through her association with publisher Nast, including lessons in leadership:

He was the head of everything. The Condé Nast Publications, he was Condé Nast! [*laugh*]. And a nicer man never lived. [*laugh*] He really was a wonderful man to work with. You notice that I said "work with" and not "for" because that's . . . Now, you see, that was a slip and that gives you the picture right there. He was absolutely marvelous. He was so appreciative if you did something good and when he was critical he was so right and so gentle and so careful about it, you know. He just was a remarkable, remarkable man, and of course talented, uhm, so talented![32]

Helen had other mentors at *Vogue,* including Dr. Mehemed Fehmy Agha, one of the most influential magazine art directors of the twentieth century, and Edna Woolman Chase, *Vogue*'s editor-in-chief. In later years, Helen remembered her time at *Vogue* fondly, despite the fact that she was fired in 1937 and replaced by her assistant, mentee, and (former) best friend—Alice Dickey Thompson.[33] This was Thompson's first betrayal of Valentine, but it would not be her last.

In 1938, a year after leaving *Vogue,* Helen had two works published: a children's bilingual picture book titled *Mary and Marie,* and an etiquette handbook called *Better Than Beauty: A Guide to Charm. Better Than Beauty* was coauthored (pre-betrayal) by Helen's *Vogue* assistant, Alice Thompson.[34] The dedication at the beginning of *Better Than Beauty* reads: "to A.T. and H.V. We dedicate this little book to two women who undoubtedly could profit by reading it."[35]

In 1939, Helen was hired as promotion director for *Mademoiselle*—known as "Millie" to its staff—by its editor-in-chief, Betsy Talbot Blackwell.[36] Blackwell and Valentine developed and implemented a new marketing strategy, educating clothing manufacturers and retailers about the buying desires and abilities of college-age women. Once convinced, the clothing industry responded with "college shops" and lines of clothing targeted to younger women. Helen might have stayed at *Mademoiselle* indefinitely if not for a meeting with publisher Walter Annenberg in early 1944.

Meet Walter Annenberg

On March 13, 1908, when fifteen-year-old Helen Valentine was a student at Manhattan's Ethical Culture School, Moses and Sadie Annenberg welcomed a baby boy named Walter Hubert into their home in Milwaukee, Wisconsin. "Moe" and Sadie already had five daughters, and three more daughters would follow Walter.[37] As the only male child, Walter held a special position in this large Jewish family—so special, in fact, that his mother and sisters affectionately referred to him as "Boy."[38]

Walter's mother, Sadie Cecelia Friedman, was born in New York and raised in Chicago in a middle-class home. His father, Moses Louis Annenberg, was born in Kalwichen, East Prussia (near the Russian border), where his Jewish family experienced discrimination. Moe's father left the family to prepare a new life for them in Chicago; a few years later, the family traveled by boat to join him. Moe and his brother Max entered the capitalist fray of late-1800s Chicago, fighting (often literally) their way from poverty to wealth, during which time Moe became an American and a newspaperman.[39] His first newspaper job was as a solicitor (paper boy) for the *Chicago Evening American*, a paper owned by William Randolph Hearst. Moe rose through the ranks at Hearst's company, and by 1906, he had saved enough money to found the Chicago News Company, a newspaper distribution service, which later became the Milwaukee News Company.[40]

In 1920, when Walter was twelve, Moe moved the family to Long Island, New York, having accepted a position with the Hearst organization overseeing nineteen newspapers and several magazines. Soon after, Hearst asked Moe to take over his company's newest acquisition, the *New York Daily Mirror*. Moe reportedly used underworld connections to ensure that the newspaper was able to compete on the street with the *New York Daily News*.[41]

During this period, Walter's family rose from middle-class comfort to upper-class affluence, moving into a thirty-two-room mansion with a bowling alley. In an effort to upgrade his moniker to match his mansion, Moe renamed himself M. L., emulating his boss, William Randolph Hearst, who went by W. R. He also began to acquire his own media properties, including the *Daily Racing Form*, the General News racing wire, and the Nationwide News Service.[42] Nationwide News Service was actually a horse-racing information clearinghouse known as "The Trust" by organized crime.[43] M. L. was well on his way to earning the title "kingpin of the nation's gambling industry," counting mob members Lucky Luciano and Meyer Lansky among his friends.[44] In 1926, the elder Annenberg finally ended his affiliation with Hearst in order to devote his energies to his own companies.

While M. L. Annenberg amassed his fortune—at times apparently through less than reputable means—he was doing whatever he could to give his children, particularly Walter, the kind of life that he had been denied as a youth. When Walter was fourteen, Moses sent him to the Peddie School, a Baptist boarding school in Hightstown, New Jersey; Peddie, unlike the more elite prep schools of the period, did not restrict attendance by Jews.[45] After Walter graduated from Peddie in 1927, he briefly attended the Wharton School of Finance at the University of Pennsylvania. At Penn, he again experienced discrimination as a Jew, despite the fact that he didn't define himself in that way. Barred from the elite fraternities, Walter joined Phi Sigma Delta, the college's Jewish fraternity.[46]

Walter was unhappy at college and returned home after a year to work as an accountant for his father's company, the Cecelia Investment Company (named for Walter's mother, Sadie Cecelia Annenberg). After Walter went to work for him, M. L. bought several "scandal sheets" and *Screen Guide* magazine; he also founded *Click* magazine. Walter was less than enthusiastic about his father's holdings; in fact, he found some of them embarrassing. One of Walter's biographers describes the difference in business orientation between father and son as that of quantity and quality.[47]

M. L.'s publications ran the gamut from the gaudy to the tawdry to the illegal. His profitable photo magazine, *Click,* was an example of the gaudy *and* tawdry. Designed to compete with *Look* and *Life,* it featured celebrity cheesecake pictorials and sensationalist copy. The Catholic Church condemned it and Canada banned it. Walter wanted his father to get rid of *Click,* but M. L. agreed only to revamp it, shifting its focus from pulpy to patriotic—one example of a more general shift in magazines that occurred during the World War II years.[48] Although the Catholic Church and Canada eventually lifted their bans, *Click* never shed its sleazy image.[49]

In the late 1930s, the U.S. government, under the orders of President Franklin Delano Roosevelt, began investigating M. L. for income-tax evasion, a tactic sometimes used to shut down criminal businessmen who had been able to avoid arrest for other types of illegal activities. The Annenberg family, however, claimed that they were targeted because of their Republican-leaning newspapers' critical coverage of Roosevelt and his administration. M. L. pleaded guilty, was indicted for tax evasion in 1939, and sentenced to prison in 1940.[50]

Walter was thirty-two when his sixty-two-year-old father was incarcerated. Two years later, in 1942, the elder Annenberg died of a brain tumor while in prison and thirty-four-year-old Walter inherited the family publishing dynasty. By then, the group was known as Triangle Publications, the name change an attempt to offset some of the bad publicity of the elder Annenberg's conviction. Triangle's holdings at the time of M. L.'s death included the *Wisconsin Daily News*, the *Philadelphia Daily News*, the *Philadelphia Inquirer*, the *New York Morning Telegraph*, the *Daily Racing Form*, *Screen Guide*, *Click*, and several wire services and "scandal sheets." M. L.'s imprisonment, followed by his death, left Walter in control of Triangle and its stock holdings.[51]

The gender inequity of the distribution of M. L.'s estate, which benefited Walter, the "Boy," far more than his mother and sisters, became a source of family discontent that increased over time. In particular, Walter found himself at odds with his oldest and only college-educated sister, Esther (known as "Aye"). The strife among Walter and his sisters came to a head when he forced all of his sisters off Triangle's board of directors for, as described by his nephew Ron Krancer, "[getting] on his nerves."[52]

M. L. Annenberg's death served as a turning point for Walter. His father had intimidated and dominated him all his life. Although he rose to the rank of vice president while M. L. was alive, Walter had not had any real responsibility up to that point. He was known as a rich young "man about town," and his youthful lifestyle resembled the wealthy young heirs of today who have a seemingly endless supply of money and time at their disposal (e.g., Paris and Nicky Hilton, the Kardashian siblings, and so on.). However, this changed with his father's death, as well as his 1938 marriage to Veronica Dunkelman.[53]

Walter inherited a business that wasn't just tawdry—it was also in debt. Spending fourteen-hour days running Triangle Publications from the *Philadelphia Inquirer* offices, Walter tried to salvage his father's business and recoup the family's reputation. Over the next several years, he sold off some family real estate as well as the wire services. He also began to implement the kind of editorial changes that he had proposed, unsuccessfully, while his father was in charge. He revamped *Click* by hiring new staff (including Estelle Ellis, who later became promotion director at *Seventeen* magazine) and directing them to cover "more serious" stories.[54]

During the war period, celebrity-filled "screen" (i.e., movie) magazines, a previously popular genre, lost both readers and advertisers to women's fashion and service magazines.[55] The Condé Nast–owned magazine *Glamour of Hollywood* quickly responded to this trend by shifting its focus from fandom to fashion, removing the "of Hollywood" from its title.[56] At the suggestion of Dr. Mehemed Fehmy Agha, Walter decided to transform his movie magazine, *Stardom*, into a women's fashion magazine.[57] Recognizing that a good editor-in-chief would be key to the success of this new endeavor, Mehemed and several other advisors encouraged Walter to consider *Mademoiselle*'s promotion director, Helen Valentine.[58]

When Walter Met Helen: An Old-Fashioned Arranged Marriage

Early in 1944, Walter Annenberg approached Helen Valentine—first through emissaries and then in person—with a business proposition involving a merger of his resources and her talents. At their first meeting, he offered her the editorship of his failing movie magazine, *Stardom*, with the mandate to reinvent it as a women's fashion magazine. As Valentine later described, this was an offer that she could easily refuse:

> [Dr. Agha] called me one day and said that there were two gentlemen who wanted to see me and they would like to come to my house some weekend and talk with me, they were in the publishing business. And so these two gentlemen came to see me one Saturday afternoon and we talked about everything under the sun and it was a sort of strange meeting, they didn't really come to the point at all, you know. But when they left, my husband said to me, "Well, you're going to be offered a job any minute now," [*laugh*] you know. Well, they were two people who were working with Walter Annenberg and what they wanted was for me to come and take over their magazine *Stardom*, which was a movie magazine, as you can imagine by the name, and turn it into a woman's magazine. They said that Mr. Annenberg would like to meet me and talk to me about it, so we made an appointment and Mr. Annenberg

> took me to lunch and he told me what he would like me to do and I said to him, "I'm not in the least bit interested. I do thank you for offering it to me, but I'm not interested. There's nothing in the world that you could offer me that would make me want to do it."[59]

However, Valentine took the opportunity to promote her own idea, one that she described to *Newsweek* as having been in development since her own daughter, Barbara, was a teenager.[60] Instead of a fashion magazine for adult women, she proposed an original concept: a service and fashion magazine written just for high school girls.[61]

Valentine's idea for a teenage service magazine developed during World War II, a time in which citizenship and global responsibility were at the forefront of cultural awareness. Valentine described the influence of this period as she recalled her sales pitch to Annenberg:

> But I said, "I've got an idea cooking around in the back of my head if you're interested—I'd like to tell you about it," so he said, "Certainly." So I said, "Well, you know, I've been thinking a lot about the young people in this country today and one of the things that startled me was, I saw a picture of a meeting at the U.N. [United Nations] and it was a photograph taken before the doors opened and there was this long line of people outside and ninety percent of them were very young," and I said, "This is what started me thinking about the young people in this country. People have an idea that the only thing they're interested in is their next date, but it isn't so. They are really thinking about very important things and we ought to be thinking about them in those terms." And he looked at me, you know, [*laughs*] wide-eyed, and he said, "In other words, you think you'd like to do a magazine for them," and I said, "Absolutely, directed only to them." So he thought for a few minutes and he said, "Come and do it."[62]

Walter Annenberg's biographies tell a similar tale of this first meeting, but with minor variations. Although Annenberg credits Valentine with being the first one to bring up the idea of a magazine for teenagers, he alludes to having had the same idea himself. Describing a walk that he took down Fifth Avenue earlier in 1944 with his sister, Enid Annenberg Haupt, he remembers noting the window displays of junior-size clothing and remarking to Enid that "there isn't a magazine for girls in that age group."[63] Walter's sisters and mother certainly believed that *Seventeen* was born of his business genius; they later described it as one of "Walter's epiphanies."[64]

And "Baby" Makes Three—Or *Seventeen*

Written news reports of the period make one point clear: *Seventeen* magazine was Helen Valentine's baby—and in the beginning Annenberg acknowledged her primary role in the magazine's birth. An article about *Seventeen*'s debut in *Tide,* an advertising and retail industry publication, stated:

> For getting the *Seventeen* idea across, Annenberg and his general manager, Kenneth M. Friede, give all the credit to Mrs. Valentine who, though 51 and a grandmother, is as vivacious as the typical *Seventeen* reader. Mrs. Valentine agreed to take over on one condition: that the publication be edited as a service magazine to meet the needs of teen-age girls.[65]

Indeed, *Seventeen* quickly became so much a part of Helen's life that references to it as her "baby" were common in media reports,[66] in the magazine itself,[67] and in the magazine's promotional literature.[68] By giving the magazine such a maternal term of endearment, Valentine signaled her role as the magazine's nurturing, life-giving creator. Overseeing the development of this magazine was not just a job for her; it was a mission.

Valentine christened the magazine *Seventeen* upon the suggestion of a friend.[69] She loved the name's simplicity, and its evocation of "the age when a girl is no longer a child, yet isn't quite a woman"—her target readership.[70] In order to avoid copyright infringement, Annenberg contacted writer Booth Tarkington, author of the popular 1916 coming-of-age novel, *Seventeen,* to request his consent. Tarkington gave the magazine his okay and his blessing.[71]

Both Annenberg and Valentine had aspirations for *Seventeen* and for its teen readership. However, while their goals were similar, their visions were informed by different concerns. For Annenberg, the goal was the pursuit of respect—for himself, his family's reputation, his company, and his magazine.[72] The younger Annenberg had always differed philosophically with his father's publishing policy of reaching for the "lowest common denominator."[73] Once in charge, Walter began to shift Triangle's business strategy from quantity amassing to quality assurance. In the case of *Seventeen,* this translated into a desire to be affiliated with a respectable publication.

Annenberg gave Valentine two editorial mandates: that the magazine be "sensible" and "wholesome." Although he initially took a hands-off approach, Annenberg felt strongly enough about wholesomeness that he gave her specific directives about the kind of copy that he did *not* consider wholesome. For example, according to his biographies, he forbade the use of the word *pimple* in any article headlines, and restricted advertising that he deemed age-inappropriate—for instance, alcohol, cigarettes, and hotels.[74]

Annenberg hoped that wholesome content would set him apart from his father, restore his family's tarnished reputation, and earn him respect from his social circles and the general public. He was immediately successful in obtaining the respect of his mother, who, after viewing the first issue of *Seventeen*, sent a note that read: "My sweetheart Boy, I am so very proud of you my dear because you do use your head."[75]

Helen Valentine was also interested in respect, although not so much for herself and her family (who were not afflicted by a Moe), but for *Seventeen*'s readers. She was determined to create a service magazine that respected the young woman reader as a "whole human being."[76] Insistent that *Seventeen*'s editorial tone didn't talk down to the reader, Valentine reportedly told Annenberg in the initial stages of their negotiations: "There's room today for a publication aimed at teen-agers. They've been neglected by the established fashion publications. Everyone treats them as though they were silly, swooning bobby soxers. I think they're young adults and should be treated accordingly."[77]

As *Seventeen*'s editor-in-chief, Valentine drew on her previous experiences in publishing, particularly her years as promotion director at *Mademoiselle*—a (young) women's magazine designed to be both "fashion-conscious" and "thought-provoking." When she moved to *Seventeen*, she made sure that every issue contained "weighty reading" on serious issues.[78] *Seventeen*'s readership was quickly approaching voting age, and Helen believed that they needed the kind of information that would allow them to make educated decisions as voters and citizens.[79] As Estelle Ellis, *Seventeen*'s first promotion director, explains, Valentine saw teens:

> Not just as consumers but as citizens of tomorrow . . . of what their rights were and what their needs were. So we were . . . we were doing articles that respond-ed to their emotional needs as adolescents trying to separate themselves from their family at a time when they're growing up and maturing but also, who are they going to be and what must they know in the way of culture, [*small sigh*] government, legislation, the war, Dumbarton Oaks, all of that.[80]

Valentine also wanted to introduce her young readership to "high culture" in literature, art, and music. She believed that girls' artistic sensibilities had not yet been obliterated by commercial culture and that they could still be "serious responders to music and art."[81] Valentine illustrated the magazine with the work of well-known artists and photographers such as Ben

Shahn and Francesco Scavullo. In 1947 she hired graphic design artist Cipe Pineles as art director at *Seventeen,* a move that would bring artistic acclaim to the magazine—as well as a lifelong friend and confidante to Valentine and promotion director Estelle Ellis.[82]

It Takes a Village

Valentine thought it important to respect not only *Seventeen*'s readership but also its staffers. Her personnel policies granted *Seventeen*'s editors considerable autonomy within their areas. She also regularly praised her staff in recognition of their abilities, efforts, and achievements.[83] Her staff, in turn, rewarded Valentine with the kind of affection usually reserved for intimates.[84] Estelle Ellis describes Helen's maternal and mentoring nature:

> She was the whole person. First of all, in a time where many women who were achieving were barracudas, she was a gentle, loving, kind, quality human being and nourished the young people who worked with her. Number one. Number two, she was married, she had her own children. She made it possible for me to think that you could do both and she did do both and she encouraged me and she was there when my first child was born. My husband called her before he called my mother and she held his hand during the very difficult first pregnancy that I had. So this was a very uncommon lady for her times.[85]

Despite the fact that he was fifteen years her junior, Walter Annenberg saw himself as "Father" to Helen Valentine's "Mother"; he once signed a letter to her as "Old Dad."[86] Like many a real father, Annenberg spent much of his time at the office (in this case, at Triangle's offices in Philadelphia), leaving most of the hands-on work of magazine making to the mostly female staffers onsite. Communication between Annenberg and Valentine took place via telephone, mail, and periodic lunch meetings at Annenberg's offices in Philadelphia.[87] Annenberg's visits to *Seventeen* during these early years were rare; some former staffers report never having seen him on the premises.[88]

Valentine headed the editorial side of the magazine, overseeing the workplace and reporting directly to Annenberg (or business manager Kenneth Friede in Annenberg's stead). As the magazine's creative leader, her mandate was to communicate her vision for the magazine to the staff; as the boss, her job was to make sure that her staff implemented that vision. In order to do that, she had to recognize, hire, and mentor staff who were able to work within these parameters.[89]

In the world of magazine publishing, the editor-in-chief's right-hand (wo)man is either the managing editor or the executive editor. The difference between these two positions is largely semantic, with the position of "managing editor" carrying more authoritative/authoritarian connotations than the term "executive editor."[90] However, both types of editor operate as the closest assistants to the editor-in-chief, making sure that her mandates are carried out.[91] At different times in Valentine's editorship, she had either a managing editor or an executive editor. Charlotte Ware originally held the position of managing editor, later sharing power with executive editor Alice Thompson (Valentine's former assistant at *Vogue*); soon thereafter, however, Ware found herself replaced by Thompson.

For the position that Valentine had held at *Mademoiselle* magazine—promotion director—she hired twenty-five-year-old Estelle Ellis.[92] Ellis was among the youngest of *Seventeen*'s staffers, fewer than four years out of college and newly married to Samuel Rubinstein. Ellis's job as promotion director was among the magazine's most important positions, involving the development of a sales campaign for the magazine. Hired in part because of her youth, Ellis's mission was to define and communicate *Seventeen* magazine and the teenage market to business. To this end, Ellis created the magazine's prototypical teenage girl, named her "Teena," and introduced her to the business community.[93]

Other important original *Seventeen* staffers of note were art director Jan Balet, a recent immigrant to America who left Germany in protest of Hitler's regime;[94] beauty editor Irma Phorylles, a twenty-nine-year-old "bachelorette" who wrote witty copy that often reminded the reader of the connection between beauty and romance; and fashion editor Eleanor Hillebrand, a twenty-seven-year-old newlywed (a.k.a. "Mrs. Bruce" in *Seventeen*'s periodic editor portraits) whose duties ranged from shopping for the featured clothing to hiring the models and overseeing fashion shoots.

One of Hillebrand's most important hires was photographer Francesco Scavullo.[95] Although Scavullo eventually became an iconic figure in the fashion magazine industry, in 1944 he was twenty-three-year-old Frank, shooting covers and photo spreads at *Seventeen*. Like the "Cosmo girls" that he would someday famously photograph for Helen Gurley Brown's *Cosmopolitan* covers, the "Teenas" who adorned his *Seventeen* covers represented the face of both the magazine and its teenage girl ideal.

Another member of the early *Seventeen* family was thirty-nine-year-old Alice Dickey Thompson Beaton, Helen Valentine's former friend and co-author, the assistant at *Vogue* who had worked her way into her mentor's job, leaving Valentine temporarily out of work.[96] Valentine's adult daughter, Barbara Valentine Hertz, and her daughter's husband, David Hertz, familiar with Helen's history with Alice, were "appalled" to learn that Helen had hired "a woman who had stabbed her in the back."[97] But she did—and it was a decision that would later backfire.

Alice wrote interchangeably under the bylines of "Alice Thompson" and "Alice Beaton"; the former was her married name by her first husband, E. Austin Thompson; the latter, her married name by her second husband, John Beaton. Although Alice Thompson's name did not appear on the masthead during the first year, she played an important part in shaping the early issues of *Seventeen,* writing the monthly column "For Seniors Only." A Quaker, Thompson shared Valentine's progressive politics, especially in regard to issues of racial, ethnic, and religious equality, and her articles addressed those topics with the fervor of a preacher.

Like many of *Seventeen*'s other staffers, Thompson balanced her work life with a full home life—one that included her second husband and two children from her first marriage. Her teenage son, Ted Thompson, occasionally contributed articles to *Seventeen*. Even before Thompson officially joined the staff as an editor, her full work and family schedule merited mention in *Seventeen*'s September 1945 birthday issue, which explained that Thompson: "leads the life of Reilly . . . the hard-working branch of the family. A crackerjack copy writer, she can't think in a room done in blue. Happily married, she has a daughter who keeps the house swarming with Teenas, and Alice says it is a mystery to her why anybody ever calls teen-agers 'difficult.'"[98]

These were some of the people whose labor shaped *Seventeen* during its important early developmental period—mostly college-educated, from the manor born to the foreign born. It was a workplace run almost exclusively by women, many of them relatively young, many Jewish, several of them recent immigrants, very few of them people of color.[99] What was it like as a workplace? Alberta Eiseman, a young immigrant from Italy who worked as an editorial assistant, reminisces:

> We were a very unsophisticated lot but we did a lot of work and it was a very good place to be for somebody young and anxious to write because they didn't pay much, heaven knows, but they did let you write. If you had any desire and talent, they'd let you write and after a while they'd give you a byline.

And that's what you really wanted.[100]

Ingrid Loewenstein Sladkus, another editorial assistant (and recent immigrant from Czechoslovakia), concurs:

> Oh, it was delightful, it really was, I mean there were little intrigues here and there that got more and more interesting as I got older, but it was a wonderful place and everyone was very welcoming to me. I was just a kid from high school, you know, but they made me feel like I was going to have a job to do and they were very nice and the editors were always very . . . I don't know how I can describe them, but they were certainly willing to be of help and to get me going in my career.[101]

Sladkus also remembers Helen Valentine's accessibility to all her employees, regardless of their position. Looking back after decades of working for other media organizations, including the *San Francisco Examiner,* Ingrid commented:

> I think it's remarkable that Helen Valentine would take an interest in a 17-year-old like I was and actually have me come for the interview and actually give me a job [. . .]. She was always friendly, very busy but always had a minute to chat with me or something like that and everybody liked her very much.[102]

Announcing "Baby's" Birth

As is usually the case with the birth of babies, Annenberg and Valentine were eager to share the news of their impending newborn—and to alert all interested parties of the economic opportunity at hand. The first announcement appeared in *Women's Wear Daily* on August 9, 1944. The full-page ad featured a picture of a smiling teenage woman with the headline: "17—The New Magazine That's Needed Now!" The text proclaimed:

> Teens are the talk of the times. Department stores from coast to coast are opening (or expanding) Teen-Age Shops. Apparel manufacturers are making more imaginative and appealing teen-age fashions. Cosmetics houses are designing special teen-age lines. Movies and the theatre alternately laugh at or weep over this fascinating younger generation. Everywhere there is talk of the teens.
>
> Now . . . here comes a magazine dedicated to this vital group . . . a medium tailored to fit their needs, their interests, their way of life. A gay, good

> taste, good humored magazine that talks straight in the language of the intelligent young woman of today.
>
> If you also talk their language . . . if you make, sell or promote anything they wear, use or buy . . . better find out more about SEVENTEEN—it may prove to be your lucky number Seventeen—the sweetest market ever sold.[103]

Just one week before Baby made her public debut, a *Business Week* article announced her impending arrival and alerted its readership (business people) to the potential value of *Seventeen*'s readership (teenage girls), explaining: "*Seventeen* will advise high school girls on fashions (in full color), beauty, movies, food, fun, and other teen-age interests. It also expects to advise advertisers on what it claims is a $750,000,000 annual market among the country's 6,000,000 high school girls."[104]

Two months after *Seventeen*'s launch *Newsweek* reported her debut a success, noting that: "The teen-agers' response to this venture into a hitherto unexploited field—their fashions, hobbies, etiquette, school problems, amusements, and behavior—was electric. The first issue, which featured a forty-five-photo double-page spread of Frank Sinatra, sold its press run of 400,000 copies and brought 500 letters from readers."[105] The business community may have ignored the presence of the teenage girl up until this point, but it was quick to take note of her once *Seventeen* magazine arrived.

Seventeen's immediate success in the marketplace alerted Walter Annenberg to the magazine's potential. One month after *Seventeen* began publication, Annenberg wrote a letter on Triangle stationery, addressed to editor-in-chief Helen Valentine, with cc's to five other involved parties: "Mssrs. First, Friede, Oschay, McGivena, and Agha." Annenberg's letter described *Seventeen*'s developmental trajectory as follows:

> The magazine SEVENTEEN was born as a result of a series of decisions as to what to do with the none too successful screen magazine STARDOM. In the late fall of 1943, we determined to try and get some of the vast amount of fashion advertising which was going begging because of the magazine paper rationing problem. We had heard that such books as MADEMOISELLE, CHARM and GLAMOUR were turning down countless pages each issue, and the lure of going after some of this overflow business was understandable.
>
> Accordingly, we requested our editors to set up a twenty page fashion section in STARDOM; these efforts after three issues did not prove fruitful.
>
> Along about that time, Mr. Annenberg discussed the publication with Leo McGivena, one of the country's top publication promotional men, and

> McGivena suggested that Dr. M. F. Agha, one time art expert for the Condé Nast publications, be contacted. Dr. Agha, who now is an art consultant for several publications and many department stores, had a conversation with Mr. Annenberg, and thereupon Mr. Annenberg engaged Dr. Agha to take STARDOM under his wing. After a few weeks, Dr. Agha flatly told Mr. Annenberg that the combination of a motion picture book with a fashion section would not get any place; that it certainly would not attract fashion advertising. The Doctor took the position that others had tried this in the past, and had failed, and urged that we remain either a movie book, or go into a complete fashion publication. We were, of course, attracted to the logic in the enormous potential that a fashion book offered. After reaching a definite decision to move in this direction, Mr. Annenberg communicated with an executive of The Blum Store, [a specialty shop] in Philadelphia, in whom he had a great deal of confidence. Mr. Annenberg asked this individual who in his opinion was the outstanding woman in the fashion magazine field with whom he had contact. The Blum Store executive readily answered, "If Helen Valentine, the promotional director of MADEMOISELLE is available, that's your woman." Whereupon, Mr. Annenberg requested Kenneth Friede, Triangle Publications executive, to contact Helen Valentine, and see if she would be interested in editing her own magazine; editing it with an absolutely free hand. After several conferences, Mr. Friede was able to report that Helen Valentine was receptive, and she was engaged to do the job.
>
> Helen Valentine recommended a new name for the magazine, and urged that we consider the title SEVENTEEN, which was suggested to her by one of her intimate friends. Mrs. Valentine further insisted that the book be edited to the tastes of teen-age girls, a field that had practically no coverage. To this the Company agreed.
>
> The proposed magazine met with instant favor among the prospective advertisers, and the many merchandise people in stores right across the country. The response of the public on the first two issues is certainly a compliment to the judgment of all those who had a hand in the book's creation.[106]

This letter offers observers a contemporaneous account of the magazine's origins unblurred by the fog of time, the vagaries of memory, and the ascendancy of certain storytellers. It sets a reference point against which future stories about *Seventeen*'s history, told by the different parties involved, can be considered and analyzed. This is important because different people's perceptions and reports of the same events and circumstances were not always congruent, and the passing of time only exacerbated these discrepancies. Later, disparities of privilege would influence whose narratives became part of the public history of *Seventeen*'s origins.

But for now, by weaving together the observations of people who were there at the time, news reports of the day, and Annenberg's letter, we can produce a rough tapestry of *Seventeen*'s genesis. The main threads pop out in vivid color: Walter Annenberg wanted to make money and improve his family's reputation by revamping his fan magazine into a women's fashion magazine; he approached Helen Valentine, who suggested a different tack—that she edit a service magazine for teenage girls. Annenberg agreed, Valentine did just that, and the result was the immediately successful *Seventeen* magazine. A marriage made in New York City produced a beautiful and profitable baby. And if this were a fairy tale, they would all live happily ever after.

But they didn't. And, if we look closely at the tapestry, we can see the threads of dissonance. As the two most important people to have "a hand in [*Seventeen*'s] creation," Annenberg and Valentine may have appeared as cocreators, but this was never a marriage between equals. Annenberg benefited from multiple privileges that ultimately placed him in a position of authority over Valentine. Before Valentine entered his life, Annenberg was privileged by both class and gender—if not by ethnicity. As the only son amongst many daughters, he alone was bequeathed control of Triangle Publications, rewarded by his father's belief in primogeniture—the right of the oldest son to inherit a family's entire estate.

Annenberg ran Triangle and *Seventeen* as a patriarch, one who maintained some distance from the women's work but also had the "final say" and whose decisions were final. Thus, although he wrote in his letter that Valentine could "edit *Seventeen* with a free hand," Valentine's "free hand" only operated insofar as the results pleased Annenberg—a situation that later chapters will illuminate. Annenberg was the owner of *Seventeen* and Valentine was his employee; since he controlled *Seventeen*'s budget, Annenberg could enforce his dictates. In the end, *Seventeen* may have been Valentine's baby, but once she was in "Boy's" employ, he "owned" both of them.

CHAPTER 2

Seventeen Magazine at War

Teena in the World of Opportunity

SEVENTEEN Says Hello

It isn't everyone who can be born at the age of Seventeen . . . but here we are, brand new, and yet—we're Seventeen in spirit.

SEVENTEEN is your magazine, High School Girls of America—all yours! It is interested only in you—and in everything that concerns, excites, annoys, pleases or perplexes you.

SEVENTEEN is interested in ***how you dress***. We're not much on the tricky stuff, but we believe clothes must be right for you and the time, place and occasion for which you'll wear them.

We care about ***how you feel and how you look***. Those two always go together. Keats said "Truth is Beauty." We have no quarrel with that—but for practical purposes health is beauty. With good health as a beginning, we hope to give you plenty of pointers on how to build a new you—which, if it doesn't knock 'em cold, at least will make people pleasantly aware of you as a person.

SEVENTEEN is interested in ***what you do***. Are you a music fiend, a bookworm, a movie fan? Do you like art, history, poetry or humor? Do you squander your leisure, or do you consider time a precious commodity?

We're keenly interested in ***what you think***. Are you so baffled by the confusions of reality that you take refuge in a world of your own? Or do you feel that the world is your oyster—just waiting to be opened and produce its pearl?

But—most important of all—***SEVENTEEN*** is interested in ***what you are*** . . . the kind of human being you are. Are you tense and ill-at-ease or comfortable and relaxed? Have you a chip on your shoulder or a smile on your lips? Are you interested only in yourself and your closest family and friends, or do you care what happens to people you'll never see? You're going to have to run this show—so the sooner you start thinking about it, the better. In a world that is changing as quickly and profoundly as ours is, we hope to provide a clearing house for your ideas.

> As a magazine, we shall discuss all the things you consider important—with plenty of help from you, please. Write us about anything or everything. Say you agree with ***SEVENTEEN*** or disagree violently, say we're tops, say we're terrible, say anything you please—but say it! [Helen Valentine, *Seventeen*, September 1944, 33 (original emphasis retained)]

Signed with a flourish in her dramatic, distinctive script of stand-up-straight-at-attention letters, *Seventeen*'s editor-in-chief Helen Valentine extended this welcome to the reader in the magazine's very first issue. Valentine's letter, however, was more than a simple "hello." Using carefully chosen words and literary devices, she set the tone and editorial philosophy of the new magazine, guiding her readers' expectations and preparing them for what awaited them in the pages of *their* new magazine.[1]

Helen's letter summarized and ranked the magazine's values. Using bolding and italics, she highlighted the relationship between ***SEVENTEEN*** and ***"you"***—"High School Girls of America." By the use of capital letters, *SEVENTEEN* asserted its authority over the reader, represented in all lower-case lettering ("you"). These style elements were somewhat at odds with the tone of the letter, which stressed nurturance rather than dominance.

An editor's voice becomes part of a magazine's tone—and this is particularly true when the magazine is the editor's own creation.[2] Valentine's use of nurturing words such as "care" and "interested" communicated to the reader that *Seventeen*'s authority emerged out of a benevolent and abiding concern for (and about) the teenage girl. This burgeoning relationship would *not* be like that between a dictator and the dictated—or, perhaps more saliently for the reader, between a parent and a child or a mother and a daughter. Instead, Valentine set the tone for the magazine by speaking to the reader in a way that echoed the dialogue between an older sister and younger sister or favorite aunt and favored niece.[3]

Valentine's letter invited the reader into a quasi-personal relationship; however, she was also negotiating a business relationship. Convincing the teen reader to "buy" into this relationship (and magazine) would require the reader's attention (and—hopefully—subscription). Valentine ended her letter with an appeal for the readership's input—on "anything or everything." Indeed, unlike the typical parent-child relationship, she even gave her permission for the reader to "disagree violently" or "say we're terrible."[4]

Valentine listed the magazine's areas of interest, setting out *Seventeen*'s parameters in bold italicized type, with "how you dress" first, "how you feel and look" second, and "how you think" last. Teens' concern for looks and dress—the body—are the most closely tied to the interests of advertisers (i.e., the clothing and cosmetic industries), the necessary investors for a magazine's economic success. How teens feel and think—psychological and intellectual concerns—are less advertiser-oriented; nevertheless, Helen focused much of her editorial coverage on them.

Valentine's interest in "what you do" offered a bridge between the body and the mind of the reader—as well as between advertiser and editorial interests. Leisure activities such as listening to music, reading a book, and watching a film are both physical *and* cerebral. They also often involve a "buying opportunity"—for an album, novel, theater ticket. It is not surprising, then, that the editorial and advertising content in *Seventeen* routinely encouraged the reader to consume these and other products.

As Valentine explained to the reader, "what you think" and "what you are" had to do with the future of the world and the world's future citizens—her readers as "whole human beings." These concerns shift attention from the individual to the social: interpersonal relationships, community concerns, national responsibilities, or global citizenship. *Seventeen* offered a good deal of advice on these topics during its first few years of publication. Valentine saw teens as adults-in-training and through this letter of introduction, she offered *Seventeen* to the reader as both training ground and personal trainer.

A one-and-a-quarter-page black-and-white photograph accompanied Valentine's letter, illustrating the relationship between the magazine and its readership (Figure 2.1). The focal point of the photograph is a birthday cake with icing that reads "Happy Birthday Seventeen." Three brunettes of varying ages encircle the cake, each classically pretty by white Western European standards. The woman in the middle leans forward and blows out the candles. Judging by her sophisticated coiffure, dark lipstick, and deeply hollowed cheeks, she appears to be well into adulthood. As the representative of *Seventeen,* she commands center stage and takes the most active role in the scene. The two younger women who flank her represent *Seventeen*'s readership. They smile and look on, but they leave the work of blowing out the candles to their older counterpart. The young woman to the left, standing closest to the adult, appears to be in her late teens. To the right, leaning forward toward the cake and into the picture, the youngest girl, apparently in her early teens, wears a pageboy haircut and a ruffled frock—symbols of youth. Of the three women, she stands farthest from the cake, but her body communicates her desire to participate in the festivities. This scene, like

Figure 2.1. September 1944 Seventeen, photographer George Karger

Helen's letter, represented her vision of the relationship between *Seventeen*'s editor and her teenage readership.

That relationship would develop over the next year. The first thirteen issues of *Seventeen*—from birth to first birthday—are of particular interest. First, they offer a look at *Seventeen*'s "baby pictures." Second, it was during these early years that Walter Annenberg allowed Valentine and her staff relatively free rein over the creative direction of the magazine. Finally, they were created during and shaped by World War II.

You *Can* Tell a Book by Its Cover

Picking up a magazine, you first see a cover, which functions as an advertisement for what lies within. What can the covers of the first thirteen issues of *Seventeen* tell us about the magazine? An initial observation is that the original *Seventeen* differed dramatically from the teen and women's magazines of today. Measuring 10 ⅜" by 13 ⅛", the magazine as a material object took up more physical and visual space than contemporary magazines. And in this case, size *does* matter. A large magazine, the size of early *Seventeen,* was unwieldy, designed to be examined in one place—a bed, table, or even the floor—and perhaps by more than one person at a time. Today's smaller magazines, on the other hand, are portable—meant to be toted about in a purse or backpack and examined between other daily tasks and errands.[5]

By contemporary standards, *Seventeen*'s early covers were spare and simple, as illustrated by its debut September 1944 cover (see frontispiece). Photographer Francesco Scavullo's first cover appeared two months later, in November 1944; in the ensuing years, Scavullo would wield considerable artistic control over the cover models and their "look," crafting and portraying the face of both *Seventeen* and the teen girl ideal. For the period from September 1944 through September 1945, twelve of the thirteen covers featured a young woman who looked her "teen" age. While the models were classically pretty by Euro-American standards, it was in a "youthful" (albeit upper class) way. Their skin shone with health, fair as Snow White's and unblemished by the acne that *Seventeen*'s "real girl" readers might battle. Their hair—ranging in shades from golden blond to auburn to dark brown (no platinum blond or raven-haired beauties among them)—was uniformly shoulder-length, smooth, and straight (save for a bit of a flip at the bottom, courtesy of a well-placed curler). Scavullo railed against the home-perm curls marketed in the magazine's advertising pages, and as long as he was in charge of *Seventeen*'s covers, no chemically produced curls would mar his photographs.[6]

Signs of World War II appeared on two of *Seventeen*'s first thirteen covers. The cover of the June 1945 issue features a patriotic theme and departs from the usual layout design. No human appears on this cover. Instead, a letter signed by U.S. military leaders—Generals Arnold, Eisenhower, MacArthur, and Marshall, and Admirals King, Leahy, and Nimitz—is set against a background of deep red, framed on one side by a wreath of starred-and-striped leaves. The letter asks the readership to support their troops and ensure a peaceful future by investing in war bonds. The inside cover acknowledgment, which usually gave buying information for clothing featured on the cover, explains the letter as "a direct appeal from the men who are leading our forces to victory...they ask only our fullest and most realistic support."[7] Although this appeal is patriotic rather than consumer-oriented, it still involves a request from the government and the editorial staff for teens to buy war bonds—to be good citizen consumers.

Figure 2.2. Cover, February 1945 *Seventeen*, photographer James Abbe, Jr.

The cover of the February 1945 issue also addressed the war (Figure 2.2). It features a young woman, the first dark brunette cover model (perhaps darker hair signaling serious subject matter), wearing a blue sweater and matching beret and carrying a Red Cross flag. Behind her, muted images of Red Cross ambulances race across the backdrop. The cover acknowledgment on the title page describes the picture: "The Red Cross, symbol of all that's good in civilization. The banner bearer wears a Vic-Deb fur felt beret designed for SEVENTEEN by Sally Victor, $6.95. The wool sweater has an elegant roll collar and enormous charm, $10.95. The Teen Shop, B. Altman & Co."[8] This cover illustrates *Seventeen*'s exemplary consumer citizen. It was possible (indeed admirable) to be both stylish and patriotic—to wear one's new clothes while doing good works. During the war era in particular, *Seventeen* promoted these two ideologies—consumption and citizenship—to its readership.

Three of *Seventeen*'s first-year issues featured special themes: April 1945's "Girl Meets Boy" issue, June 1945's "Your America" issue, and September 1945's "First Birthday" issue. Sometimes the thematic covers departed from the standard layout. For instance, the Birthday issue included a special cover line noting: "NOW WE ARE ONE YEAR OLD—THANKS TO YOU"; the "Girl Meets Boy" issue shook things up by inviting a boy to join the cover girl in a friendly game of cat's cradle (a string game popular at the time).

Holiday-related issues of *Seventeen* represented youthful beauty "in season." The November 1944 and December 1944 covers celebrated Thanksgiving and Christmas. The November "Thanksgiving" cover (Figure 2.3) features a young woman wearing a brown dress that sets off her deep brown eyes, standing in front of a table spread with nuts, grapes, oranges, apples, and gourds—abundant fruits of the Thanksgiving season. The model's gold charm bracelet shows off both a fashion of the time and her family's affluence. Behind her, a framed painting hangs above the banquet table. Although the picture is blurred, its African folk style and the dark skin of the people portrayed (contrasted against the stark white of their attire) suggests that they are people of color.

According to family sources, Valentine had wanted to include African American girls as models, but Annenberg refused her request.[9] Perhaps Francesco Scavullo, the cover's photographer, shared Valentine's progressive politics and creative vision of a racially integrated *Seventeen*.[10] Whether intentional or not, the juxtaposition of the three main visual elements of this cover—the affluent white girl, the overflowing banquet, and the portrait of "black folk"—creates dissonance. Deliberately or accidentally, Scavullo inserted irony into this particular *Seventeen* cover.

The cover of the December issue displays a similarly colorful—although not at all ironic or dissonant—holiday portrait. Contrasted against the dark green background, a young woman wearing a snow-white gown sits holding

Figure 2.3. Cover, November 1944 Seventeen, photographer Francesco Scavullo

a small white dog with a red bow crowning its head. The dog's red bow and the model's red bow mouth, together with the tree-green backdrop and the pure white dress, signify "Christmas," no words necessary.

Whether spotlighting beauty, fashion, citizenship, relationships, holidays, war, or milestone magazine birthdays, *Seventeen*'s covers reflected the content of the pages to follow. And the number of those pages increased significantly from birth to first birthday. The first issue was eighty-eight pages; twelve issues later, the magazine had almost doubled in size to 168 pages. *Seventeen* boasted in a promotional document from 1945, "Although the baby is only one year old, she certainly is big for her age!"[11]

Looking Inside

During *Seventeen*'s first year, the table of contents listed articles under the topical categories of, from top to bottom, "What You Wear," "How You Look" (expanded to "How You Feel and Look" in June 1945), "Getting Along in the World," "Your Mind," and "Having Fun." In January 1945, "Fiction" was added. The value that *Seventeen* put on each of Valentine's original reader concerns (fashion, beauty and health, self in relation to others, the life of the mind, and activities) can be measured by the magazine's allotment of page space to articles under each of the five original categories in the table of contents. In the first year, *Seventeen* devoted the majority of its editorial space—in almost equal proportion—to articles about "Having Fun," "Your Mind," "What You Wear," and "Getting Along in the World." Articles about "How You Feel and Look" as well as "Fiction" stories, on the other hand, made up a tiny minority of the total discourse (Table 2.1).[12]

The distribution of features in *Seventeen*'s first year reflects a magazine that valued service and citizenship as much as fashion and fun. In fact, the balance between service and fashion could shift toward the former on occasion, especially in *Seventeen*'s special themed issues. For example, the magazine devoted 35 percent of the editorial space in the July 1945 "Your America" issue to articles that fell under the rubric of "Your Mind"—most of them about politics and patriotism. Conversely, "What You Wear" features in this issue fell to just 15 percent of the total editorial content.

The April 1945 "Girl Meets Boy" issue offers a similar example of the influence of a special issue on editorial content. This issue diverged from the norm in that it was written for both girl and boy readers. As the magazine explained in its previous month's issue, "The April issue of SEVENTEEN will be coeducational. The male sex is, after all, as important as the female, so members of both groups are cordially invited to share it."[13] For this issue, the editors reduced features on "What You Wear" to just 15 percent and expanded the features about "Getting Along in the World" to 31 percent. This initial "Girl Meets Boy" issue acknowledged but downplayed

Table 2.1. Editorial Content in Seventeen

	September 1944 to March 1945						
	9/44	10/44	11/44	12/44	1/45	2/45	3/45
Issue Size–	91 pp	95 pp	103 pp	123 pp	123 pp	163 pp	163 pp
Special Issue	First			Xmas			
What You Wear	23%	24%	22%	19%	**24%**	19%	20%
How You Feel/Look	12%	9%	9%	10%	7%	10%	7%
Fiction	0%	0%	0%	0%	10%	9%	12%
Getting/Along/World	15%	23%	19%	20%	20%	21%	**27%**
Your Mind	25%	16%	19%	24%	16%	**22%**	17%
Food & Home	0%	0%	0%	0%	0%	0%	0%
Having Fun	**26%**	**29%**	**31%**	**27%**	23%	19%	17%
Percent of total copy	52.50%	50%	53%	48%	45%	41%	42%

Note: Issue size equals actual page count plus ad space on covers (inside front, inside back, and back cover). Categories receiving the greatest editorial coverage appear in boldface type.

romance, instead stressing the need for young men and women to learn about each other as human beings and "fellow" citizens. Helen Valentine, writing in her article "The World Is Yours," explained the reasoning behind the special "Girl Meets Boy" issue, and directed the readers to specific articles of note:

> This Girl-Meets-Boy Issue of SEVENTEEN tries to help you over a few of the hurdles [. . .] We believe that friendships between boys and girls are not only possible but that these friendships must form a vital part of everyone's life (Are Boys People?, Page 96). We believe that necking is a subject which must be honestly understood and frankly discussed (Star Dust or Indigestion?, Page 97). We believe that boys and girls need to respect and protect their bodies (The Time Is Now, Pages 74 and 75). We believe that the old division between woman's work and man's is beginning to crumble and should disintegrate further (Why Don't Parents Grow Up?. . . Jobs Have No Gender, Page 18; also If He Could Only Cook. . . , Pages 76 and 77). We think that boys and girls should not concentrate too closely on their own tiny group but should think of themselves in relation to all people (A Code for Everyday Living, Pages 64 and 65).[14]

	April 1945 to October 1945						
	4/45	5/45	6/45	7/45	8/45	9/45	Avg
Issue Size–	171 pp	171 pp	171 pp	123 pp	171 pp	171 pp	163 pp
Special Issue	Girl/Boy			America		1st Bday	
What You Wear	15%	16%	19%	15%	26%	25%	20%
How You Feel/Look	7%	5%	9%	8%	8%	6%	8%
Fiction	16%	10%	7%	12%	11%	13%	8%
Getting/Along/World	**31%**	15%	21%	8%	10%	13%	19%
Your Mind	18%	21%	18%	**35%**	**26%**	17%	21%
Food & Home	0%	0%	0%	0%	0%	0%	0%
Having Fun	14%	**32%**	**25%**	21%	20%	**26%**	24%
Percent of total copy	41%	40%	41%	46%	43%	41%	45%

Clothing, Shopping, and Style

While fashion coverage dropped in some special issues, it's not surprising that the August 1945 issue, with its back-to-school focus, had the highest proportion, at 26 percent. Still, this same issue included an equal proportion of articles about "Your Mind." Thus, in the early issues of the magazine, the appeal to fashion did not take precedence over the appeal to service.

"What You Wear" features were generally composed of photographic and/or illustrated fashion spreads of clothing or accessories, often associated with seasons, holidays, or events/venues (school, dates, church, dances, work). These images illustrate teen girl fashion trends of the war period, a time during which dresses and skirted suits were the norm but pantsuits and short sets were also common. The popularity of pants and shorts reflected the influence of war on fashion; apparently, while the "boys" were away, the girls did play—in their left-behind (masculine) clothes. *Seventeen* praised "suits" for their menswear-inspired detailing, tailoring, and fabric. The magazine even counseled readers to raid the closets of their male relatives, as in the fashion spread "Daddy, May I Borrow Your Tie?"[15] The July 1945 frontispiece took the menswear look even further, sailing into a kind of gender-bending fashion fantasy. Picturing a young woman in "pirate pants," the accompanying copy described "Lady pirates" who must have been "done up so . . . with shirt and knee-high pants, girdled by a broad, swashbuckling belt."[16]

The August 1945 issue of *Seventeen,* however, signaled a postwar shift in women's clothing, as fashion designers began to move away from the menswear look toward a hyperfeminine silhouette.[17] Apparently, when military men returned to America, women's call to duty went beyond returning to them their jobs, as well as their comfy suits and pants. *Seventeen*'s fashion feature, "Sweaters Come Into Their Own," heralded this shift, particularly the return of the "female form":

> Up until lately a sweater simply hasn't been chic unless both you and your best friend could get into it simultaneously. It had to come within a quarter-inch of your knees; and if you had any waistline, you kept it a shameful secret. Well, the reprieve has come! We have had the Word that the female form is no longer among the missing. So come out from under that thing you've been tenting in, and see how exceedingly ornamental a sweater can be![18]

From its first issue, *Seventeen* enjoyed and profited from a close and reciprocal relationship with the emerging teen clothing industry. Valentine was so devoted to the success of the teen specialty industry that she restricted *Seventeen*'s fashion pages to teen-sized clothing only. In addition, the magazine routinely published articles like "Are There Skeletons in Your Closet?" which promoted the teen clothing industry to the readership—as well as *Seventeen*'s own efforts on their (both readers' and manufacturers') behalf:

> Until the last few years when high school shops began to crop up in department stores, there had actually been no place for you to buy your clothes. You had certainly left the children's department far behind, but you just as certainly weren't ready to buy your clothes in either the regular misses' departments or the small-sized women's shops. [. . .] there didn't seem to be any alternative for you. Thank goodness there is now. And better still, there will be more and more and more and more, especially when peacetime settles the fabric shortage. We are trying to help you by working closely with the teen-age manufacturers and designers who make the clothes you look so well in. It isn't only the styling of these clothes that makes them right for you and for no other age group. It's the sizing too. The growing and sprouting and developing of the teen-age figure are all carefully considered and catered to

> in the cutting of teen sizes 10 to 16. (Incidentally, don't confuse these with Misses' sizes 10 to 20.) Here, in the editorial pages of *your* magazine, we feature only *your* sizes.[19]

From its first issue, *Seventeen* role-modeled shopping in the monthly "What You Wear" column, "We Go Shopping." In November 1944, the name changed to "Let's Go Shopping," the newfound imperative communicating to the reader that she was definitely invited along. Written by beauty editor Irma Phorylles, "Let's Go Shopping" detailed in narrative form an imaginary teen girl's shopping adventures, which, in an example of "covert advertising," included the names of specific stores and brands purchased.[20] The first installment, for instance, promoted department store Lord & Taylor, as well as other shopping destinations and manufacturers. Written as a dialogue between an (exasperated) teenage daughter and her (exasperating) mother, it begins:

> Mother, do you notice anything different about me? No... my HAT! Well. I know I didn't last year, but ALL the girls are wearing them now! Lord & Taylor has these HEAVENLY knit caps for only $3.95! Oh, and Mummy, wait till you see the bag I bought there to wear with my reefer! It's plaid wool, and carries all my JUNK, and it looks POTS more than $3.95! Well, Bunny had to get warm slippers and robe for boarding school, and she got them right in L & T.[21]

Although usually accompanied by her best friend, Bunny, the April 1945 "Girl Meets Boy" issue found our Teena shopping with her boy pal, Pete. References to boarding school, "Mummy," and a lifestyle that included monthly spending sprees at upscale department stores such as Saks Fifth Avenue (especially under the economic duress of wartime constraints) signaled that this teen shopper lived in an upper-class world. Although many readers might not have lived in a parallel universe, they could at least enjoy the experience vicariously. And for those lucky girls with resources, the column always included ordering information.[22]

Seventeen's editors recognized that not all of its readers could afford to go on the kind of shopping sprees that the ideal "Shopping" Teena enjoyed. For these readers, they offered advice on how to dress frugally yet stylishly. They suggested sewing as a way to afford your clothes and wear them too. The July 1945 fashion spread "Pattern Wardrobe," for example, featured four pages of back-to-school clothes made from patterns and rhetorically asked the reader: "How about making the whole works yourself . . . you save money, besides which you get exactly what you want."[23] In fact, unlike contemporary fashion magazines, *Seventeen* included "patterned" fashions in every issue. This was due in part to a government-led war effort to encourage female "citizen consumers" to sew their own clothes, investing any saved money in war bonds.[24] Helen Valentine even gave a speech on sewing as a valuable skill at a meeting for the "National Junior Sewing Project" held by the American Women's Voluntary Service in April 1945.[25]

Through both fashion spreads and articles, *Seventeen* offered all of its readers, working class through upper class, an education in how to be a good consumer—"good" meaning active, but also thoughtful and responsible. For instance, fashion spreads sometimes promoted economical clothing, such as March 1945's "Cost: All Less Than $12," which featured "good buys" from the Jr. Deb Centre at Macy's.[26] In addition, how-to articles on shopping and building a functional and fashionable wardrobe began appearing in the second half of *Seventeen*'s first year. Articles such as "Clothes Quandary: Its Cause and Cure,"[27] "She Never Has a Thing to Wear,"[28] and "Are There Skeletons in Your Closet?"[29] directed the reader to prepare in advance for her shopping trip by assessing her own body type and figure flaws, inventorying and critiquing her existing wardrobe, and then planning a pragmatic buying strategy that would use her clothing budget to its best advantage. These articles took a balanced approach to buying choices, advising quality over quantity. For example, the February 1945 quiz, "Clothes Harmony," instructed the reader through a series of "correct" answers to "Allot as much money as your budget will stand" for "a major addition to your wardrobe, such as a coat," and generally buy "things with basically good lines and of fabrics that will last for more than one season."[30]

Seventeen's advocacy of responsible consumption was one example of the editors walking a thin line between their consumer and service mandates, advising the reader that fashion was neither all-important nor unimportant. As they state in "Clothes Quandary":

> Stressing clothes and appearance beyond all else would be superficial and silly. It's equally silly to look upon clothes as just something to protect you from the elements. First impressions are not to be sniffed at, and the way you look and dress does either much to get things going smoothly or curdle them from the start. This goes equally for when you're introduced to old family friends, your blind date, or a prospective employer.[31]

Body and Face

While "What You Wear" articles and fashion spreads sold clothing and accessories (body wear), the articles in "How You Feel And Look" sold health and good looks—and the products to achieve them (body care). Although they represented a relatively small percentage of the overall editorial content, the articles that appeared under this heading offered the highest concentration of detailed editorial advice. Often written by beauty editor Irma Phorylles, these articles dispensed health and grooming guidance that covered the body from head ("Acne"[32]) to toe ("Your Feet: Friend or Foe?"[33]), from nutrition ("Lucky Seven"[34]) to diet ("Up and Down the Scale"[35]), and from menstruation ("The Moon and the Mood"[36]) to melanin ("Don't Blister, Sister"[37]). These editorials often stressed the relationship between the body, beauty, and romance.

Seventeen's body advice was moderated by an appreciation for its readership's youth. Beauty articles warned against looking too adult, arguing instead for healthy living, simple cleanliness, and good grooming (and a touch of lipstick). The ideal teenage girl look, as promoted by *Seventeen,* was definitely more virginal than vampish. However, since virginity was a temporary status on the way to marriage (at least in fairy tales), the desire for heterosexual romance underlay much of the body discourse. In addition, the body work encouraged by *Seventeen* often necessitated some sort of product purchase, be it soap, shampoo, or saddle shoes. Thus, consuming was part of a teen girl's body work—perhaps less visible than grooming (it didn't have its own table of contents category) but no less important an endeavor.

According to *Seventeen,* feeling and looking good began with a healthy body—not the anorexic-chic physique of more modern times, but a more accessible fit-and-trim silhouette. Phorylles described the ideal body type, circa 1940s, and the means to achieve it, in her September 1945 article "New Term . . . New You":

> You'd like to have a reasonably small amount of flesh attractively distributed on and according to your bony structure. Firm, clear, healthy flesh. The kind that comes from three definite meals a day with a minimum of feeding between them. [. . .] It is also achieved by a good balance of exercise—tennis, swimming, basketball, or any of the other active sports that keep your outdoors and working hard.[38]

In that same article, Phorylles explained that a "good body" is not a stopping point, but instead a beginning point. The body is merely a canvas; to become a work of art, it must be properly beautified and embellished.

Grooming—the care, maintenance, and proper display of specific body features—must be a full-time "body project"[39]: "Diet and exercise will help you to a better-looking body, and a finer-looking skin, but we aren't going to stop there. Not on your life, we aren't. What about grooming for instance? For a very large instance. Grooming is a smooth, solid picture that is composed of countless little parts."[40]

Teaching girls how to gild their lilies and polish their wares was a significant part of *Seventeen*'s lesson plan. To that end, the January 1945 issue heralded the arrival of an intermittent feature: the beauty makeover. Over the next three months, *Seventeen* ran a series of articles that taught "real girls" how to improve their appearance. Although Helen Valentine mentioned in her September 1944 credo letter the magazine's intent "to give you plenty of pointers on how to build a new you," this series ostensibly arose out of the magazine's response to reader requests. As the editor's note accompanying the first article in the series, "Is That Your Face in the Moon?," explains:

> Your letters are the seeds from which our beauty articles grow. So many of you have asked us what to do for a face which is not a perfect oval, that we are starting a series which will tell you what you want to know. In each article we shall take a different type of face and show you what a famous authority can do with it.[41]

Written by the prolific Phorylles, this series, ironically entitled "Becoming Friends with Your Face," brought in beauty industry professionals such as Elizabeth Arden and Helena Rubinstein to teach the tricks of their trade to the *Seventeen* reader. Photo spreads document the process as these beauty Houdinis waved their mascara wands and—voilà!—transformed the plain Jane face of a real girl into the perfect Teena face of the ideal girl.

Because grooming almost always necessitates the purchase of grooming aids, most of the beauty articles offered somewhat generic product suggestions (lipstick, shampoo, nail polish, and so on) while always admonishing that less is more on a teen girl. Teena's goal was to achieve a look that was neither too much nor too little, but *just right*. On occasion, *Seventeen* recommended actual product brands, but this was not typical, at least early on. However, in January 1945, the magazine introduced a new monthly feature called "Dressing Table Talk," which spotlighted brand-name cosmetics for purchase.[42]

Seventeen's fashion and beauty articles reflected the norms of a fashion magazine, asking the reader to assess herself or her wardrobe and advising her on self-improvement through consumption. However, the remaining table of contents categories focused more on the reader's personality and character, sometimes even challenging the beauty and fashion directives.

Teens in the World

Articles organized under the table of contents section "Getting Along in the World" explored the reader's self in relation to others at home, school, work, and her community, and seem to most closely correspond to Valentine's early reference to "What You Are." These articles offered direct advice on how the teen reader should think and behave in her various venues and relationships. Although some articles covered the expected terrain of contemporary teen magazines, such as boy-girl relations (e.g., "First Date Quiz"[43] and "How Do You Rate as a Date?"[44]), others encouraged the reader to question the status quo, including the existing gender and racial stereotypes and boundaries. For example, while the magazine always counseled respect for one's parents, it also encouraged standing up for one's beliefs—particularly if those beliefs mirrored *Seventeen*'s. Alice Thompson wrote about the merits of a family debate in the July 1945 "For Seniors Only" column, subtitled "It's Not an Easy Thing":

> But if you air your views, whether about your allowance or about world politics, you may find some good mental stimulation in your family's arguments. You may even prod Mother out of her housewifely confines to take a greater interest in history-making events. Or you may help her to rid herself of some worn-out old prejudices. And you may give your whole family a new awareness of the fact that the little girl they remember has grown into a thinking young woman. Then you will be on your *own*!"[45]

The magazine also encouraged the reader to challenge her parents on the issue of gender bias. For example, the March 1945 installment of "Why Don't Parents Grow Up?," subtitled "Jobs Have No Gender," took on the topic of chores, informing the reader that "Preparing food, serving, washing dishes, cleaning the living room and bath—should be shared by *all* the citizens of your home, according to the time and energy each has available."[46] The May 1945 article "Lassies at the Lathe" attacked gender stereotypes at school by featuring a high school carpentry class for girls. As the caption explained:

> The boys guffawed when the senior girls at Teaneck High first started their course in carpentry. But these girls have taken to lathes and band saws with such ease that the tilt-top tables they make look quite professional. They've

made themselves so at home in this corner of an alleged "man's world" that even they are surprised.[47]

This article offers a good example of the sometimes contradictory discourses competing within the pages of *Seventeen* during this first year—in this case between the "feminine beauty" and "gender equality" threads.[48] Although just pages earlier in this same issue, Irma Phorylles wrote about the *vital* importance of nail grooming in her article "Give Me Your Hand," "Lassies at the Lathes" describes "nail polish [as] a constant casualty. A bit of sandpaper, and off it comes. But what's a little nail polish? This work is too fun to worry about such trivialities."[49]

The importance of school and work, and the relationship between the two, was a common thread that ran through every issue of *Seventeen*. Articles about school stressed doing well in high school generally, but also specifically, as with the article "I Can't Work with Figures," which admonished girls to become adept at math.[50] The June 1945 issue featured several articles encouraging college attendance, including "Send Yourself to College" and "State College BA"—an *eleven-page* article detailing the enrollment policies at seventy-four state universities.[51]

Interestingly, although articles about school were common in the first thirteen issues, *Seventeen* actually published more articles on the topic of work during this period. Alice Thompson often addressed employment issues in the "For Seniors Only" column, advising the reader that making a living should be considered de rigueur for all women. From the column's very first installation, Thompson encouraged the magazine's readers to consider careers in such male-dominated fields as medicine, science, law, engineering, and business. In the January 1945 column (subtitled "With Chance for Advancement"), Thompson provided detailed information on entry-level jobs in advertising, public relations, magazine publishing, photography, and costume design that could eventually lead to an upper-echelon position.[52] Such specific career counseling was common in the pages of *Seventeen* during its first year, as was the promotion of employment in fields and positions that were not thought of as female venues, including television production ("Vocation in Video"[53]) and aviation ("Cadet Training Helps Win Wings"[54]). *Seventeen*'s writers also loved to promote the career that they knew best, magazine production ("I Want to Work on a Magazine"[55]). Another job that warranted attention—ostensibly due to reader requests—was modeling. However, *Seventeen*'s article on the topic, "Cover Girl," reads as a cautionary tale; the subheading warns: "Modeling Is a Very Strange Career—The More Popular You Are, The Sooner You're Through."[56] The one "career path" never pitched by *Seventeen* during the first year was homemaking. As twice-married Alice Thompson warned the reader in her very first column:

> What kind of work do you want to do? However "subject to change without notice," you should have more than a hazy idea of how you will earn your living. A marriage license is no longer a stay-at-home guarantee. Your only real security is what you go out and get for yourself.[57]

Seventeen also included articles on money management as a part of "Getting Along in the World"; the writers recited some variation of the following mantra over and over again: School leads to work and work leads to money and money leads to independence. In articles like "Do Your Dollars Act Like Pennies?"[58] *Seventeen* advised the reader on saving strategies and good money sense. In fact, during the war period, the magazine promoted financially responsible consumption as well as a kind of anti-consumption.[59] Financially responsible consumption messages encouraged the reader to shop frugally and thoughtfully, being cognizant of both the value of the product and the money that was used to purchase it. Anti-consumption messages suggested ways for readers to make things from items found in the home and how to care for the things they already owned. For example, "She Never Has a Thing to Wear" gave directions on caring for lingerie, sweaters, different types of fabric, and shoes in order to extend their use.[60]

Finally, "Getting Along in the World," according to *Seventeen*, included the community beyond home, school, and work. The articles that addressed the reader's relationship to her community often related to the war and the changes it wrought. In particular, articles like "First Aid for the Army"[61] and the monthly feature "Serving the U.S." highlighted and encouraged community volunteerism in support of the war. Other articles suggested that the reader keep busy doing good works. Keeping teens properly occupied, in fact, had become a society-wide mandate during this period, the war having exacerbated fears of teen delinquency, fueled by the concern that absent fathers and less parental oversight might lead—or were leading—to juvenile criminal behavior. "Teen canteens" and "teen towns," formal meeting places for youth to gather and socialize after school hours, arose as a solution to this perceived delinquency crisis.[62] *Seventeen* responded with articles about this teen trend, including "How to Swing a Canteen"[63] and "Teen Town at

Jacksonville,"[64] as well as a monthly feature "Next on the Agenda," which debuted in the August 1945 issue.

Articles encouraging excellence of character appeared under both the "Getting Along in the World" and "Your Mind" rubrics and were woven through with a common thread that challenged prejudice and discrimination of any kind. Alice Thompson took on the subject in a special "For ~~Seniors~~ Human Beings Only" column, subtitled "I'm Not Prejudiced, But . . . "[65] Using Nazi Germany as her jumping-off point, she decried *all* prejudices—specifically mentioning those based on gender, religion, race, and national origin—and assigned blame to socialization: "We're brought up to dislike 'wops,' or 'kikes,' or 'micks,' or 'niggers,' or 'bohunks,' or 'Mexes.' Every part of the country has its own set of pet prejudices. Each of us acquires them and they grow stronger as we grow older because it makes you feel good to be better than someone else."[66] Thompson challenged the reader to fight discrimination by considering every human being individually, and not as the member of a group. She ended her essay with an ominous warning that "If we don't stop ourselves, if we can't beat this ugly thing called prejudice, it will catch us all—and that does mean you."[67]

Home. School. Work. Community. These were the parameters of the world as addressed in the articles of "Getting Along in the World." But this was a contained world, ending at the edge of the manicured lawns of middle- and upper-class America. A more realistic title might have been "Getting Along in *Your* World." Or even more accurately, "Getting Along in *Teena's* World"—the world of the ideal U.S. teenager: a world where "home" assumed a house, parents, siblings, and an education in American schools that would lead to the pursuit of the American dream—fulfilling work and fair wages. A social life that included hanging out with friends and dates with boys. The outside world—the world beyond middle-class America, the world of *others*—that was the literary territory covered by the articles in *Seventeen's* categorical section "Your Mind."

The World of the Mind

Written with passion and sincerity, often by *Seventeen* principals such as Helen Valentine and Alice Thompson, the articles in "Your Mind" urged the reader to notice the world beyond her own, the world not covered in "Getting Along in the World," the world of ideas and diversity. Simultaneously staunchly Americanist and expansively global, these articles were shaped and informed by World War II, as seen through the prism of editor Valentine. The "Your Mind" articles were guided by the ideals of a "higher calling" and "citizenship," shifting focus from "what's best for me and my world" to "what's best for America and the world." Thus, with an almost evangelistic fervor, *Seventeen* exhorted its readers to be the best American and *global* citizens that they could be.

Seventeen preached overcoming prejudice as a necessary element of good citizenship. As one strategy to achieving this end, the writers encouraged their readers to stray from their comfort zones (even if just in the abstract) and to meet and get to know people who were "different" from themselves (or, more correctly, from the assumed reader-self: a middle-class American white girl). Articles under the "Your Mind" rubric facilitated these introductions by featuring people whom the typical reader would not likely meet in her own home town. For example, *Seventeen* ran a series of articles that highlighted the lives of high school girls in other countries—or, more specifically, in the United States' war-allied countries, regions, and territories: first Great Britain, followed by China, Russia, India, France, Latin America, Canada, Turkey, Hawaii, and Sweden.[68] These articles detailed the lives of girls from other places, including their war work, schooling, family structures, gender roles, and career aspirations, as well as less serious topics such as social lives and—when applicable—boy-girl relationships (in many of the countries, romantic relationships were not condoned until adulthood). In that vein, the feature on Hawaiian girls had a very interesting—and progressive—take on ethnic intermarriage, stating, "Many generations of intermarriage of all races and nationalities have produced a polygenetic people. There is no race prejudice or discrimination among the Orientals, Caucasians and Polynesians represented. There isn't even a realization that they represent the most democratic of all melting pots."[69]

In the near future, this kind of discourse, positively portraying the breaking down of ethnic/racial boundaries, would create considerable dissonance between liberal-leaning Helen Valentine and her conservative publisher, Walter Annenberg.[70] But in the early years of the magazine, under Valentine's direction and especially during the war, the progressive discourse prevailed. On the other hand, the magazine trod lightly when it came to illustrating racial desegregation. Pictures of dark-skinned "foreigners" (such as the girls-in-other-countries series) were often the only counterpoint to the light-skinned American "Teenas" who dominated the fashion photographic landscape of *Seventeen*. The first picture of a nonwhite American girl appeared in the March 1945 issue, in an article about the School of American Ballet featuring a small inset photo of "willowy, vital Betty Nichols, pretty negro girl [and] dancer in Billy Rose's 'Carmen Jones.'"[71]

The "Your Mind" monthly feature "Teens in the News" also offered an occasional opening for pictures of American teens of color. For example, the April 1945 installment featured a paragraph about and picture of Chinese American teens, writer Christina Chan and her artist brother, Plato Chan. Two months later, "Teens in the News" highlighted African American teen Thelma Porter, winner of a beauty-charm contest in her New York borough of Brooklyn.[72] And in this same issue, an article about canning included a small inset picture of a young African American woman at work.[73] Valentine's insistence on the inclusion of pictures of African American teenagers, however minimal, would become a point of contention between her and Annenberg in the intervening months and years.

When *Seventeen* spoke of overcoming prejudice, it seemed to speak to a generalized readership of young white women. However, an article about battling prejudice elicited a response from a reader that reminds us that this wasn't always the case. "T. F." from Chicago wrote: "I've just finished reading the article 'What Kind of a World Do You Want?' I wish I could really tell you how I feel. You see, I'm a Negro and my people are one of the many victims of prejudice."

T. F. thanked *Seventeen* for printing the article, which she said helped her to better understand the mechanics of prejudice, but she also included a suggestion, challenging the editors to go even further in their fight against ignorance and discrimination: "Could you have an article written on the part the colored boys are taking in this war? They're not all smiles the way pictures show them. They work hard. They sweat and shed blood, too. They give their lives, and above all, they're human."[74]

Seventeen's war and citizenship discourses were often intertwined; Valentine's December 1944 frontispiece essay, "First Christmas," offers a great example of this:

> Here it is—SEVENTEEN's first Christmas, but somehow the usual greetings choke in our throat. It isn't easy to sing out a merry message when the world is saddened by separations and destruction and death. But, like the star that once brightened a dark sky, hope shines again in the eyes of those who have been liberated from the prison of Fascism. Fortunately, for them and for us, valor toughens the spirit of those who fight against oppression—confident

> that freedom is close at hand. This Christmas let us celebrate by giving friendship—and understanding—to people of all faiths in all parts of the world. Let us send them help and comfort and love, so that they may know they have brothers and sisters across the sea. This new-found sense of universal kinship should do much to gladden us now and make merry the peacetime Christmases to come.[75]

One aspect of diversity that did not receive much coverage in *Seventeen* Magazine was Judaism or Jewishness. Despite the fact that Annenberg, Valentine, and many of the magazine's staffers were of Jewish heritage, there was no seasonal Hanukkah magazine cover and few warnings against anti-Semitism. Gender and race prejudice could, seemingly, be challenged—but not the religious dominance of Christianity in America.

Numerous articles in the "Your Mind" section focused on the war, their titles asking the reader questions such as "What Are You Doing About the War?"[76] and "Military Training—Should It Be Compulsory?"[77] Liberally (in both senses of the word) doling out information on the political process, *Seventeen* informed the reader about the importance of voting,[78] a free press,[79] and the "Community Forum" movement.[80] A proponent of the creation and development of the United Nations, *Seventeen* published a detailed exposition of the Dumbarton Oaks plan.[81] In addition, John Ashworth, a propaganda analyst for the Office of War Information, wrote a series of articles for *Seventeen* on the UN and related political topics, including "Discussing Our Foreign Policy,"[82] "The Bretton Woods Plan,"[83] "The Fight Against Inflation,"[84] and "Blueprint for a Better World."[88] Although the U.S. government issued Ashworth's day-job paycheck, *Seventeen* assured the reader that "When he writes for SEVENTEEN, he expresses his own views, of course, and not those of the Government."[86]

Seventeen neglected to mention, however, that during the war, the government was routinely expressing its views to magazine editors through the *Magazine War Guide (MWG)*.[89] Some of the government's promoted topics that received corresponding coverage in *Seventeen* during this period included high school graduation,[90] canning,[91] inflation,[92] home safety,[93] Christmas mail to the troops,[94] Red Cross membership,[95] nurse recruitment,[96] teacher recruitment,[97] the Dumbarton Oaks plan,[98] and victory garden farming.[99] One *MWG*-suggested topic that did not receive coverage in *Seventeen,* despite its seeming relevance, was the increase in venereal diseases in the under-twenty population. *Seventeen* apparently drew the line at such explicit sex education in its own "war work." And while *Seventeen* definitely accommodated the government with the inclusion of articles addressing suggested topics, they still represented a tiny percentage of the magazine's articles.

Finally, the "Your Mind" section included somewhat lighter fare, such as book and music review columns and articles about "high culture" and science. Books recommended in *Seventeen*'s monthly literary review column covered the same topical territory as the magazine itself. The recommendations ran the gamut from fiction to nonfiction and from serious topics of history, politics, and career exploration to the fluffier fare of etiquette, popular culture, and romance. Still, the magazine occasionally exhibited a judgmental attitude about what constituted valuable reading material, taking a stand against silly mindless frivolity and for serious cerebral heft. Take, for example, this excerpt from the April 1945 "Books" column, which sounds as if it were written by a prudish Marxist librarian:

> The word "Escapist" is a popular polysyllable meaning "Read 'em and Leave 'em." "Flip Through 'em and Forget 'em." As a matter of fact a *lot* of those "one night stand" books that you see at the Little Booke Nooke Around the Corner would be better off if they were carefully collected by the Boy Scout Waste Paper Squad, and dumped back into the hopper for another try. For there's actually enough opiate content on most public book-shelves today to put us all into a comotose [sic] state for the rest of our lives.[100]

Girls Just Want to Have Fun

Of course, sometimes even the most serious, goal-oriented teens had to have some fun, so *Seventeen* also included monthly features on entertainment and entertaining, as well as comics and puzzles, all grouped under the rubric of "Having Fun." The backbone of this substantial section was its monthly features, which included "Mental Gymnasium" (brainteasers), the music and film review columns "Music on a Platter" and "*Seventeen* Selects," "Radio Column," and a comic by artist Betty Betz and fiction editor Anne Clark that humorously educated the readership in how *not* to behave in problem situations (starring a bumbling "anti-Teena"). The August 1945 comic, "This Couldn't Possibly Be You," offers a great illustration of the overall series (Figure 2.4), beginning with its captioned poem:

As soon as school begins you find
Your class contains girls of the kind
Framed here for everyone to view—
We're awfully glad they are not you![101]

Some of the monthly features that first appeared in the "Having Fun" category were holdovers from *Stardom* magazine that disappeared as *Seventeen* grew into its own identity. For example, the first issue of *Seventeen* featured a *Stardom* celebrity column entitled "Hollywood Table Talk" but it vanished within months. Another *Stardom* holdover, the movie review column, was retained, but under the new name of "*Seventeen* Selects." Although *Stardom*'s entertainment-industry focus diminished considerably under *Seventeen*'s editorship, *Stardom*'s legacy continued on in the "Having Fun" articles on the lives and careers of the era's most popular entertainers. These articles gave readers a peek into the lives of two rather different groups: famous male entertainers and teenage girl actresses (or the teenage daughters of adult entertainers). Dixon Gayer, who wrote *Seventeen*'s music review column, "Music on a Platter," also interviewed and wrote articles about jazz musicians such as Xavier Cugat, Cab Calloway, Woody Herman, Charlie Spivak, Hal McIntyre, Artie Shaw, and Louis Prima.[102] Because many of these artists were men of color, their pictures introduced some racial and ethnic diversity into *Seventeen*'s photographic landscape.

The "Having Fun" section illuminated *Seventeen*'s distinction between activities done for the sake of enjoyment and activities that were considered "work." Activities that might be considered pleasurable—grooming, shopping, relationships, and reading—appear *not* in the "Having Fun" section but in other sections, portrayed not as leisure activities but as forms of labor that needed to be pursued in order to achieve ideal femininity. *Seventeen* also identified different kinds of work as fun. For example, celebrity articles almost always represented paid labor in the entertainment industry as both glamorous and enjoyable[103]—but less flashy occupations also qualified as fun. The May 1945 article "What a Way to Earn a Living!" highlighted eleven workers (more than half of them women) engaged in interesting work in the sciences.[104] Finally, *Seventeen*'s editors presented their own work as fulfilling and enjoyable, as in the "First Birthday" issue article "Editors Are Frequently People"[105] (Figure 2.5).

In its first year, *Seventeen* also framed the work of the home as fun—a leisure endeavor, rather than a required task. Cooking, in particular, was presented as something that teens did for enjoyment. Included among the entertainment articles of "Having Fun" was the intermittent feature "*Seven-*

Figure 2.4. "This Couldn't Possibly Be You," August 1945 *Seventeen*

Drawing captions

1. You know *you* wouldn't comb your hair / When you're at luncheon *any*where!
2. Her dress might do for masquerade— / At school it does not make the grade
3. What makes her think school is the place / For frou-frou, flowers, bows and lace?
4. You know by now that she is clever— / Must she go on and on forever?

Figure 2.4. *(continued)*

5. She numbs your ears with tales of fun / She had beneath last summer's sun

6. There goes the snob, with nose on high. / Than be like her, you'd rather die!

7. Each lad she sees must be her beau. / She cannot bear to let one go

8. Soft words and gifts are not the way / To get a "D" mark changed to "A"

Figure 2.5. "Editors Are Frequently People," September 1945 *Seventeen*, photographer Francesco Scavullo

Drawing captions

1. Maybe you thought Helen Valentine was a platinum-plated Lady in the Dark, barricaded behind mink-lined doors... Well, surprise!... she has a giggle and a granddaughter!
2. Hillebrande the Haughty, Eleanor the Elegant... bejeweled, bored... is actually happiest in shorts walking her cocker spaniel at her dream of a farmhouse up in Connecticut
3. You probably had her down as a burly, brutal type with a bullwhip. Well, kiddies, Charlotte Ware is little and lush, and her artist husband (now in China) calls her peanut!
4. You can stop looking for I. Phorylles in a cloud of incense and fancy bubble baths. Irma likes frou-frou along with the best of you, but her favorite fragrance is of boots and saddles

teen Cooks," in which teens were invited into "Macy's Home Centre" to test recipes, often for parties or festive events. Following the editors' assertion that "chores have no gender," *Seventeen* invited boys into the kitchen, too, for an opportunity to prepare and serve food to an audience of girls. Through this experience boys learned that cooking could be enjoyable; as one young man exclaimed, "I never thought I'd make a salad—and like it."[106]

The reader could expect to find stability and continuity in the organization of the magazine's table of contents—with the exception of one issue. *Seventeen*'s December 1944 issue expanded to include a special category entitled "Gift Ideas," which featured seven articles with suggestions for Christmas presents to give and to request. As noted above, this December holiday issue included no mention of Hanukkah, despite the shared Jewish heritage of editor Valentine and publisher Annenberg. *Seventeen*'s world mirrored the world in which it was created and produced—an American society whose roots were firmly entrenched in a kind of generalized Christianity that pervaded and propelled both culture and commerce.

Seventeen's Magazine's First Birthday

In celebration of *Seventeen*'s first birthday, Triangle Publications hosted a "birthday anniversary" cocktail party for staff and advertisers at the Waldorf-Astoria Hotel in New York City, extending an open invitation in the *New York Times*.[107] In the magazine's September 1945 "Birthday" issue, Helen Valentine revisited her introductory letter from the September 1944 issue and reflected back over the past twelve months, reviewing the promises made in her early credo. Again using creative literary devices to communicate her message to the reader, Valentine reprinted the original letter in italics and identified her "current" thoughts in regular type.

> ***Happy Birthday***
>
> In my right hand a pencil—in my left a slice of the birthday cake you see on the opposite page. And in my heart a warm feeling of gratitude that our first birthday has brought SEVENTEEN so many friends. You've made it a busy but wonderful year. We sometimes wonder what gave us the courage and incentive to start SEVENTEEN. Probably it was the deep-seated conviction that you high school girls really needed, really wanted a magazine of your own—the very special kind of magazine which we outlined in our original credo:

***SEVENTEEN** is interested only in you—and in everything that concerns, excites, annoys, pleases or perplexes you.* We still are—and always will be!

***SEVENTEEN** is interested in **how you dress**. We're not much on the tricky stuff, but we believe clothes must be right for you and the time, place and occasion for which you'll wear them.* We tried to live up to this. We hope you liked our fashions.

*We care about **how you feel and how you look.** Those two always go together. Keats said "Truth is Beauty." We have no quarrel with that—but for practical purposes health is beauty. With good health as a beginning, we hope to give you plenty of pointers on how to build a new you—which, if it doesn't knock 'em cold, at least will make people pleasantly aware of you as a person.* Well, have we been of any help? Your letters seem to say yes.

But, to our way of thinking far more important, we've tried to be useful in other ways too. A year ago this month we said to you:

***SEVENTEEN** is interested in **what you do.** Are you a music fiend, a bookworm, a movie fan? Do you like art, history, poetry or humor? Do you squander your leisure, or do you consider time a precious commodity*? Today, with all there is to do, this last question seems to be doubly pertinent.

*We're keenly interested in **what you think.** Are you so baffled by the confusions of reality that you take refuge in a world of your own? Or do you feel that the world is your oyster— just waiting to be opened and produce its pearl*? In fact, have you that knife right at hand? It's time to start prying.

*But—most important of all—**SEVENTEEN** is interested in **what you are**... the kind of human being you are. Are you tense and ill-at-ease or comfortable and relaxed? Have you a chip on your shoulder or a smile on your lips? Are you interested only in yourself and your closest family and friends, or do you care what happens to people you'll never see*? We'd all *better* care about all peoples, now that we know it's really one world! And in that very first issue I reminded you that you are going to have to run this world of ours—so the sooner you start thinking about it the better. From the thousands of letters you have sent us I would say that you *are* thinking about it—and thinking straight. You're interested in boys and books, clothes and current events, people and politics, cooking and careers... in fact, you're interested in everything. Your curiosity about your world and everybody in it has made our job easier, happier. We like finding out that reprint orders for the Dumbarton Oaks article have kept pace with requests for dress patterns... that you like to read about *both* Toscanini and Harry James.

> Our hope for a better world rests with you. We know you'll do a good job. Every member of our staff wishes you well and thanks you warmly for making this such a very happy birthday—H.V.[108]

Thus, a year went by at *Seventeen* magazine—a very eventful year for the United States and the world beyond, one that included the death of President Franklin Delano Roosevelt, the new presidency of Harry S. Truman, the dropping of the atomic bomb on Japan, and the end of the Second World War. It was also a year that saw the creation of our fledgling magazine, *Seventeen*. Although the "teen-ager" existed prior to *Seventeen*'s entry into the marketplace, the two developed somewhat in tandem thereafter, with *Seventeen* presenting itself as an authority on the teen girl ideal and offering copious amounts of direction on its achievement.

Several factors influenced the magazine's early content and its depiction of the ideal teen girl, among them the editorial vision of editor-in-chief Helen Valentine, the environment of World War II, and the economics of running a financially solvent magazine. Valentine's vision was informed by her own experience as a working wife and mother and by her progressive politics. Approaching her readership as thoughtful, teachable young women, she schooled them in the values that had served her own life well: education, career, family, community service, gender equality, universal kinship—as well as charm and style.

World War II offered an ideal environment for Valentine's progressive doctrine to express itself in the pages of *Seventeen*. The war created opportunities that, for its duration, made gender and racial boundaries more permeable, certainly in regard to occupational opportunities and ideologies of "brotherhood" across nations. On the other hand, some boundaries stood firm—including the relative invisibility of Jews and Judaism in the magazine's text. While *Seventeen* included occasional pictures of teens and adults of color, the magazine's "Teenas" were always white—and celebrated Christmas, not Hanukkah. While Walter Annenberg would soon take it upon himself to patrol the magazine's color barrier, it was a barrier not of his making but one that already existed in American society; as *Seventeen*'s financial manager, one of his primary concerns was not to offend advertisers.[109]

Indeed, *Seventeen* had to be financially successful in order to continue to thrive, and advertisers held the key to the magazine's success. Thus, an immediate need in ensuring *Seventeen*'s growth was handed over to a "nanny" to capture the attention and economic support of business. And that's where Estelle Ellis and her promotional campaign came in.

CHAPTER 3

Teena Goes to Market

Seventeen Magazine Sells the Ideal Consumer to Business[1]

> And this was really a wilderness time, it was like discovering a whole new country. Because there was no awareness—not only of teenagers—but there was no awareness of teenage girls, there was no awareness of how they dressed, or the clothes they needed. There wasn't even anyone producing clothes for this age group. There were no cosmetics being created for this age group. So it's hard to believe it, but at that time, it was totally . . . new terrain. New territory, new country to be discovered.[2] [Estelle Ellis, *Seventeen* magazine's first promotion director]

Seventeen staffers ventured into the "wilderness" of the 1940s, promoting the concept of the teenage girl in numerous venues and to different constituencies. In the magazine, they advised the high school reader on how to be an ideal teen girl. But *Seventeen* also promoted the teen girl through its education of adults, particularly those in the advertising and retail industries. Because the magazine could not succeed without the financial support of advertisers, selling businesses on the idea of the teen girl as a consumer was among the first tasks at hand.

Seventeen's young promotion director, Estelle Ellis, served as liaison between the magazine and the business community, developing a campaign that introduced the teen girl to business(men), a match that, it was hoped, would lead to a long-term relationship between buyer and seller. For their part in raising awareness of teens as consumers, the original *Seventeen* staffers can claim (and have claimed) their place in the conception of the contemporary youth culture. As Ellis unequivocally states in her business materials: "*Seventeen*'s phenomenal publishing success created an awareness of the burgeoning youth market, setting off the 'youth quake' that reverberated throughout the second half of the twentieth century."[3]

Meet Estelle Ellis

Although they shared a common Jewish heritage and both were born of immigrant parents, Estelle Ellis's family background was very different from that of *Seventeen*'s editor, Helen Valentine, and publisher, Walter Annenberg. Valentine was born and raised in affluent Manhattan; Annenberg spent his adolescence in a Long Island mansion. Ellis, on the other hand, grew up in a working class neighborhood in Brooklyn, where her father, Russian immigrant Peter Ellis, worked as an electrician, and her mother, Latvian immigrant Bessie Caplan, ran her own in-home sewing business.[4]

Peter and Bessie raised Estelle and her sister during the Depression years when, for many Americans, work and money were scarce. Perhaps because of this, Estelle never questioned whether she would eventually work or not; from her vantage point as a young working class woman, paid employment was a fact of life. Certainly, as opposed to Helen Valentine, she didn't have the luxury of contemplating the "choice" between being a homemaker or a "working girl." But she was also influenced by Bessie, who raised her daughter to be a "careerist," that period's term for a working woman.

Popular culture provided another source of inspiration for Estelle. The 1930s and '40s produced a plethora of literature and movies with positive "careerist" role models, and actresses such as Katharine Hepburn (in *The Philadelphia Story* and *Adam's Rib*), Greer Garson (in *Pride and Prejudice*), Judy Garland (in *The Wizard of Oz*), Myrna Loy (in *The Thin Man* series), and Vivien Leigh (in *Gone with the Wind*) portrayed characters who were strong, smart, sassy, and savvy. Estelle aspired to be a "girl reporter" like those she watched in the films of her adolescence, the most famous one being Hildy Johnson, played by Rosalind Russell in the 1940 classic film *His Girl Friday*.[5]

While Estelle dreamed of a future based on what she saw on the movie screen, her goals for her immediate future were more pragmatic. Although neither of her parents had much formal schooling, her mother encouraged Estelle to pursue higher education, which Estelle saw as a means to an end: employment. She approached her decision to attend Hunter College in New York City in a no-nonsense way; as she later recalled:

> I was the first child in the family to get to college and I was part of a generation that was not sensitive to the issues of does a women work or doesn't a woman work. The fact that I got to college certainly carried with it the promise that I would quickly earn some income to be able to help support

> my family, my mother and father, and so at no point was there any question about whether or not I would work.[6]

Ellis's experience as a student at Hunter differed significantly from Valentine's experience at prestigious Barnard College. At the time of Ellis's enrollment, Hunter's "campus" was strewn across the city and students had to trek from site to site in order to attend classes. Ellis recalls her college years as laborious (versus glorious):

> [I] traveled by subway to Hunter College, before they had one building. Went all the way up to the Bronx, then went to a factory building here on Park Avenue. It was murderous. I have no sense of having gone to a college. Going to my classroom was like going to Macy's on Thursday night when I worked there, I mean it was no different. I can't even begin to tell you anything about my college years because all I was was a drone.[7]

Ellis graduated from Hunter in June of 1940 with a political science major and journalism minor. While there, she met Samuel Rubinstein, the man she married. Her first job out of Hunter was as the assistant—or as Ellis describes it, "Girl Friday"—to the promotion director of *Popular Science* magazine.[8] This job was the first in a more than half-century-long career in marketing and promotions.

Popular Science became Ellis's "classroom" where she was introduced to marketing ideas and strategies that she would later apply in her work as promotion director at *Seventeen.* In particular, she learned about the emerging concept of magazine genres and their role in the targeting of specific audiences.[9] She also observed the strategy of getting educators to use magazines as teaching tools, an idea she imported while at *Seventeen.* In her oral history, Ellis describes her education in marketing at *Popular Science*:

> The man who was the president of *Popular Science* Publishing Corp understood the value of having a magazine that schools could relate to and he was very jealous of the position that *Mademoiselle* had as a magazine for college girls and he observed that and he determined that the time had come to produce a magazine for high school girls and he thought that the same logic would apply. He would instead relate to home economics classes and he would have his in with educators and he'd be able to tell advertisers that he could reach young women in high school and he would then be able to reap the benefit of the early recognition that the young woman consumer was a valuable person to be marketing products to.[10]

Using *Mademoiselle* as an exemplar, *Popular Science* spun off *Design for Living* magazine in September 1941, targeting high school girls, home economics teachers, and advertisers. Ellis was recruited to assist *Design for Living*'s editor, Tess Buxton. As Ellis explains, her value to the new enterprise was based on her youth: "[S]ince I was the only young face around there, he let this lady borrow me to become her promotional assistant or to do her promotion for *Design for Living,* identifying me with the age group."[11]

Ellis loved her work in promotions so much that she referred to herself as a "promotion groupie."[12] And as groupies are wont to do, she sought out models of excellence to emulate. It was during this period that Ellis discovered and began following the work of Helen Valentine, promotion director at *Mademoiselle.* As she describes it: "But I, during this period already, had some sense of the fact that *Mademoiselle* had the best promotion director of them all. [. . .] I began to collect all her promotion material, this lady called Helen Valentine."[13]

Unfortunately for Ellis and the staff of *Design for Living,* the magazine published only four issues before the bombing of Pearl Harbor precipitated restrictions on the use of paper. Ellis then found a job as an advertising copywriter—not her first choice in work. She dreamed of promoting one of the elite fashion magazines produced by the prestigious publication houses of that time period, particularly Street & Smith (publisher of *Mademoiselle* and *Charm*) and Condé Nast (publisher of *Glamour* and *Vogue*). According to Ellis, however, these types of jobs were out of her reach, for reasons that had nothing to do with her talent, drive, or intellect:

> I can look back and think that I wasn't of the social class or of the religious persuasion that they were looking for. [. . .] But the point was, I was also not of the social class. They were hiring debutantes. As you know, in those days they were hiring rich kids out of the Ivy League schools who were very happy to work for practically nothing to be part of the chic world of the fashion magazine. [. . .] Well, I was a kid from Brooklyn with a big behind and no knowledge of what social smarts were. I wasn't their candidate. [. . .] A kid who came from Brooklyn didn't get a job at Condé Nast or Street and Smith.[14]

This class-related employment pattern persists; today, entry-level jobs at women's fashion magazines continue to be filled by young upper-class women whose family finances can supplement their otherwise meager salaries.[15] But while Ellis's working class origins may have slowed her progress into the elite world of fashion magazines, she was not stopped. She developed a persona that communicated education and good breeding and often enabled her to "pass" for someone from a completely different background. As she explains in her oral history:

> I never sounded like a Jewish kid from Brooklyn . . . You might say how the hell did I ever develop this voice and this diction and the way I talk, which makes so many people who meet me from out of town (because I did a lot of traveling in my business career) say, "You cannot have come from New York." You know, they just assume that I came from somewhere else because I don't speak as a New Yorker nor as a Jewish person from Brooklyn.[16]

Ellis re-entered the magazine publishing world with a job at Walter Annenberg's Triangle Publications. Initially hired as the fashion and beauty editor at *Screen Guide*, a movie magazine, Ellis was soon promoted to women's editor of photomagazine *Click*. At *Click* she had her first glimpse into Annenberg's quest to repair his family's reputation:

> You know, the whole thing [*Click* magazine] was instituted to create a respectability for a publication that the advertising agencies in this country were not taking seriously. Number one, because of its heritage, and number two, because Walter Annenberg was identified with racing form publishing.[17]

Ellis learned a lot about the magazine business at *Click*, but her most important life-changing event occurred in a chance meeting in a building elevator when she found herself face-to-face with her professional idol, Helen Valentine. The story of how twenty-five-year-old Estelle Ellis met fifty-one-year-old Helen Valentine has become so much a part of Ellis's own historical lore that she tells it often. She begins the story at her own beginning, at a place and time when Valentine had just been hired by Annenberg to edit Triangle's newest publication, *Seventeen* magazine:

> And that was the beginning. And there I was, in that area where she [Valentine] started her magazine, and by somebody looking out after my good interests up there, I met her—this woman who I had been dying to work for and never was allowed to meet—on an elevator, and I told her with what passion I viewed her work and she said, "What do you do?" and I told her and she said, "I'd like to see your stuff." So the next morning I showed her my stuff and the next thing I knew I was hired to become the first promotion director of *Seventeen* and I worked with this woman for 13 years. The first issue we put out together was September 1944 and it was the first issue of *Seventeen* and that's really where it begins for me.[18]

Selling the Teen Girl as a Consumer

Ellis's job as promotion director at *Seventeen* involved developing the sales campaign for the magazine; her mandate was to define and communicate the importance of the teenage girl/market to business.[19] Her approach to the campaign was innovative for its time, and drew from the lessons learned by both herself and Helen Valentine in their previous experiences at other magazines. In particular, Valentine benefited from seeing the economic windfall of identifying and targeting the market demographic of college-age women at *Mademoiselle*. *Seventeen* magazine imported this strategy and applied it to their high school–aged "younger sisters."

In contrast to their publishing competition, *Seventeen* and *Mademoiselle* paid close attention to their consumer, and they urged business to do the same: "Retailer," they implored through their promotional campaigns, "know thy buyer." Ellis describes the shift in focus from merchandising to marketing as the difference between a producer orientation and a consumer orientation. "Merchandising," she explains, "is solving problems by thinking of products, not people; marketing is making the human connection."[20] This marketing perspective allowed *Seventeen*'s creators, and particularly Ellis and the promotion staff, to view their role in introducing business to the teen girl consumer (and vice versa) as an altruistic endeavor—an extension of the original service mission of the magazine. Ultimately, as Ellis sees it retrospectively, they were meeting the needs of both businesspeople and teenage girls. She explains:

> [W]e were helping corporations move away from their production-orientation and we were helping them grow their business by thinking of consumers and not thinking only in terms of the equipment that they had and the products they could produce, but rather insisting that they evaluate what people need and then they should produce that. And we said that was the difference between consumer-orientation and production-orientation and it was reshaping industry.[21]

But serving business was only half the equation. According to Ellis, *Seventeen* was also extending a service to the teenage girl consumer by "seeing people and translating people's wants and needs and patterns of life and their value base and their priorities and translating that in terms of who needs what now."[22] From Ellis's perspective, she was in the business of helping teen girls receive what they wanted and needed—products, but also cultural identity and value in a society that was moving from a producer-driven to a consumer-driven economy.

Ellis's position as promotion director required her to communicate a twofold (and sometimes contradictory) message about *Seventeen* and its teen readership. First, she had to inform businesspeople about the editorial mission of the magazine, with its vision of teen girls as "whole human beings"; then, she had to sell them on the teenage girls as consumers: of clothing, cosmetics, food, and entertainment. As promotion director, Ellis remembers being given considerable input into the magazine's editorial direction, despite the fact that her position technically fell on the advertising side of the office:

> Now, ordinarily promotion directors don't get a chance to do anything except hype a magazine, but *Helen* understood right from—and that's why she wanted me—Helen knew that if I was part, an integral part of her vision for this magazine, that I would be a translator of her ideas to businessmen who weren't reading any of these magazines and who certainly didn't, you know, have *any idea* about what this market was about. So she said she wanted me to be the translator—which meant that I was an integral part of the editorial development of this magazine right from the start, which was a very rare thing for anyone in promotions, 'cause sometimes promotion was on one side, editorial was another, and there was a kind of a snobbery. But in this case, in Helen's case, since Helen herself came out of promotions, she recognized that what I could do for her was to articulate . . . our vision.[23]

When Ellis speaks of "our vision," she refers to herself and Valentine. But where was Walter Annenberg's vision in the creation and promotion of *Seventeen*? Annenberg had previously articulated his own vision of *Seventeen* as a "wholesome" magazine, and one area where he had considerable input was that of advertising. From the beginning, Annenberg set restrictions for what kinds of advertisements the magazine would accept for publication. He deemed liquor, beer, and cigarette ads as unacceptable. Similarly, he nixed ads for hotel honeymoon suites and bridal gowns—both of which he thought might signal an encouragement of early marriage. He okayed cosmetics ads, but rejected hair dye ads, rationalizing that while makeup could be washed off (at a parent's request), dye was (semi)permanent. As Annenberg later explained, "To me, not having that advertising was a matter of character. And it was good business. Parents, especially mothers, liked having their daughters reading *Seventeen*."[24]

According to Ellis, Annenberg's relationship to *Seventeen* made for a harder and more confusing sell to advertisers, who often couldn't reconcile *Seventeen*'s wholesome mandate with the Annenberg family's rather unsavory publishing reputation. The memory seems to amuse her: "[Annenberg] owned the *Philadelphia Inquirer* and *Racing Form*. And [advertisers] kept saying, you know, as a matter of fact, one of the funny parts was, "How can we take you seriously, you'll put in a racing form in the middle of *Seventeen*! [*laugh*]"[25] Ultimately, however, this was somewhat of a moot point, since retailers and advertisers were less concerned about the editorial mission of the magazine than they were about the magazine's readership—and what that readership could do for them. Thus, Ellis's most important sale was of teen girls as consumers.

In order to establish their consumer identities, Ellis had to articulate teen girls' buying preferences to retailers and advertisers. This mandate relates back to *Seventeen*'s marketing philosophy. Instead of saying to retailers, "You make [name your product] and we can sell it to teen girls," *Seventeen* said, "Teen girls need [name the product] and if you make it, they will buy it." According to Ellis, this consumer-focused marketing approach—a strategy that *Seventeen* took directly from the playbook of *Mademoiselle*—was particularly innovative for the time. She uses the metaphor of a "loop" to explain how it worked:

> I traveled the entire country from coast to coast, banging on doors, seeing not only advertising agencies and telling the story of young women, but I was telling the story also to retailers. And making that loop which was critical since they had no business—there was no industry creating clothes or cosmetics and [Valentine] knew that this was the *mother lode* of business, that if we could *persuade* industry that this was a market that they should respect, that we would get the kind of advertising that would sustain this publication, even as it was sustaining and making prosperous *Mademoiselle* with college girls. *But* the lovely loop was, how do you tell this to department stores [*voice becomes loud*] who do not *allow* teen-agers to come into the stores because they're not, they don't see them as teen-agers. So I beat a tambourine . . . to let stores know that there was a market here that they should be . . . cultivating. So that just as there were college shops, then there were going to be teen shops. And there was going to be the development of teen shops. Now, once you've got retailers saying, "Hey! These are good customers that we want in our store," then advertisers wanted to be in that magazine because they wanted to influence with their product the retail store. And that was the whole, that whole little loop.[26]

It is easy to see that the loop system benefited retailers, advertisers, and *Seventeen* magazine, but Ellis also claims that it benefited teens. She frames her case for selling teens as consumers in terms of "respect." Selling products to teen girls as consumers would lead to the increased status of teens in a consumer-driven society; as they became more valuable to the economy, they would become more valued citizens. In her words: "these young people were entitled to be respected by the retailers of this country, by the advertising agencies of this country, by the manufacturers of products!"[27]

Ellis's message was that teens had buying "needs" that business could fill. But just who were these "teens"? And what were their specific "needs"? *Seventeen* staffers thought they had a pretty good vision of their readership, but that vision wasn't enough for Helen Valentine. Valentine instructed the promotional staff to gather demographic research data to "validate and give authority to the message."[28] A few months after the magazine's first issue, *Seventeen* hired David Hertz (Valentine's son-in-law) of the Princeton, New Jersey consulting firm Benson and Benson, Inc. to survey a sample of its subscribers and their mothers in order to get a more nuanced picture of its readership. A year later, *Seventeen* paid the consulting firm, Opinion Research Corporation (ORC), also of Princeton, to compile additional survey information, this time from a national cross section of teenage girls, on their food consumption (shopping and eating) and preparation.[29]

The Birth of Teena

With demographic research in hand, Ellis had an inspiration that would shape *Seventeen*'s promotional campaign for the length of her tenure. Although the survey data offered valuable descriptive information about *Seventeen*'s readers and teen girls in general, Ellis believed that statistics alone were not illustrative enough to represent—or sell—the teen reader to business. She decided to build a promotional campaign around a *persona*—to construct an embodied ideal with parts that integrated the creators' vision, the advertisers' desire, and the readers' statistics. Thus, Ellis created "Teena, the prototypical teenage girl." Ellis describes the birth of Teena:

> [I]t was a way of creating a persona for this market because people don't understand raw statistics! They understand, you know, the human story. And I always went for the human story. So by making Teena a *person,* I could define

> her . . . it was personifying the market! . . . So, you know, you have to humanize, you have to personify. People just don't fall in love with statistics!"[30]

Business would eventually fall in love with Teena. First, though, Ellis and her staff had to develop their prototype—Teena—and then introduce her to the marketplace.

In developing Teena, Ellis began with two important characteristics: wholesomeness and youth. Much like the biblical Adam and Eve or Frankenstein's monster, Teena was the product of her creators, so she had to be as wholesome as both Annenberg and Valentine envisioned. In addition, Ellis needed to communicate to advertisers and retailers that Teena was not merely her mother's mini-me; instead, she was a distinctly different consumer. Translated into product preference, Teena needed youthful, ladylike (i.e., not dowdy or sexually provocative) clothes and makeup geared to her special age group. Ellis explains the dilemma that this initially created for both advertisers and the magazine staff, using the case of cosmetics as an example:

> So, you know, if you go back in time, pre-'44, all of the ads for cosmetics were for mothers, for their age group, and we didn't want those kinds of ads in our publication. Because, you know . . . it would *dilute* the message and also it would be dissonant. And visually dissonant in imagery![31]

For those advertisers who failed to understand the consumer distinction between teens and adult women, Ellis developed a booklet entitled "Who Is Teena? Judy Jeckyll [*sic*] or Formalda Hyde?" that explicitly spelled out who Teena was—and who she was *not* (Figure 3.1).[32] Illustrations of two very different teen girl personas, Judy Jeckyll (*Seventeen*'s editorial Teena/ideal reader) and Formalda Hyde (the advertisers' misrepresentation), accompanied the magazine's narrative about the identity mix-up:

> When we first saw Teena she was in high school. She was somewhere between thirteen and eighteen years of age . . . she wore simple, clean-cut clothes, was a member in good standing of the soap and water set . . . and she spoke to friends and family alike in what we all recognize as basic English.
>
> Because we spoke her language too, we decided to cater to her tastes and take care of her needs through a magazine she could call her own. And we named it—SEVENTEEN. But by the time SEVENTEEN appeared on the newsstands we had a feeling Teena might be leading a double life. She seemed to be one girl in our editorial pages and quite another when we leafed through our advertising—kind of a split personality.

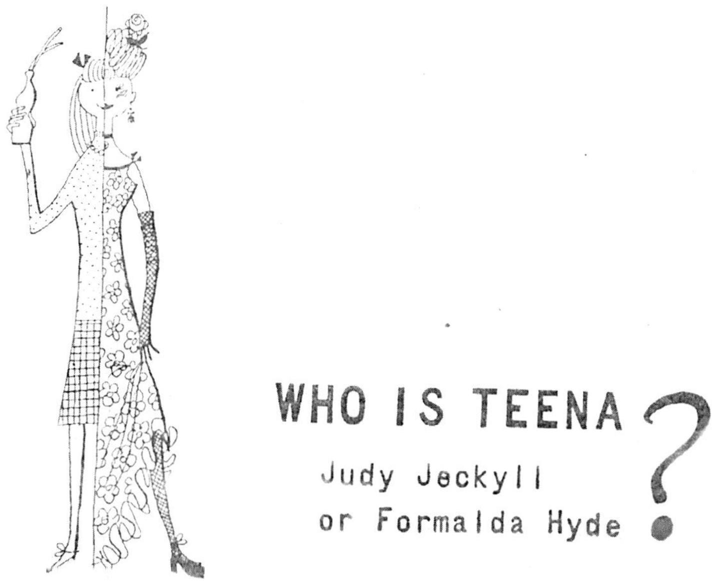

Figure 3.1. *Seventeen* Promotional Document: Judy Jeckyll and Formalda Hyde booklet, personal collection of Estelle Ellis

This was particularly noticeable when our editors (women who should know the ways of women) held Teena's interest with realistic articles on politics, democracy and the post-war world, while some of our advertisers did their best to woo her with a mumbo jumbo called jive talk.

They even tried to sell her on spike heels . . . fussy hats . . . sloppy . . . sweaters, and dresses with a life-begins-at-forty look. This really had us baffled since we had repeatedly told them that Teena and her teen-mates were buying up the youthful wholesome clothes featured on our editorial pages.

We became all the more confused when we remembered that Teena poked fun at glamor girls who piled on the war paint . . . wore bird nest hair-do's and sprouted claw-y fingernails. Why then did smart advertisers– try to sell Teena cosmetics via over-done and all too frequently overage models?

[–only smart advertisers advertise in SEVENTEEN]

IT JUST DIDN'T MAKE DOLLARS AND SENSE

$$

No more sense than the "over-exposed" photos and drawings some of our lingerie and hosiery advertisers put in *Seventeen*. For while we'd be the first to ad-

> mit our girl Teena knows all about the birds and bees, we've been around her long enough to know she's not the kind of girl you can win with "cheesecake."
>
> We finally figured it out! It was undoubtedly a case of mistaken identity. A few of our advertisers took Teena for someone else! If that happened to you—and you would like a fresh introduction—write the SEVENTEEN Advertising Advisory Board, 11 W. 42nd Street, New York 18, N.Y.
>
> P.S. We've got Teena's number—have you? If not, look her up in SEVENTEEN – the young girls service magazine.[33]

Marketing Teena

Having chastised and re-educated the business community, Ellis translated the statistics collected on the teen reader into characteristics of the embodied Teena, using several communication strategies and vehicles. She published the survey findings in book form under the titles *Life with Teena: A Seventeen Magazine Survey* and *Life with Teena, Volume II: Food,* distributing them to advertisers, retailers, and manufacturers.[34] Both books used the reader/teen girl survey results to tell a story about the prototypical Teena. The first volume of *Life with Teena* described the average reader's vital statistics, as well as her aspirations, her shopping habits, possessions, and preferences, and her relationship with *Seventeen.* In answer to the question "Who is Teena?," Chapter 1 answered:

> Our girl Teena is sixteen years old. She's five feet four and a quarter inches tall and tips the scales at 118 pounds. She goes to a public high school, expects to graduate next year at the age of 17 and go on to college with a B.A. or B.S. in mind. Her chances of going to college are good, since Teena's mother is in favor of higher education! And her father can afford to foot all her college bills. He's a professional man . . . a business man . . . a white-collar worker. Teena could work her way through college if she had to . . . she earns money even now, minding babies after school. And it's not just "pin money" she's working for either . . . when Teena works she earns $13.48 a month—all of which she keeps for her own expenses. This, in addition to a regular family allowance—$2.13 a week. Which she spends on movies, bus fares, cokes, school supplies, lunches, candy, etc.[35]

Businessmen learned from this description that the average teen reader had the number-one characteristic that it takes to be a good consumer—

money. In fact, she was doubly blessed financially because she had access to her own earned disposable income and that of her father. There were hints that she was a good long-term investment, since college attendance increased her chances of landing an educated husband. Subsequent chapters revealed that Teena "is a homemaker at heart," helps others with their shopping selections, including her family members, girl friends, and boyfriends, and that she assists mom with domestic activities, including grocery shopping, menu planning, and meal preparation. Teena uses cosmetics, goes to the movies, and participates in athletic activities. Her favorite magazine? *Seventeen,* of course! And she shares it with her mom, her sister, her friends, and even her brother![36]

Because *Life with Teena, Volume II: Food* included data from a national cross section of teen girls, it described the average *teen girl* (as opposed to the average *reader*) while also providing businessmen with a contrast between the two. "Chapter 1: Profile of Teena," introduced the average teen girl: "Teena is somewhere between thirteen and nineteen years of age. She lives everywhere in the USA—in big cities, in small towns, in the suburbs or on the farm. She is one of three children in a family and is as likely to be the daughter of a professional or a proprietor as of a laborer."[37]

A footnote compared Teena II (the average teenage girl) with Teena I (the average *Seventeen* reader), noting that the latter "is more likely to be the 16-year-old daughter of a professional, a white collar or skilled worker." Thus, the average reader tended to be a little older and with more disposable cash than the average teen—an obvious selling point for the magazine. She was also more likely to be an urban/suburban resident of the East Coast or the Midwest.

Volume II focused specifically on Teena's role as a domestic worker and consumer. The text noted that Teena often does the grocery shopping for the family, but that she is a different kind of "shopper" from her mother: "Teenagers have fewer brand prejudices than their mothers, due in great part to their youth, inexperience and the wartime shortage of various brands. It is evident from the foregoing breakdowns that many of the young girls questioned have not as yet chosen their brand favorites."[38] This was a particularly important point to make to grocers, but it was also made to retailers in general. Teena, *Seventeen* told businessmen, is still impressionable and hasn't become "branded" by certain companies. This claim implied that businesses could influence Teena if they reached her in time—and that the pages of *Seventeen* are where the two could meet.

Ellis used two other promotional strategies to introduce Teena to businessmen: direct mailings and advertisements. For the "calling card" direct mailing, *Seventeen* sent postcards featuring drawings and text about Teena to retailers and advertisers. In advertisements, *Seventeen* promoted Teena in major industry publications of that time period, including *Women's Wear Daily, Drug Trade News, Tide, Printer's Ink, Advertising Age, Retailing Home Furnishings,* and *Cosmetics and Toiletries.* Although the Teena of this campaign also drew on the statistics of the average reader, she had been given a makeover—one that accentuated her most marketable features (particularly as a consumer) while downplaying her less salable characteristics (citizenship and intellectuality). The promotional ad Meet Teena introduced her in classic story form:

> **Meet Teena . . .**
>
> No one thought she could read!
>
> Once upon a time—and not so long ago—a High School Girl (we'll call her Teena) looked into the family magazine rack for something to read. She found a magazine chic enough for mother, another rugged enough for father, a third just right for brother Bill, yet nary a one for her! Teena got the sad, sad feeling that publishers didn't know she could read. Or if they did, they didn't seem to care. So she started a one-girl campaign—protested loud and strong (she had 6,000,000 teen-mates to back her up), and it wasn't long before people were talking about Teena the High School Girl who reads . . . influences the buying habits of her family . . . chooses the clothes she wears, the lipstick she uses, the food she eats. Others still more farsighted thought of Teena in terms of future buying power—a career girl, a college student, a mother! The happy ending writes itself. Teena got what she wanted—her own magazine *SEVENTEEN.* If you want to talk to Teena, do it through *SEVENTEEN.*[39]

This ad, written in the tradition of the fairy tale, introduced Teena to business. Of course, as with fairy tales in general, it was neither wholly truthful nor realistic. Instead, it contained the truths that its authors wanted to get across to their audience. In this fairy tale, *Seventeen* resulted from the popular demand of millions of teenage girls, when in fact the magazine's birth was the direct result of decisions made at the producer level.[40] The text of this introduction previews some of the themes of the Teena campaign: Teena the high school girl who has many "teen-mates"; Teena the girl who reads—and has influence. Teena the girl with a future—as a college student, wife and mother, and, of course, consumer.

To get the advertiser to "buy" *Seventeen,* the magazine had to sell itself as the premier teen girl authority. A major part of the promotional campaign involved making a convincing case that *Seventeen* was the expert on Teena—and her millions of teen-mates.

> ***Seventeen* gets them young**
>
> We speak from authority—for we know more than 3,000,000 of these girls intimately. They read *SEVENTEEN* each month. What's more, they believe what they read because they saw it in *SEVENTEEN.*[41]

This advertisement stresses a foundational concept of the Teena campaign: *Seventeen* and teen girls have a special relationship, in which *Seventeen* knows these "young" women "intimately." Establishing intimacy was important, as *Seventeen*'s position of influence over Teena was predicated upon Teena's vulnerability as she made the bumpy transition into adulthood. And *Seventeen* marketed this special relationship to the advertiser:

> **What's buzzing in Teena's bonnet?**
>
> It's a smart advertiser who knows!
>
> Teena the High School Girl has a peck of problems. She's what older folks call an awkward adolescent—too tall, too plump, too shy—a little too much of a lot of little things. But they're *big* things to Teena. And though she doesn't always take her troubles to mother, Teena writes her favorite magazine for the tip-off on the clothes she wears, the food she eats, the lipstick she wields, the room she bunks in, the budget she keeps, the boy she has a crush on. *Seventeen* seems to have all the answers—that's why like Teena, smart advertisers use *Seventeen.*[42]

In the previous ad, *Seventeen* presented itself as Teena's mother substitute—and then offered up its progeny as bait to the highest bidder(s). In order to be economically viable, *Seventeen* had to serve both its readers and its advertisers—two distinct constituencies with differing interests. *Seventeen* smoothed this tension by asserting that the needs of the reader and advertiser were intertwined. As the text from an advertising pamphlet entitled "*Seventeen* Comes to the Aid of the Advertiser" illustrates, this ability to bring reader and advertiser together was sometimes presented as *Seventeen*'s higher calling:

> *SEVENTEEN,* the young girl's service magazine, believes strongly that in helping its advertisers it is helping its readers! [. . .] For *SEVENTEEN* feels

> keenly its responsibility as a national advertising medium—a responsibility that begins with helping the teen consumer find the products "SEEN IN *SEVENTEEN*" in home towns throughout the United States.[43]

The "calling card" promotion, in particular, established the close relationship between *Seventeen* and Teena. Of the nine different postcards, all carried the caption "You Can't Tear Her Away From *Seventeen*" and featured drawings of Teena in a variety of settings. In the postcards, Teena is portrayed as a young white girl with long straight brown hair and a slender—but not skinny—build, with perky round breasts and a small waist. Whenever her face is shown (sometimes it is obscured by the *Seventeen* magazine she holds), she is smiling. The accompanying copy extols the special relationship between Teena and *Seventeen*. Through the pictures and copy, we learn that Teena prefers reading *Seventeen* to almost all other activities—including dating. On one postcard, Teena reads the magazine while ignoring three male suitors who look on; on another, Teena reads the magazine while at a school dance. *Seventeen* also accompanies her in other activities, including playing in the orchestra, bathing in the tub, and walking in her graduation procession. At times, she is so engrossed in the magazine that she puts herself in danger; in one picture, Teena is reading *Seventeen* while snow skiing and is so mesmerized that she almost collides with a tree[44] (Figure 3.2). Read literally, this is a powerful relationship: Teena is so enamored by *Seventeen* that she becomes oblivious to all else—even romance and danger.

In order for the sales transaction between *Seventeen* and the advertiser to be finalized, however, establishing a relationship between magazine and reader was insufficient. *Seventeen* had to convince the advertiser that the magazine *influenced* Teena and her millions of teen-mates. *Seventeen* made this point in text from the calling card campaign: "She only has eyes for her favorite magazine. And there are 850,000 others just like her—high school girls who use *Seventeen* as their shopping guide; high school girls who check the magazine's editorial and advertising papers before they buy."[45]

The crucial sales point is that Teena looks to the entire magazine—both editorial and advertising copy—for advice and direction. This point is so important that *Seventeen* used actual sales data to support its assertions. For instance, one calling card exhorted "But don't take our word for it! Ask Harvey's of Nashville. Their two column, $625 insertion drew 36,000 inquiries"[46] and a print ad exclaimed, "Confidentially . . . We've got pull—but do tell everybody. Our December cover sold 2,500 teen-age evening gowns."[47]

Figure 3.2. *Seventeen* Promotional Documents: Teena Calling Cards, Estelle Ellis Collection, Archives Center, National Museum of American History, Behring Center, Smithsonian Institution

A 1945 article about *Seventeen* in the industry publication *Tide* indicated that Ellis's sales job was not an easy one—at least initially: "[*Seventeen*'s] reader market, the teen-age girl, was regarded by many advertisers as a dubious, if personable, purchasing agent."[48] However, just two years later, *Advertising Age* proclaimed the teen girl the advertising industry's new "pin-up girl."[49] *Seventeen* helped Teena achieve this status by highlighting her value and ability as a consumer extraordinaire. One of the crucial points that Ellis communicated about Teena was that she had access to money. The following print ad describes the source of her money—and how she spends it:

> **Teena goes to town**
> to buy a new dress to wear back to school; to look for a radio to play in her room; to market for groceries to help mother out; to get a new lipstick to build up morale. For Teena the high school girl has money of her own to spend—money enough for movies, sodas, records and clothes. And what her allowance and pin money earnings won't buy, her parents can be counted on to supply. For our girl Teena won't take no for an answer when she sees what she wants in *Seventeen*.[50]

Seventeen established several points in this text. First, Teena has money that she's ready and willing to spend. In accordance with the findings of the reader surveys, the text depicted Teena as possessing her *own* money, whether earned through outside work (e.g., babysitting, after-school job) or through domestic work (her allowance). The latter source reminds us of Teena's economic dependency on her parents. However, at least in this context, Teena was described as a strong-willed and insistent girl who will get the extra money she needs from her parents if necessary. Of course, this also presumed that Teena belongs to a family that has the financial resources to fund her buying—but this *was* often the case, according to *Seventeen*'s survey data.

This promotional ad also described the kinds of products that Teena is in the market for: clothes, electronics, cosmetics, and entertainment. It informed potential advertisers that Teena has many interests and can't be pegged into just one buying slot—and this diversity of consumptive possibilities certainly broadens her value as a buyer. One place that Teena is shown frequenting is the grocery store (Figure 3.3):

> **Teena goes to market . . . are you on her shopping list?**
>
> Teena the high school girl is a homemaker at heart! When school is out you will find her trotting down to the neighborhood market to bring home the bacon—shopping for the groceries her family needs. A girl with grown-up responsibilities, Teena fixes supper when mother wants a stand-in. She plans the menu and prepares the food when it's her turn to entertain the gang. A big help around the house, Teena knows how to cook, clean, sew and shop. A peek into her market basket proves she knows her groceries too. If you want your product included in that basket, you'd do well to tell her about it in the magazine she reads and believes—*Seventeen*.[51]

Promotional Teena, as a housewife in training, practices her skills at home and on her friends. In a strategy that does not exist in the marketing of contemporary *Seventeen* (covered in the Epilogue), the early magazine put a lot of effort into wooing grocers and food manufacturers to become suitors of Teena. When Teena was described as "bring[ing] home the bacon" in this context, the allusion was clearly to domestic labor and not to workforce labor.

The demographic information revealed that most of the readers were from middle-income families, and *Seventeen* used this middle-class status as a selling point, as the following print advertisement illustrates:

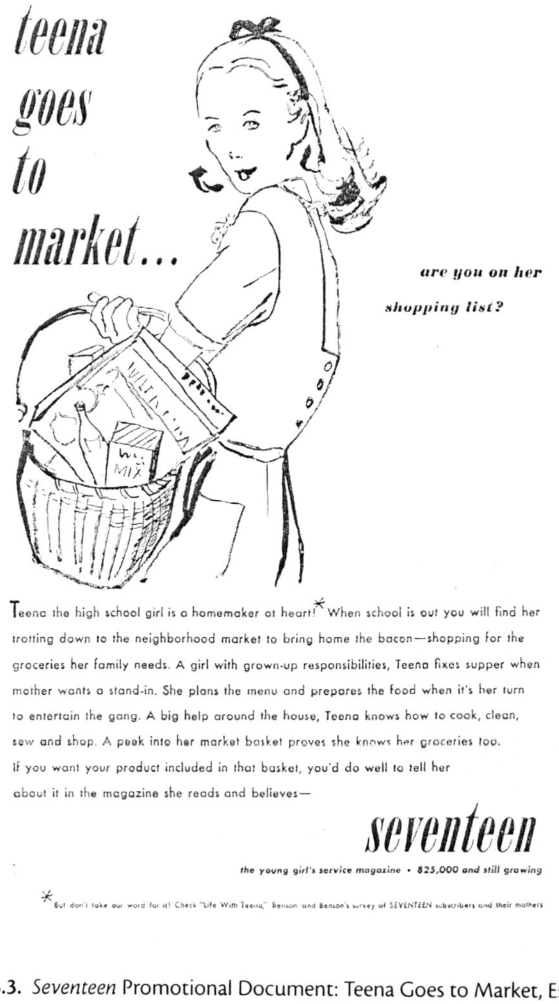

Figure 3.3. *Seventeen* Promotional Document: Teena Goes to Market, Estelle Ellis Collection, Archives Center, National Museum of American History, Behring Center, Smithsonian Institution

Teena wasn't born with a silver spoon in her mouth

. . . chances are she doesn't have "Grandmother's silver" to inherit! Reason enough fourteen of the nation's top silver companies are selling Teena their patterns and their names in *SEVENTEEN* each month. Buying for herself today and a family of her own tomorrow, Teena (there are 7,999,999 more at home just like her) is the nation's most potent consumer. Industry is reaching her in the magazine that keeps pace with each new generation of teens.[52]

Seventeen suggested to advertisers (in this case, sterling silver manufacturers) that *not* being wealthy can actually make Teena a better buyer. It also suggested—in a much-recited promotional mantra—that there were millions of girls *just like Teena*. The only change that took place in each recitation is the number of millions proclaimed, a number that increased relative to the magazine's readership. This was a key point in the campaign: Teena wasn't just one person, one model, one icon. She represented millions of real American teenage girls.

Additionally, describing Teena as a "potent consumer" conjured up the kind of fertility that is associated with young bodies. According to the promotional literature, another characteristic of Teena that makes her a good consumer is her youth. An ad that featured two young women exuberantly running across a field (attired in frocks) was accompanied by copy that reads:

> **The Age of Action**
>
> Teen-age—that time in a lifetime when you run after the things you want! Teens need more because they do more . . . want more because they see more . . . get more because they have the stamina of youth. Their vitality can be industry's inspiration—it inspired a vital magazine! *Seventeen.*[53]

The words describing teens in this passage are all extremely active: run, do, want, need, see, get! According to this ad, nothing can deter a teen from the physically challenging activity of consumption. *Seventeen* presented teens—and especially teen girls—as being specially suited for power shopping, forming a "vital" link between the magazine and retailers.

All that youthful energy needed to be directed, however, and that is where *Seventeen* and the advertiser come in. The advertiser (via *Seventeen*) was charged with the task of educating Teena on the ABC's of buying—of filling her mind with buying knowledge. For as the headline of one advertisement provocatively stated, "*Seventeen* Sells You a Blank Page."[54] The double meaning is clear: *Seventeen* was selling "space"—in both the pages of the magazine and the mind of the reader. According to *Seventeen*, however, Teena *knows* she needs help and welcomes the assistance:

> **Teena is a good listener. . .**
>
> Tell her your sales story!
>
> Teena the high school girl has a mind of her own—but it's open to suggestions. Shopping without mother for the first time, our girl Teena has her ears

> cupped for information and help. She's attentive, receptive—to new ideas, new products and new names. At a fast-growing fashion-conscious age, Teena and her teen-mates comprise a market 7,000,000 strong—a market that is strong in its buying power and positive in its brand preferences. The labels that Teena looks for today are the labels she'll remember and reach for tomorrow. To make her aware of your brand name and your label, sell her on your product now in—*Seventeen.*[55]

These promotional themes suggest the tension between the independence/dependence of the teenage years. Teena has a mind of her own ... but she must fill it with the input of others. She doesn't need mother anymore ... but she needs *Seventeen* (and its advertisers). She is one . . . in a million. For the advertisers, Teena's youth also held the promise of a lucrative adulthood. Much like a young calf on the loose, Teena needed to be "branded" now, so that she wasn't lost in the future. *Seventeen* made this point even more overtly in the following ad, which showed Teena holding a crystal ball:

> **Look Ahead With Teena**
>
> She's a girl with a future!
>
> You don't have to be a crystal gazer to know that Teena the High School girl is within a few years of a job . . . a husband . . . a home of her own. Open-minded, impressionable, at an age when she's interested in anything new, Teena is a girl well worth knowing—surely worth cultivating. The lipstick that satisfies her now is the one you'll find in her purse when she's old enough to "remember when." The brand names she's made conscious of today are the ones she'll cling to—and trust—tomorrow. It's easier to sell Teena in her teens than to unsell her when she's 21-plus. Teena the girl with a future can be your future too, if you sell her in the magazine she and her teen-mates beg, borrow and buy—*Seventeen.*[56]

Business was told that Teena, like fertile soil, needed "cultivation" (a word that Ellis continues to use when speaking of teens). They were also reminded that this kind of toil takes work—but that the teen girl territory was "worth" the effort. Seeds sown in the teen years would reap a future adult consumer harvest.

The chain of consumption did not end once Teena has been influenced by *Seventeen* and branded by the advertiser. In fact, this was the point at which Teena became most valuable in the entire process as her role shifted from follower to leader—from influenced to influential:

> **Teena is a Copycat**
>
> —what a break for you!
>
> Our girl Teena (unlike her older sister) wants to look, act and be just like the girl next door. She and her teen-mates speak the same language . . . wear the same clothes . . . eat the same foods . . . use the same brand of lipstick . . . go in for the same gimmicks . . . and lately even read the same magazine (*Seventeen*, of course!). For Teena and her teen-mates come in bunches—like bananas. You'll see them shopping together, sipping Cokes at the corner candy store together, going to movies, market and club meetings together. Sell one and chances are you'll sell them all—all 6,000,000 of them—especially when you sell them in the magazine they're sold on . . .
>
> *Seventeen.*[57]

One purpose of this ad was to differentiate Teena, as a high school girl and market segment, from "her older sister." By "older sister," *Seventeen* was making reference to college-age women—and the emerging genre of magazines marketed to them (e.g., *Mademoiselle*). Because *Seventeen* was competing for advertising with other fashion magazines, it had to establish both its readership and itself as distinct entities in the publishing world so that advertisers would see that they could only reach the teen-age buyer via *Seventeen*.

This advertisement also identified the unique consumer value of Teena and her teen-age girl cohorts: they're "copycats." This meant that an advertiser only had to sell one Teena on a product in order to reap the benefits of selling to the whole group. Although the majority of teen girls were represented as followers in this ad, one of them was depicted as influential. It's impossible to discern whether this copycat characteristic represented a "real" phenomenon of youth or a self-fulfilling prophecy; nevertheless, it was a part of the cultural lore of the time period, as this quote from a 1946 article in *Business Week* illustrates: "the teen-age market—a special area that has come into its own during the war. It's a jackpot market, because, unlike her older sisters, every teen-ager wants to look almost exactly like every other teen-ager."[58]

The portrayal of teenage girls as followers conflicts with descriptions of Teena as independent and strong-willed in other advertisements in this promotion, but it was an important point to make to the advertiser. Selling Teena to the advertiser was much easier if the advertiser thought that she was an "exponential" purchase; thus, all teen girls (even the followers) are represented as influential over others (Figure 3.4):

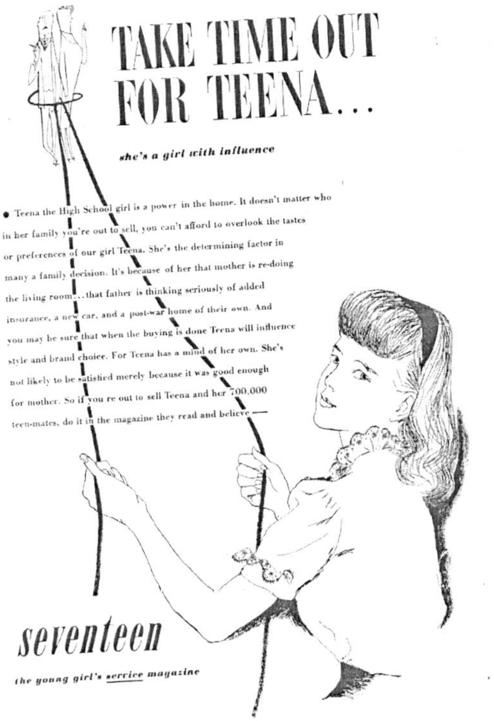

Figure 3.4. *Seventeen* Promotional Document: Take Time Out for Teena, Estelle Ellis Collection, Archives Center, National Museum of American History, Behring Center, Smithsonian Institution

Take Time Out for Teena...

She's a girl with influence

Teena the High School girl is a power in the home. It doesn't matter who in her family you're out to sell, you can't afford to overlook the tastes or preferences of our girl Teena. She's the determining factor in many a family decision. It's because of her that mother is re-doing the living room... that father is thinking seriously of added insurance, a new car, and a post-war home of their own. And you may be sure that when the buying is done Teena will influence style and brand choice. For Teena has a mind of her own. She's not likely to be satisfied merely because it was good enough for mother. So if you're out to sell Teena and her 700,000 teen-mates, do it in the magazine they read and believe—

Seventeen.[59]

The accompanying picture depicted Teena holding a lariat that has captured her parents. The object of branding—a symbolic cow—became the lead "cowgirl" in the family. Teena finds her power in this role. In the wild, wild world of shopping, she—not her father or mother—is the family consumption leader. Thanks to the education she has received from *Seventeen* and its advertisers, she has become a savvy consumer and the usual familial roles flip-flop as her parents seek her advice on what to buy. And, as the next advertisement makes clear, Teena's influence in the buying arena knows no bounds:

> **Bank on Teena**
>
> the high school girl—
>
> To get her family to take a trip . . .
>
> To persuade her father they need a new car . . .
>
> To convince her mother they can't live without new living-room furniture . . .
>
> To sell her teen-mates on the record, the blazer, the candy bar or lipstick she bought for herself. For our girl Teena has a way with her friends and her family. Persuasive . . . persistent, she knows how to get what she wants. And you can make her want the product you sell if you tell her about it in the magazine she reads and believes—
>
> *Seventeen.*[60]

To paraphrase a popular Broadway tune from the 1950s, it seems that "whatever Teena wants, Teena gets"—for herself, and even for others. Of course, in the world in which our Teena lives, there is one significant person who has been glaringly absent thus far—but he's an important component in her buying cycle, as illustrated in the following ad:

> **Girl meets Boy**
>
> —and they're going to the movies
>
> [. . .]
>
> Characters: 8,000,000 teen-age girls and the boys they influence
>
> Story: Girl meets boy . . . boy dates girl . . . girl gets boy to take her to the movies
>
> Plot Development: This is where you come in! You write the happy ending when you sell the girl who sells the boy on more movies—on your movies in particular.[61]

Once Teena lassoed herself a boy, her influence extended into a new arena—the date. In *Seventeen*, Teena seems to reign as queen of this kingdom, too. On the surface, she has the power to direct the date by "getting" the boy to do her bidding (in this case, take her to a particular movie). However, read more closely, her power is superficial. Teena may get her way, but her ideas and desires are not her own—they have been fed to her by the advertiser through *Seventeen*. Even her relationship with "the boy" lacks her real influence, as another "Girl Meets Boy" ad reveals:

> **Girl meets Boy**
>
> —and it's only the beginning! There's nothing like the start of a beautiful friendship to start a girl on a buying spree . . . to start her thinking of the cosmetics and toiletries that will improve her looks. A girl meets a boy and she reaches for a lipstick, she fusses with her hair and she pressures her parents for mascara, for perfume, for a dressing table of her own. She motivates and initiates buying in the millions [. . .].[62]

It is really the boy who is the more influential component in this duo; he—albeit indirectly—influences Teena to go on a "buying spree." From the advertiser's standpoint, the boy (or romance, more generally) is a catalyst for more buying—and an opportunity for continued influence of Teena. He is the link that transforms the consumptive process from linear to circular—a marketing loop much like the one that Estelle Ellis proposed. Teena goes to *Seventeen* for direction, the advertiser influences her to buy, she influences others to buy—and then a boy makes her feel inadequate, which sends her running back to *Seventeen*. As some scholars have noted, consumer behavior is predicated on creating a feeling of inadequacy in the buyer.[63] The "logic" of advertising requires that the tension created by this feeling of inadequacy can only be reduced through the consumption of products. Thus, romance played an integral part in the selling of Teena to the advertiser—but only as a part of the process. In the creation of Teena as the prototypical teenage girl, gender socialization took a back seat to the primary goal of consumer socialization.[64]

Teena's Happy Ending

Once upon a time, Estelle Ellis and *Seventeen* introduced advertisers to "Teena, the Prototypical Teenage Girl." As a result of the magazine's matchmaking efforts, advertisers learned all about Teena, including that she was quite a shopper—and a young woman of influence. They also learned that they could influence her to buy their products. Their courtship took off—but how did their relationship progress? In celebration of its fifth birthday in 1949, *Seventeen* published this print ad, a retrospective birthday card in praise of both Teena and the advertiser:

> **You Can't Blow Away 5 Years!**
>
> Sixty Issues Later . . .
>
> - Fashion manufacturers are creating clothes styled and patterned exclusively for the teen-age girl
> - Retailers are expanding teen shops, hiring advisors, organizing high school boards, planning ads, windows and department displays to attract Teena and her friends to every department in a store
> - Cosmetic and toiletries companies are packaging special products for the teen consumer . . . are selling their sales staff on the importance of catering to the adolescent [. . .]
>
> Sixty Issues Later . . .
>
> *Seventeen*, the magazine that first fell in love with Teena, knows she has captivated industry as well . . . is proud to have been chosen by industry to sell the nation's 8,000,000 teen-age girls.[65]

Five years after Estelle Ellis and *Seventeen* introduced Teena to business, the economy was making a place for her, as retailers and merchandisers rushed to meet the consumer "needs" of the teenage girl. The promotional Teena whom they met and to whom they responded, Ellis's prototypical teenage girl, differed from editorial Teena in ways that were both complementary and contradictory. Editorial Teena was based on Helen Valentine's image of teen girls as "whole human beings"/readers of a magazine intended for their edification and education. This original vision represented ideal Teena as a multidimensional girl: one who balanced beautification and romance with citizenship and intellectual pursuits. The promotion campaign's Teena prototype needed to attract a very different audience—businessmen and advertisers. This constituency's interest in teen girls was in their potential as consumers; whether these same girls were active citizens or community activists mattered not to business—unless it could be mined for profit. Thus, promotional Teena was obsessed with beauty, boys, fashion, and domesticity—and most especially with shopping for the products associated with those pursuits.

This Teena's depiction as a future stay-at-home housewife reflected *Seventeen*'s bow to the aspiration of its readership and to the desire of domestic advertisers, and did not reflect Valentine's original vision. Indeed, the real women of *Seventeen*'s workplace—editor-in-chief Valentine, promotion director Ellis, and nearly every other female staffer—were wives and mothers who worked outside the home. However, the editorial staff's personal beliefs and editorial concerns were superseded by economic decisions.[66] Promotional Teena introduced domestic goods retailers and manufacturers to a readership that engaged in present-day domestic consumption and dreamed of future domestic bliss. Read more broadly, Teena wasn't just going to the market, she was going *on* the market—as a commodity.

In the early development of *Seventeen,* Ellis—a young working class girl from Brooklyn—held, ironically, the position of matchmaker between wealthy businessmen and middle and upper class teen girls. Indeed, the teen-age girl ideal that Ellis created and communicated through the persona of Teena differed from her own experience, particularly in regard to social class and gender roles. Certainly, Ellis wasn't the progeny of a professional father with deep pockets to pick; she couldn't have been described as a "homemaker at heart"; and as a financially independent businesswoman for her entire adult life, her "need" for a boy was not economic. Ellis's Teena campaign was based on a feminine ideal that predated *Seventeen,* one that permeated Western society and that socialization imprinted on every citizen—Ellis included. Ellis didn't create a new reverence for feminine youth, beauty, domesticity, whiteness, and wealth; she merely compiled these characteristics into a teen-age girl prototype and then sold Teena, her teen-mates, and *Seventeen* in a marketplace that immediately recognized their value.

CHAPTER 4

Teena Means Business

Seventeen's Advertisers Court the Teen Girl Consumer

> *Teena means business*
>
> Don't pass her by!
>
> You can't afford to overlook the high school girl. She's buying for herself today . . . she'll be buying for a family of her own tomorrow. She's in the market for clothes she can wear, cosmetics she can use and food she can bring home for mother. And you may be sure the products she's buying in her teens are the ones you'll find on her bathroom and pantry shelves when she's set in her ways. She's an important girl and bound to be quite a woman. Sell her now—for now and the future—in the magazine she reads and believes —*seventeen.* [*Seventeen* promotional document][1]

Baby cannot live on bread alone.

If subscriptions and newsstand sales were the bread and butter of *Seventeen*'s existence, advertising was its mother's milk. This wasn't unique to *Seventeen*; it is an economic reality for most mainstream magazines—and particularly so for women's fashion magazines, with their symbiotic relationship with the fashion and beauty industries.[2] Advertisers—not readers—held the key to *Seventeen*'s economic survival, making Estelle Ellis's position as promotion director one of the most important at the magazine. Ellis's message of *Seventeen*'s privileged relationship with the newly identified teen girl consumer was apparently well received by the business community, who came bearing gifts of advertising revenue to the newborn magazine.

As *Seventeen* grew, so too did its advertising, proportionally. In its infancy, the magazine's pages were almost evenly split between editorial copy and advertising copy. By the end of the first year, however, this ratio had changed to about 45/55—45 percent of space devoted to editorial content, and 55 percent to advertisements. Advertising that appeared in *Seventeen* magazine fell into seven different product categories:

- Body care (cosmetics, grooming, feminine hygiene, and medicine)
- Body wear (clothing, undergarments, shoes, accessories, jewelry)
- Entertainment (movies and records)
- Education/Employment (correspondence courses, vocational schools, colleges);
- Snacks (sodas and candy)
- Miscellaneous (pens, paper, wallets)
- Domestic (linens, cookbooks, hope chests, sterling silver)

Seventeen's advertisers brought more than revenue to the magazine, and they sold more than products to the teen girl. They joined the editorial staff in creating the feminine teen ideal, offering the readers pictures to emulate, advice to follow, and a glimpse into the future of an ideal "womanhood." While some elements of what constituted ideal femininity remained constant across time, other elements emerged or disappeared with the progress of the war.

Advertising During World War II

Every issue of *Seventeen* during the magazine's first year of publication carried advertisements that referenced war or contained signs of it. The most common signs were the tiny war slogans tucked away in the corners of ads for clothing, cosmetics, and colas. They often referred to war bonds and implored the reader to "Back the Attack with War Bonds!," "Buy More War Bonds," and "Hold Those Bonds!" Some advertisers warned against waste—of resources or words. Soap makers Lux and Swan, for example, urged the reader not to waste soap, "for soap contains material vital to the war effort."[3] Flame-Glo Lipstick cautioned the reader to "Seal your lips—You can talk about love, but Uncle Sam asks that you keep military secrets to yourself!"[4] These warnings represented an alliance between Madison Avenue, the U.S. government, and mainstream magazines, working together to elicit support for America's war effort.[5]

Manufacturers used their ads to apologize for the scarcity of their products, pleading for patience from the reader/consumer. These appeals, made by makers of blouses, sweaters, girdles, linens, Kleenex tissues, and cosmetic cases resulted from the U.S. government's control over resources deemed essential to the war effort. Because of their usefulness as war materials, silk, wool, synthetics, rubber, paper, and metals were either removed from the public sector or rationed.[6] Some manufacturers tried to make the best of the situation, using their ads to sell waiting as something that consumers could do in service to their country. Featherknit sweaters, for instance, encouraged patriotic patience: "We hope to resume production of Featherknits for you soon, but Featherknits are now being made exclusively for G. I. Joe. Lucky gals may still find some F's at their favorite shops. Plucky gals will be glad to wait for Victory, when Featherknit Sweaters will be even more glamorous than ever."[7]

Waiting for the future, however, was hard for manufacturers—particularly for girdle makers, whose products were made of many of the materials that were among the most rationed. Foundation maker Jantzen took an interesting tack in addressing this problem, making women's bodies part of the body politic. As they exhorted the reader:

> Your hips are everybody's business! Your figure has become a matter of national importance! The slimmer you are, the less fabric required to girdle you, the more slimming, trimming, smoothing, soothing Jantzen foundations can be turned out into the world. So do get out and do active things like walking, dancing, digging, swimming—it's a lot of fun and it's slimming.[8]

While these companies sold wartime virtue alongside their products, others used the war as an advertising backdrop. Several clothing advertisers posed their teen models with war planes or weapons. The Peggy Paige dress company created one of the strangest pairings, positioning two young women in front of a Bofors gun (a large cannonlike artillery), declaring both girls and gun to be "America's Secret Weapon" (Figure 4.1).[9] Other advertisers—including Dr. Pepper and Judy Kent (a teen clothing company)—showed civilian women with servicemen at USO clubs.[10] This setting alluded to the most common way that advertisers signaled the war in their ads: through the inclusion of servicemen as signs (and reminders) of romance.

Dating and Daintiness

Wartime ads superimposed military themes upon the age-old theme of dating and romance, with images of soldiers and sailors assessing young women's slenderness and "daintiness."[11] Wartime ads featuring servicemen

Figure 4.1. Peggy Paige Advertisement, February 1945 *Seventeen*

and civilian women differed little from the nonwartime ads in their appeal to romance and male approval. The military men portrayed in war-era ads "served" as the token representatives of romance. Like Ken dolls dressed up as G.I. Joes, only their clothes had changed; they still functioned as Barbie's male counterpart. And Barbie was still, mostly, Barbie.

An ad for Joan Lord Fashions shows desire at a distance: a sailor on a ship looking through binoculars at a young woman on shore.[12] Similarly, in an ad for Heart Throb Fashions, a soldier signals his approval of a young woman (and her attire) with a wolf whistle.[13] Sometimes the gaze was more intimate; many ads featured servicemen and civilian women looking adoringly into each other's eyes. Ads for Keepsake Diamond Rings—which appeared in almost every issue—took the familiar story of (service)boy meets girl to its logical end, portraying soldiers and their adult girlfriends in loving embrace, with captions that proclaimed, "Together again! Joyously greeting a bright tomorrow . . . your love and hers forever sealed with the traditional symbol of the engagement!"[14]

The dating theme merged with that of "daintiness" in wartime ads.[15] During *Seventeen*'s first year, seventeen companies placed twenty-four advertisements that mentioned daintiness; fifteen of these ads targeted women generally, and nine spoke to teens specifically. Advertisers sold daintiness along with their products in these categories: clothing, foundations, feminine hygiene, deodorants, cleansers, and cosmetics.[16] For the most part, these advertisers advised girls to maintain their daintiness by wearing clothing and undergarments that accentuated (and/or controlled) the female body shape and by keeping that body in a state of "wholesome" cleanliness that belied physical reality. For them, a "dainty" body was a body free of natural scents, whether the result of physical activity (i.e., sweat) or biological function (i.e., menstruation). Nonspi deodorant spoke directly to teen girls about the relationship of daintiness to an active social life:

> Personal daintiness is always essential to popularity. Teen-agers with their natural interest in dances and parties, must be fastidious in their grooming. Frequent participation in active sports and strenuous dancing demands a good anti-perspirant to avoid offending. Dependable perspiration control will prevent much unhappiness and embarrassment for teen-agers as well as their mothers and older sisters.[17]

Accompanying many of these ads was a warning that a loss of daintiness would lead to a loss of male approval. A Lux lingerie soap ad, featuring a young woman in an embrace with a uniformed suitor, warns:

> Romance in the air . . . Don't let undie odor rob you of your share! Romance comes when you seem truly precious and wonderful in his eyes. Even a hint of perspiration odor may break that magic spell. Of course underthings absorb perspiration and others notice this odor long before we do ourselves. Play safe with daintiness—Lux lingerie after *every* wearing.[18]

Table 4.1. Product Advertising Content in *Seventeen* Magazine

	September 1944 to March 1945						
	9/44	10/44	11/44	12/44	1/45	2/45	3/45
Special Issue	First			Xmas			
Body Wear	57%	63%	60%	74%	82%	77%	80%
Body Care	21%	25%	27%	19%	8%	17%	14%
Entertainment	14%	12%	9%	3%	8%	1%	2%
Educ/Empl	4%	1%	3%	1%	2%	2%	1%
Misc	4%	1%	<1%	2%	<1%	<1%	<1%
Snacks	1%	0	1%	1%	0	2%	2%
Domestic	0	0	0	0	0	1%	0
Percentage of Ads	47.5%	50%	47%	52%	55%	59%	58%

	September 1949 to March 1950						
	9/49	10/49	11/49	12/49	1/50	2/50	3/50
Special Issue	5th Bday	Home	Parents	Xmas	School		
Body Wear	82%	70%	73%	57%	60%	73%	78%
Body Care	11%	17%	14%	19%	17%	16%	13%
Entertainment	2%	2%	3%	10%	11%	1%	2%
Educ/Empl	1%	3%	1%	2%	5%	1%	1%
Misc	0%	0%	1%	1%	0	2%	0
Snacks	<1%	1%	<1%	<1%	<1%	<1%	1%
Domestic	4%	7%	7%	10%	6%	7%	5%
Percentage of Ads	64%	57%	61%	46%	43%	58%	60%

Table 4.1. *(continued)*

	April 1945 to September 1945						
	4/45	5/45	6/45	7/45	8/45	9/45	Avg
Special Issue	Girl/Boy			America		1st Bday	
Body Wear	70%	68%	56%	53%	76%	68%	68%
Body Care	22%	19%	32%	34%	16%	25%	21%
Entertainment	3%	3%	3%	7%	4%	4%	6%
Educ/Empl	1%	<1%	2%	2%	<1%	<1%	2%
Misc	<1%	2%	2%	<1%	1%	0	1%
Snacks	3%	3%	2%	4%	2%	3%	2%
Domestic	1%	0	1%	2%	0	1%	<1%
Percentage of Ads	59%	60%	59%	54%	57%	59%	55%

	April 1950 to September 1950						
	4/50	5/50	6/50	7/50	8/50	9/50	Avg
Special Issue	Girl/Boy	Yours	Pretty		School	6th Bday	
Body Wear	73%	75%	53%	28%	90%	80%	69%
Body Care	17%	12%	28%	52%	7%	11%	18%
Entertainment	1%	4%	6%	6%	1%	1%	4%
Educ/Empl	1%	3%	3%	4%	1%	1%	2%
Misc	0	0	1%	<1%	0	0	<1%
Snacks	0	1%	<1%	4%	<1%	1%	1%
Domestic	8%	5%	8%	5%	1%	6%	6%
Percentage of Ads	61%	62%	55%	27%	65%	59%	55%

One has to wonder how odoriferous one's undies would have to be in order to offend the olfactory sensibilities of those in less-than-intimate proximity. According to Lux, however, "undie odor" was a looming threat to both daintiness and romance. Mavis Talcum Powder made the relationship between the two an equation, saying "To the dainty belong the men!"[19]

While all advertisers tried to sell their products and their worldview to *Seventeen*'s readership, some benefited from being part of a common class of advertisements. In particular, body care and body wear products spatially and visually dominated *Seventeen*'s advertising pages during its first year (Table 4.1). Conversely, ads for products in the categories of entertainment, education/employment, miscellaneous, and snacks made up a small percentage of the overall advertising, with ads for domestic items—the least frequent type of advertisement during the first year—almost nonexistent. Body wear and body care ads dominated the magazine's commercial space not just in number but also in prestige, occupying the most influential locations within the magazine's layout and with full-page color portraits.[20] Although both types of ads sold body-related products, they diverged in their approach to the teen reader.

Body Care

Body care advertisers during *Seventeen*'s first year included cosmetics companies that still enjoy contemporary recognition, such as pow(d)erhouses Revlon, Maybelline, Helena Rubinstein, and Elizabeth Arden, as well as companies that have faded from view or no longer exist, such as Dana, Yardley of London, Vidafilm, Overglo, Woodbury, and Chen Yu. Other frequent advertisers included Lustre-Creme and Drene shampoos, Lux and Swan soaps, Arrid deodorant, and Kotex sanitary products (one of the magazine's most ubiquitous advertisers).

For the most part, and especially in *Seventeen*'s earliest issues, body care advertisers approached the teen readership as if they were their mothers—or at least their older sisters. None of the body care ads for the magazine's first issue specifically mentioned teen girls. These advertisers initially ignored—or were ignorant of—the special category being carved out for teen girls as consumers. Instead, many early body care advertisements featured adult women selling adult products.

One strategy used in these adult-oriented ads was the celebrity testimonial. Overglo cosmetics, for instance, featured a parade of celebrity spokeswomen in their ads, including Joan Leslie, Anne Baxter, Claudette Colbert, Dorothy McGuire, Rosalind Russell, Betty Grable, and Dorothy Lamour. These ads extolled Overglo's ability to give its users "youthful radiance"—an odd appeal to *Seventeen*'s readership, most of whom already possessed youth and didn't need to purchase it. Maybelline, Woodbury Powder, Lux, Arrid, and Spellbound perfume also used adult female celebrities in their ads, while Maybelline, Lux, LeSonier Powder Mitt, Irresistible Lipstick, and DuBarry Cosmetics featured brides, accompanied by text that linked the use of the product with the likelihood of marriage—something that Walter Annenberg had not wanted to promote to his young readers.

Although the use of adult celebrities and brides to sell products to teen girls made for an incongruous consumer fit, other body care ads departed from *Seventeen*'s "wholesome" editorial mandate. Perfume ads, for instance, often focused on sexuality; Violet Sec Fragrances offers an example. The full-page ad for Violet Sec perfume in the April 1945 issue of *Seventeen* (on page six—prime advertising real estate) portrayed a shadowy drawing of a platinum blond woman in a cocktail dress and long black evening gloves, sitting with a sparkling cocktail by her side. The woman gazes into the shadows, seemingly on the hunt; the accompanying caption hints of her prey, declaring "Violet *Sec*'s Appeal"—the "fragrance that turns a man's fancy."

Lipstick ads also used an appeal to sexuality. Ponds Lipstick ran a comics-style series that featured buxom women locking lips with men in kissing marathons that lasted from twenty-four hours to—in one instance—several months. Although the characters and the locales changed, the storyline and the women's beyond-ample chest size remained constant. Another cosmetics company, Dana, used adult sexuality to promote its Tabu lipstick. Its August 1945 page-ten ad (again, a prime location) featured an adult model with dark red lips and nails, wearing a low-cut dress pinned with a large bow at her chest, each loop accentuating the breast beneath it. The model lounges on a shag rug against a fantasy jungle background, a pensive look on her face. The text beneath her reads: "Dana has translated the sultry charm of TABU into the five most enchanting reds lips have ever worn. And TABU lipstick is so laden with TABU perfume, your lips wear the 'forbidden' fragrance all the while."

A few body care advertisers produced teen-appropriate copy. Yardley of London, for instance, recognized the new teen market from the beginning. In Yardley's ads, drawings of teen girls accompanied text that spoke directly to the readership, mimicking the magazine's conversational style. One ad featured a young girl practicing her lines for a play, the heading proclaiming her to be a "Stand-Out at Try-Outs." The text addresses the reader personally, communicating to her that Yardley understands the importance of being "yourself" (i.e, a teen/individual) and highlights the good fit between "you" and Yardley:

> Fun to find yourself in a part that really fits. . .
> Playing you to perfection, on stage and off!
> That's the joy of Yardley make-up. . .
> It's just right for your role.[21]

Unlike some of its competitors, Yardley understood the relevance of the emerging teenage "role" and the importance of an appropriate match between product and consumer. As opposed to the heavily made-up "vixens" of other makeup ads, Yardley depicted Teena (and, thus, its product) as "vivacious, young, never overstated."[22]

Some cosmetics companies targeted a teen's "youthful" skin as unique and warranting a special regimen. Rose Laird advertised its foundation as a cure for acne with a jivy poem entitled "The Saga of Sal":

> Miss Sally Q was in a stew
> She had "a date"—but what to do!
> Her face was kicking up like mad,
> Had spots and things—sure looked real sad!
> Her spirits sagged to lowest ebb
> When in dashed Babs, a sizzling deb,
> Her skin as smooth as a bit of down.
> Our Sal threw her a slaying frown,
> "You had spots yesterday!" she said.
> "Where are they now, you mean redhead?"
> Said Babs:
> "This creamy, peachy look you see
> Comes in a bottle chickadee!
> Protective Make-up Film, by Laird.
> You'd use it too if you really cared."[23]

While Rose Laird appealed to teens dealing with the present-day scourge of acne, cosmetic company Elizabeth Arden asked them to consider their skin in the future. One full-page Arden ad alerted teens to the importance of initiating a skin care regimen while young:

> Build your beauty on your youth! Start while you're young to establish a habit of beauty that will remain bright and shining through the years . . . don't take for granted that fresh blossom of girlhood . . . resolve to make it last . . . so in maturity your mirror will reflect a lovelier you. Begin now with Elizabeth Arden's routine for youth . . . keep your skin scrupulously clean, braced, supple, use makeup keyed to your life and your looks . . . the investment of a little care now will bring you tremendous dividends in years to come.[24]

Although the Arden ad communicated concern for the *reader's* "years to come," the real concern was for the *company's* "years to come"—cementing a lifelong relationship with the female teen consumer.[25]

Body care advertiser Kotex also spoke directly to teen girls. Kotex marketed its sanitary napkins in the form of a quiz, a format that has survived in the editorial pages of teen magazines from the first issues of *Seventeen* until today. Using this Q&A device (entitled "Are You in the Know?"), Kotex counseled the reader on a range of subjects, none of which was hygiene-related or had anything to do with its product. Instead, through the choice of question topics, Kotex illustrated the "typical" teen life and teen girl concerns, and used the answers to communicate its vision of the Teena "ideal." The reader "learned" from the Kotex ads that she should know how to match clothes and body type; be a junior hostess; care for hands and brows; keep jewelry from tarnishing; get exercise; catch the attention of a boy; play tennis; and end a date ("with a thank you" since "reserve is becoming").[26]

Deeply embedded within the quiz answers was specific information about the delicate matter of menstruation, referred to euphemistically as "certain days," "problem days," and "trying days." The July 1945 Kotex advertisement offers an illustration of the advice component of the quiz, as well as the veiled allusion to menstruation. It portrays a boy standing by a jukebox, flanked by two young women, one in rolled-up jeans, the other in a form-fitting dress; in answer to the question "Which chick will get the dance?" the copy reads: "Why should he dance with a dolly in denims—when there's a swish dish to charm the eye? A fellow likes his females *feminine* (see the girl on the right). So, wear your swooniest frock and be confident—even at 'certain' times."[27]

While most body care advertisers addressed the teen reader as an individual—a singular buyer in a great consumer universe—a few considered her in relation to her family. Tone marketed its skin-care line to both daughter and mother, noting its "correct preparations for every skin type." In addition, the copy alluded to the expectation that daughter would eventually become mother, thus—much like cosmetic advertiser Elizabeth Arden—creating a "now and later" relationship with the teen consumer, with the promise that "Tone, faithfully used in later years, will help maintain the skin at its beauty peak."[28]

Nonspi antiperspirant advertisements represented mothers as hovering over their daughters. The first of Nonspi's ads was written as a daughter-mother dialogue, the daughter asking the questions, the mother—as the spokesperson for the advertiser's message—responding as the wise voice of experience. "Mother, Can Perspiration Spoil this Dress?" the daughter inquires; Mother answers: "Yes! Underarm perspiration ruins many a beautiful dress, and underarm odors ruin many a girl's happiness too."[29] A Nonspi ad that appeared in a later issue addressed mother and daughter as co-consumers, promoting Nonspi "for teenagers as well as their mothers and older sisters."[30]

Perhaps Teena's oddest suitor was laxative maker Ex-Lax. In contrast to the Tone and Nonspi ads, which represented mothers as role models, the mothers (and fathers) in Ex-Lax's ads never knew best, as they fumbled in their attempts to help the teen overcome her unspoken malady. Ex-Lax ads represented the teen and sometimes her aunt (a "persona" the magazine's editorial tone often took) as the experts on the body, the mother as bumbler. One such ad began with the heading: "Mother was <u>such</u> a problem!" and explained:

> I just couldn't do a thing with Mother when I was little. Whenever I needed a laxative, she'd force me to take some horrid old medicine that would shake me up inside and leave me feeling *just awful*! [. . .] Finally, Mother got wise to Ex-Lax! Golly, what a happy day that was for me.[31]

Another Ex-Lax advertisement played off the tale of Goldilocks and the Three Bears. In a quest for the cure, Dad "means well" but picked one that was *too strong*, Mom "harps on the subject," picking one that was *too mild*.[32] Aunt Lu, however, picked the "happy medium," leading the teen narrator to exclaim: "You can reason with Aunt Lu! When I told her my troubles, she said, 'What *you* need is Ex-Lax!' She was right, too!"[33]

While some body care advertisers addressed the reader as a teen consumer from the beginning and others continued to talk past her, some companies—such as Drene Shampoo, Swan Soap, and Revlon—addressed adult women in their initial ads and teen girls in their later ads. This developing understanding of the teen consumer among body care manufacturers was founded on Estelle Ellis's promotional campaign, including her "corrective" pamphlet, "Who Is Teena? Judy Jeckyll or Formalda Hyde?" (detailed in Chapter 3).[34]

Drene's first three ads in *Seventeen* featured pictures of adult women and copy that addressed a generalized female consumer. Beginning in February 1945, however, Drene's ads started to feature pictures of younger women with text references to "youth" generally and "Miss Seventeen" more specifically. Swan Soap made a similar change in its ad campaign. While its first ads spoke about the product and its use in general terms, its later ads became more teen-focused, speaking to "Miss Teen." In *Seventeen*'s July 1945 issue, Swan's ad explained to the teen readership the "4 Kinds of Love and What to do about Them." (They are romantic love, parental love, clothing love, and love for Swan Soap). In later issues, Swan advised teen girls on "What Do Boys Like Most?"[35] and "Four Little [skin care] Pitfalls and How to Lick Them."[36] Swan, like Kotex, wasn't just selling a product; it was also helping to construct the teen girl ideal. This selling strategy mirrored the editorial articles on "How You Feel and Look"; both delivered the message that real teen girls *needed* direction in becoming "ideal."

The most dramatic ad campaign renovation was undertaken by Revlon, a major presence in early *Seventeen* magazine. The company's ads—full page, prominently placed, and often in color—were initially adult-oriented. The ad on the back cover of the February 1945 issue, for example, featured an adult woman wearing a red evening gown, fur stole, and wide feather hat, her blood-red-tipped fingers holding a gold compact of indeterminate use (it could easily have been a cigarette case). The accompanying copy read "Revlon color. Pulsating on lips. Vibrating on fingertips."

Pulsating lips and vibrating fingers were not part of the vision of ideal teen wholesomeness promoted in the editorial pages. However, by the summer of 1945, Revlon's advertising had undergone a major "youthification." In a two-page spread in the June issue, Revlon went back to school—college, to be precise. Under a caption that read "Revlon . . . wins the campus!" Revlon congratulated itself for being college girls' favorite nail enamel, "based on a recent survey of leading women's colleges."[37] The ad featured a picture of a college-age model posing in a long white gown, braids wrapped around her head, holding a small bouquet of flowers in one hand and an arm wrapped around a serviceman. A month later, Revlon's ad featured a scenario in which a young woman prepared to leave for college. And by *Seventeen*'s "First Birthday" issue, Revlon had finally worked its way back to high school. In that month's two-page color spread, Revlon marketed itself to teenage girls, personified in the ad by five young women, all with ribbons in their hair, eating, studying, applying fingernail polish, and showing off polished nails. The caption advises less school study, more self-study: "Comes a time to put aside the book and ponder about yourself . . . The high school's prettiest girls insist on matching lips and fingertips with long-lasting Revlon Nail Enamel and Lipstick."[38]

Body Wear

While body care advertisers doled out advice to educate *Seventeen*'s readers on the "ways of the (feminine) world," body wear advertisers used the strategy of show and tell—offering photo after photo of young women "showing the way" (usually via a department store) to the feminine teen ideal. Department stores and clothing manufacturers targeted the teen consumer from the magazine's first edition, selling clothing made especially for teens and using models that looked teen-aged. This congruence between consumer and product was due in part to the fact that the clothing industry had already begun to recognize the emerging teen niche, building this specialty clothing market over the previous two decades.[39] Thus, body wear ads in *Seventeen*'s initial issues offer a look into the state of the teen clothing industry as it continued to develop in the 1940s, as well as some insight into *Seventeen*'s influence on this industry's healthy and rapid growth.

From the magazine's first issue, the national department store Saks Fifth Avenue (with outposts in New York City, Chicago, Beverly Hills, and Detroit), as well as metropolitan department stores like the Blum Store of Philadelphia and Mandel Brothers of Chicago, showcased themselves and their teen clothing lines to *Seventeen*'s readership. With each issue, new stores joined the parade, constructing a purchasing road map that began at the buying mecca of New York City (Saks, Bloomingdale's, Macy's, Lord & Taylor) and traveled out to other major metropolitan centers such as Chicago (Mandel Brothers, Carson Pirie Scott, and Marshall Fields & Co.), Washington, D.C. (The Hecht Company), Philadelphia (Blum Store, Bonwit Teller, Gimbels, and Dewee's), Detroit (Ernst Kern Company), and Boston (Filene's). Over time, lesser-known department stores in midsized cities such as Kansas City (Harzfeld's), New Orleans (Holmes), Dallas (Neiman Marcus), Grand Rapids, Michigan (Herpolsheimer's), and Jacksonville, Florida (Furchgott's) placed themselves on this advertising map.[40]

The department store ads in *Seventeen's* early issues indicate another trend: teen girls were becoming a distinct, market(able) category, deserving of shopping places and consumer products just for them. During *Seventeen's* first year, more and more department store ads announced a new addition—the "teen shop." Although teen shops existed prior to *Seventeen's* launch—in fact, as far back as the 1930s[41]—the magazine offered the perfect advertising venue, with unprecedented access to millions of teen shoppers nationwide. Some department stores gave their teen departments creative monikers such as the "Slick-Chick Shop" at Union Store in Columbus, Ohio, but most kept to more easily identifiable names, variations of the target shoppers' demographic characteristics. Youth, age, and high school attendance were highlighted in names such as "Young Circle" (Saks Fifth Avenue); "Youthfully Yours Shop" (Scruggs Vandervoort Barney); "Teen-Age Shop" (Hecht's and Neiman Marcus); "Teen Shop" (Mandel Brothers and Schuster's); "High School Shop" (Ernst Kern, Gimbels, Marshall Field's, and Stewart's); "Hi-School Shop" (Bloomingdale's, Boston Store, Famous-Barr, and Filene's); and "Teen-High Shop" (Hudson's of Detroit).

As clothing advertisers' references to "teen shops" grew, so too did references to "teen sizes" and "teen-sized" clothing—as opposed to women's and junior size fashions. Although Helen Valentine insisted that *Seventeen's* editorial fashion pages feature only teen-sized clothing, the magazine accepted advertising for women's clothing makers and sizes. Thus, in the first issues of *Seventeen,* teen-specific clothing ads were interspersed among ads for junior and women's clothes. Companies offered a confusing array of size choices, including Junior sizes 9 to 15,[42] Sub-Junior sizes 7 to 15,[43] Princess Junior Sizes 11 to 17,[44] and Mite Sizes 7 to 15.[45] Advertisements for "chubby sizes" 10 ½ to 16 ½—clothes made for those teen girls who deviated from the body ideal—were a rarity. By the end of the first year, teen-sized clothing (sizes 10 to 16) became more common in the advertising pages, marketed not only by department stores but also by teen clothing producers, including American Debuteen, Carolteen, Derby Sportswear, Emily Wilkens, Gail Berk Classics, Joan Lord Fashions, Juniorette, Sandra Lee, Teen-Set, and York Teen. Teentimers, a New York City clothing manufacturer that began operation in 1942, was particularly responsive to the teen clothing trend. Although the company began as a manufacturer of junior wear, it changed course after learning that department store buyers were marketing its clothing to high school–age girls. Teentimers became one of the most prominent teen clothing companies in the 1940s—and a major advertiser in *Seventeen.*[46]

Body wear advertisements often mimicked *Seventeen*'s editorial voice, speaking to the teen girl directly and confidently, asserting that they really did know her—and her needs—best. An Emily Wilkens ad from the December 1944 issue reads:

> Emily Wilkens with her genius for reading the teen-age mind has dreamed up the dresses you need for holiday dates. She knows that there is nothing like a good dress properly moulded to a young figure to develop the poise you need when suddenly you discover (jeepers!) you're almost grown up.[47]

Wilkens' mention of "proper moulding" illustrates one difference between the fashion advertising and editorial content during *Seventeen*'s first year. Clothing advertisers seemed more body conscious than the magazine's fashion writers, stressing the importance of a *slender* figure. For instance, an ad for the Jr. Shop at J. P. Allen in Atlanta describes the featured dress as "whittl[ing] a waistline you usually skip lunch to get,"[48] while a Carole King dress is described as having "a full shirred skirt to make your waist look no bigger 'n a minute!"[49]

Not surprisingly, girdle makers focused almost exclusively on the discipline (and punishment) of the teen girl body. American Girl foundations promised that its "girdle makes you gurgle at new found glamour—diminishes hips—makes your derriere mind!"[50] Flexnit, a foundation company that had recently begun marketing to teen girls, offers another example of girdle ads. Featuring a shadowy drawing of a teen-age girl wearing nothing but a white girdle, the text reads: "As of this minute, every Flexnit garment is made definitely for you—to mold you and hold you in the way you should grow. Later, if your figure needs more control, there'll be a Flexnit foundation to provide it."[51]

Flexnit was talking about training Teena in multiple ways: training her to discipline her own body through the use of the girdle, training her to be a lifelong consumer of the brand, and training her to present and display her body for the approval of men. While Flexnit left this last mandate unspoken, many other advertisers didn't. An advertisement for Teen-Set frocks from Lansburgh's "Smart Teen Shop" in Washington, D.C., made the link between body and romance explicit, describing its products as "Date-appealing dresses to play up your classy chassis. Smooth swoonables that will send him out-of-this atmosphere."[52]

Body wear advertisements held out the promise of romance, routinely describing their apparel as "date-bait," "beau-bait," and "wolf-bait." They also promoted a quasi-romantic relationship between girls and their clothes in which "clothes-love" knew no apparel boundaries: "You'll get a 'crush' on all three of these crushed leather lammie-cape bags!" promised purse maker Belt-Modes[53]; "Saybrooke is the love of your life," cooed the sweater manufacturer[54]; and Connie Shoe Creations bragged that "Smooth girls love them with all their heart."[55] Clothing served as a conduit between girls and boys—girls could fall in love with their clothes, and then boys would fall in love with the (well-dressed) girl. An ad for Yearounder hats illustrated the relationship, promising that its hats will "win your heart (and HIS, too)."[56]

Some clothing advertisers were so aware of *Seventeen*'s role as conduit between themselves and the teen buyer that they photographed their models reading or carrying the magazine. Four different ads in the first year—Joan Lord Fashions,[57] Jane Holly Originals,[58] Thornton Hats,[59] and Gail Berk Classics[60]—featured a teen model clutching an issue of *Seventeen*. Thornton Hats ran ads identifying both its product and *Seventeen* in other venues, including the fashion trade newspaper *Women's Wear Daily*.[61] Of course, this could be construed as an advertisement for *Seventeen*—which, in essence, it was. But it was also a sign from the business community that they understood *Seventeen*'s role as the link between their products and the teen buyer. Indeed, in just a year's time, *Seventeen* became the advertisers' place to be in order to catch the eye of the millions of Teenas whose purses carried wallets with money to spend.

Advertising in Postwar America

Seventeen's advertising numbers tell a story of stability and consistency, whether in times of war (September 1944–September 1945) or peace (September 1949–September 1950). The overall 45/55 ratio of editorial to advertising content fluctuated slightly across seasons and special issues, but didn't vary as an annual average. There was a similar continuity in the types of products advertised in the magazine. A comparison of advertising ratios between *Seventeen*'s first year and sixth year reveals little change for most categories: body wear and body care advertising continued to dominate spatially while advertising for entertainment, education/employment, miscellaneous, and snacks remained minimal.

The end of the war did, however, bring some changes to the advertising landscape, most obviously in the disappearance of the flag-waving slogans, war bond appeals, and pictures of soldiers that had served as patriotic prompts to consumption. In addition, the postwar period ushered in a change of focus, particularly for women, from the activeness of the outside world to the coziness of hearth and home. This renewed call to domesticity permeated *Seventeen*'s postwar advertising pages, influencing some advertisement categories more than others. The long-haired model Teenas of war-period body wear ads cut their hair and changed their clothes, but their represented "lives" didn't change much. Domesticity informed fashion, but didn't transform it—in part because the beauty/romance mandate that undergirds fashion is compatible with any cultural focus. On the other hand, advertisements for body care and domestic products reflected changing times.

Although the postwar period saw a slight decrease in the percentage of body care ads, an increasing number of these advertisers targeted teenage girls specifically. Those that spoke directly to the teen girl consumer continued the strategy of selling their products wrapped in a discourse of non-product-related advice, but that advice grew increasingly focused on the boy-girl relationship. In addition, a new advertising force arose in the postwar period to join the body care advertisers in their advisory capacity to teen girls: domestic product advertisers. Indeed, advertisements for domestic products saw the greatest change between war and postwar periods, increasing in both prevalence (as measured by percentage of total advertising space) and visibility (as measured by page coverage, location, and use of color). Sterling silver companies, in particular, began to snap up *Seventeen*'s most influential advertising spaces, selling their wares by speaking directly to the teen girl consumer and by painting an idealized picture of her future. Together, the body care and domestic advertisers of the postwar period marketed more than products or even a consumer lifestyle. They constructed a complementary narrative in which their products led the way to the ideal feminine future—from love to marriage to domestic bliss.

Body Care

In the period between *Seventeen*'s first and fifth birthdays, the editorial staff made a concerted effort to woo body care advertisers, selling them on the potential buying power of the teen girl consumer. While Estelle Ellis and her staff continued reaching out to a range of advertisers through their promotional campaign, editor-in-chief Helen Valentine and beauty editor Jean Campbell specifically targeted the beauty industry. On one occasion, Valentine addressed the Fashion Group, a fashion industry organization, on the topic of grooming and beauty strategies for teenage girls.[62] She informed these industry insiders that high school–age girls needed—indeed wanted—very specific beauty regimen advice and the products to accomplish it. According to Valentine, *Seventeen*'s role was to deliver the advice while the industry's role was to supply the product. Specifically suggesting that cosmetics companies create and market age-appropriate palettes of demure pale pinks to teen girls, she also reminded the Fashion Group membership that cleanliness was the primary component of youthful good grooming.

In February 1949, Valentine and Campbell participated in a panel presentation for the Fashion Group on the necessity of perfume.[63] Together with thirteen other women's magazine editors and led by Chanel president H. Gregory Thomas, the panel proposed that perfume should be marketed for everyday use, not just for special occasions, and for teenage girls as well as for mature women. Several months later, Campbell made an appeal to the beauty industry on behalf of the teen girl as a consumer of grooming products. In an article published in the industry magazine *Cosmetics and Toiletries,* Campbell posed the rhetorical question, "Why snub 8 million customers?" She answered that they shouldn't, that the teen girl was a lucrative purchase/r, and she pointed to the rapid response of the fashion and domestic industries as evidence (and exemplar). Campbell recited the promotional campaign's major points about teen girls as consumers, including their independence from parents ("They have been liberated from the authority of adult control"), tempered with their residual vulnerability and need for adult input ("The teen-ager is the easiest to sell [. . .] She hasn't built up the blasé resistance of habit"). Best of all, argued Campbell, the teen girl had access to her own money as well as her "papa's." Asking the industry "And what do you do when it's [teen purchasing power] right under your cash register? Ignore it?"—"*Better look a little closer,*" she warned.[64]

Apparently, a significant number of body care advertisers did just that. In the magazine's sixth year, eighteen companies placed advertisements in *Seventeen* that marketed their product directly to a teen girl consumer. Of the thirteen advertisers from the first year whose ads targeted teens specifically, only four remained: Elizabeth Arden, Helena Rubinstein, Kotex, and Lux soap. Others—Yardley, Rose Laird makeup, Ex-Lax, Swan soap, Kreml shampoo, Tone cosmetics, and Nonspi deodorant—no longer advertised in *Seventeen.* Drene and Revlon continued as major advertisers but discontinued teen references in their ads. New advertisers, however, including Camay (soap); Noxzema, Tussy, and Cashmere Bouquet (skin care); Prell, Halo, and

Figure 4.2. Kotex Advertisement, September 1949 *Seventeen*. Copyright Kimberly-Clark Worldwide, Inc., Reprinted with Permission

Breck (shampoo); Mum and Veto (deodorants); Ipana (toothpaste); Modess and Tampax (feminine hygiene); and Toni (home permanents); all ran teen-targeted ads featuring pictures of teens and teen-oriented content.

Cosmetics advertisements declined in the postwar period, while advertisements for cleansing products increased—perhaps a sign that Helen

Valentine's tutorials on teen needs were being heeded. The adult vixens of the perfume and cosmetics ads of the war period all but disappeared, as did the adult mothers who had previously accompanied their teen daughters in the skin care, deodorant, and medicine ads. The body care advertisers of the postwar period sold cleanliness and hygiene and joined their body wear counterparts in addressing the teen girl as an autonomous consumer within her own world of product possibilities.

Body care, whether advocated by *Seventeen*'s beauty department or its advertisers, was never really an end in itself. Certainly, these advertisers marketed their products to teens for their obvious usages—as cleansers and hygiene aids. But often underlying the practical product promises was another kind of promise—the promise of love and romance as the result of using certain products. And to *that* end, body care advertisers became educators, offering teen girls a curriculum of romantic direction, advice, and prognostication.

Postwar advertisers doled out relationship guidance with a subtle hand. Many beauty ads included pictures of boys and girls flirting, associating their product with romance. Some advertisers, especially those selling feminine hygiene products, spoke to girls sotto voce, as if sharing secret, important information. Modess and Tampax both used this tone to promote the unobtrusiveness of their products. Modess marketed the anonymity of the box that their product (feminine napkins) came in, describing it as "shaped to resemble many *other* kinds of boxes" and intended to "help keep your secret."[65] Tampax tampons marketed their product's internal (thus secret) usage as a way to keep that "you-know-every-month business" completely under wraps and "improve your social poise on the 'difficult days.'"[66] The key selling point for each of these products was their ability to conceal a normal bodily function. Although unstated, the objects of this subterfuge were the young men who populated the teen girl's life, since other women were acutely aware of "those days."

Another feminine hygiene company, Kotex, remained a major advertiser in postwar *Seventeen* and continued its strategy of offering teen girls an education on body maintenance and relationship etiquette through the quiz "Are You in the Know?" Once again, euphemistic copy about menstruation was buried in quiz questions and answers that covered such topics as what to do about a sunburn,[67] whether you should cut your own hair,[68] and how to ascertain your appropriate weight[69] (Figure 4.2). Pictures of young men and women in dating scenarios accompanied this advice, illustrating the relationship between beauty and romance. At times, Kotex directly advised the teen reader on boy-girl relationships, answering such burning questions as "If he's talkative, what's your technique?"[70] "Should a present for her Sigh Man be personalized?"[71] and "How should you greet your date mate?"[72] In its January 1950 ad, Kotex even suggested the proper attire ("tweeds") in order to "snag the prof"![73]

While Kotex and the other feminine hygiene manufacturers identified the parameters of the ideal teen girl's body maintenance and her dating relationships, soap maker Camay set out the trajectory of her life through their campaign featuring "Your Firsts." This ad series covered the pivotal moments of a young woman's life, which all related to young men and romance. Every month, Camay highlighted different important "Firsts," from the teen girl's "First Orchid!" and "First School Beau!" to a college girl's "First Fraternity Pin!" and "First Black Dress!" Each instance of a "First!," however, ended in exactly the same way, with a picture of "another radiant Camay bride" and the admonishment to "follow the lead of the lovely Camay brides."[74]

Teena's life, in the imagery of postwar advertising, started with a bar of Camay soap and ended at the altar. In the world as portrayed by Camay, marriage was presented as both goal and future end point for the teen girl. Although body care ads of the war period sometimes used brides to promote their products, it wasn't until the postwar period that advertisers began to put teen girls directly on the path to marriage.

Sterling Silver Dreams

Body care products and their use were just the first step toward romance and marriage, however. Advertisements for domestic goods began to appear in the pages of *Seventeen* magazine in the postwar period, pitching marriage and homemaking along with their products. As precursors of the domestic ideal that would fully develop in the 1950s, these purveyors of the tools of housekeeping and hostessing equipped *Seventeen*'s teen girl readers for an idealized feminine adulthood—Destination: Domesticity.

The rise of domestic advertisements in postwar *Seventeen* mirrored the shift that took place in American society as domesticity (re)emerged as women's ideal role—and home, her ideal workplace—after a short-lived wartime sabbatical. Although advertisements for domestic products didn't begin to approach the numbers of either body wear or body care advertisements in postwar *Seventeen*, they did move from last to third place in five years' time. In addition, domestic advertisements occupied the prime sales territory in *Seventeen,* their full-page color ads located in the influential first-well section of the magazine. Much like the body care advertisers, they used their prestigious position as a bully pulpit, offering the teen readership an advanced course in Ideal Womanhood 101.

Domestic ads in *Seventeen* didn't just increase from war to postwar period, however; they metamorphosed. During the war period, the few domestic ads that appeared in the magazine's pages sold laundry soap, fabric, and bedding. Wartime advertisers promoted these items in a kind of gender-generic way—that is, as products to be used by *people* in a variety of settings. For example, an August 1945 advertisement for the Bates Company displayed its bedspreads and drapes in a college dorm room with a male inhabitant (sporting saddle shoes and letter sweater).[75] Other war period domestic ads featured fabric displayed unaccompanied by any human models.[76] During the postwar period, however, domestic ads became more gendered, promoting products to *women* for use in household settings. In their postwar scenarios, these advertisers portrayed girls and women as domestic producers and consumers, boys and men as domestic receivers, and the home as a woman's world.

In the period from September 1949 to September 1950, twenty-two manufacturers advertised the "necessities" of postpubescent feminine domesticity: silverware, hope chests, culinary products and tools, and home decorating items. Half of these advertisers marketed their products specifically to teen girls, led by the representatives of the sterling silver industry. Indeed, sterling silver advertisers became a major advertising presence in postwar *Seventeen,* their wares prominently displayed in full-page color ads in the most prestigious areas of the magazine. These ads often featured teen girl models, but perhaps more importantly—and very much like some body care ads and the editorial voice of the magazine itself—they directly engaged *Seventeen*'s readers, referring to them individually as "you," and addressing them either from a caring adult authority standpoint or as a teen girl confidante. Using this intimate conversational style, manufacturers such as Gorham, International, Towle, and Reed & Barton spooned out heaping helpings of advice about both sterling silver tableware and the domestic lifestyle, enhanced with exclamation points and typographical accentuation meant to reflect the importance of their product and its place in the ideal feminine world. In selling their products, sterling silver manufacturers drew on homemaking as a goal and a feminine ideal. Their narratives traced a trajectory for feminine success in which Romance led to Marriage led to Home led to Homemaking.

The domestic advertisers' trajectory built on that begun by the body care advertisers, whose stories promised that Beauty would lead to Romance. Considering the narrative as a whole, beginning with Beauty and ending with Homemaking, Marriage is at the center of the advertisers' postwar message. Whether they referred to it as the "happy day,"[77] the "Big Day,"[78] the "most important event in history!"[79] or "THE moment of my life!"[80] advertisers communicated to the teen reader the centrality of the (one) wedding in the life of a woman. And these postwar domestic advertising narratives presented marriage as the *only* way to achieve the ideal feminine lifestyle. Although a single woman "careerist" might have the resources to make her own purchases, in the stories told by the advertisers, acquisitions from a home to the sterling silver within it were always tied to marriage. The teen girl narrator of the February 1950 International Sterling ad makes the connection between silver, marriage (as the antithesis to career), and home ownership clear:

> Now that I'm almost grown up, I've been doing some heavy brooding about the future. School can't go on forever, and I'm certainly not the career type. I'm a little young to set the date and pick the bridesmaids. (Mother's eyebrows would go sky-high at the thought!) But a girl can't start too soon to *plan* for marriage and a home of her own.[81]

The teenage girls who inhabited the world of sterling silver advertisements spent much of their time dreaming of and planning for a future wedding, their domestic fantasies amplified by holidays and other special occasions such as Valentine's Day:

> It's the time of year, I guess, with Valentine's Day just around the corner, to get lyrical—to dream about a long, swooshy dress for a Prom . . . and having a date with the most wonderful boy! Starts a girl thinking. About the future. I could be wrong, but this little tune might wind up as the wedding march.[82]

Christmas:

> Some Christmas—and it might not be too far away—you'll be trimming your own tree in your dream-house-for-two.[83]

Graduation:

> Spring's in the air, graduation time is here—and something in your heart has burst into bloom. Suddenly you keep dreaming about that longed-for springtime when you'll walk down the aisle on your father's arm. That dream may come true sooner than you think![84]

Figure 4.3. Gorham Advertisement, April 1950 *Seventeen*

And most certainly the weddings of other young women (Figure 4.3):

> MAYBE YOU'VE DONE IT, TOO . . . sneaked away from the receiving line for a long look at the wedding gifts. You "oh" and "ah" because everything is so beautiful, and look longest at the silver. Then suddenly, you decide to stop sighing and start saving for your *own* Gorham. And by your wedding day you'll probably have a whole set of Gorham to start out with.[85]

This reference to Gorham silver demonstrates the significance of sterling silver ads at this period of *Seventeen*'s history. After establishing matrimony and homemaking as the vision of the future, the sterling silver advertisers set about assisting teenage girls in their journey toward the dream. They did this by marketing silver as the first step on the road to Destination: Domesticity. As one International Sterling ad explained, "Choosing her sterling is an exciting milestone in any girl's life, for it's the first step toward the dreamhome she'll have someday."[86] Lunt ads offered young "hostesses to be" a general timetable for beginning their collection process, advising them that "[t]he day you find the pattern that *really* pleases you . . . that's the time you should start your Sterling. Chances are this will be long before you're engaged."[87] Towle presented the best-case scenario for preparation, when its teen girl narrator said about her older sister, "Why she had her whole collection of Towle before she even had her man picked out!"[88]

To paraphrase an old nursery rhyme, "First comes sterling, then comes marriage, then comes Teena with a hostess carriage." But the advertising campaigns weren't just marketing sterling silverware as the first step; they were also presenting it as the material representation of marriage and love—a substitute to cling to until the "real thing" came along. Sterling manufacturer Gorham describes their product in terms commonly used for the matrimonial ideal: "Beautiful sterling (solid) silver, to love and live with all your life! Its very permanence—the fact that it can't wear off or wear out, ever-symbolizes the lasting, till-death-do-us-part marriage that you mean yours to be."[89]

Taking on the role of matchmaker, sterling silver advertisers promoted silverware as one half of a love match, portraying girls who had fallen in love with these inanimate objects which were apparently meant for more than spearing meat and spooning soup. Speaking of these metal utensils as knights in shining armor, International Sterling promised that "there will be *one in particular* that will melt your heart"[90] while Nobility Plate took the fairy tale to its logical end, by offering teen girls the opportunity to "choose yours like a princess."[91]

When the teen girl representatives of these ads addressed the reader, they spoke as adoringly about their chosen patterns as they might about a much-desired suitor. Towle's full-page color ads featured a different teen girl model and scenario each month. Although the Towle girls and their scripts changed, they were united in their common love of sterling. Miss February states: "The way I feel about Madeira, the TOWLE pattern I picked, proves a girl can be starry-eyed and practical too,"[92] while her October counterpart confides: "Everyone knows what I want—more of my Sterling. Ever since the happy day I chose TOWLE's Old Master and started my set with one spoon, my set has been growing. [. . .] I fall in love all over again with every piece of TOWLE's Old Master."[93]

Apparently, love knows no bounds in these ads—even the love between a young girl and her "Old Master," a theme that would emerge as a 1950s cultural narrative in Vladimir Nabokov's novel *Lolita,* whose sexy nymphet portended the future of the teen girl ideal. Transferring their desire to silverware, the girls of the sterling ads just couldn't get enough of these *objets d'amore*—and why not? For as Reed & Barton explains, "your" sterling pattern is "The Love of Your Lifetime," resulting in an attraction so strong that "you can't resist a love-at-first-sight feeling."[94] Perhaps the possibility of creating such a love match explains the *imperative* in many of these ads. Or perhaps more realistically it resulted from the silver manufacturers' awareness of the economic windfall that awaited them if their matchmaking succeeded. Whatever the explanation, almost every ad implored the reader to begin the selection process immediately, italicizing their imperatives: "*It's the thing to do,*"[95] "Start *this* Christmas,"[96] "*Choose [. . .] now!*"[97] "*Get started,*"[98] and "*Don't wait!*"[99] Gorham spoke for all the sterling silver companies when it (boldly) declared from inside the front cover of the September 1950 issue: "**You're never too young**!"

Some sterling silver advertisers seemingly address the teen reader as a "whole person," asserting that intelligence separated the girls who understood the necessity of silverware ownership from the girls who did not. Over and over, across brands, advertisers told readers that "smart" and "wise" girls recognized the importance of beginning their sterling silver collections. However, the intelligence about which they spoke was less IQ than EQ (economic quotient). The September 1950 Towle ad, read closely, serves as a "fine" example of how advertisers equated intelligence as affluence. The teen girl narrator, holding (not wearing) a pair of glasses—a sign of intelligence—looks at the reader through one of its lenses and proceeds to inform her about:

> **What every Girl Should Know (about her Sterling)**
>
> Smart enough to want Sterling—and wise enough to know:
>
> *THIS.* TOWLE Sterling means fine solid silver in beautiful patterns that are found only in the finest stores. [. . .]
>
> *Still More.* It's so easy to collect your set of TOWLE. When you choose your TOWLE pattern, your favorite TOWLE store will register it for you. Simplifies matters all around—your friends know what you want, and that's what

> you get for Christmas and for birthdays. Prices to please all your friends—only $2.95 for a teaspoon, to start with.[100]

This ad, one example of a general trend, assumed a young consumer who shopped in the "finest stores" (indeed, she has a favorite) and whose teenage friends routinely bought each other gifts, not balking at the purchase of a single teaspoon of "fine solid silver" for "only $2.95" (a minimum starting point that translates to $26.10 in 2009 U.S. currency).[101]

Another Towle ad extrapolated its sales pitch from spoon to set, speculating about the financial status of a girl for whom "a teaspoon costs as little as $2.95—sized to your allowance; place settings and serving pieces fit relatives' budgets!"[102] Since a place setting would run more than three times the cost of a spoon (and perhaps much more), the financial fit required relatives with expansive budgets and generous pocketbooks. Indeed, the girls who inhabited the sterling silver ads often talked of their silver collections as a financial investment, much like their parents' stocks and bonds. The narrator of the December 1949 Towle ad writes her list of New Year's resolutions and includes among them: "*I will prove to myself that I'm smart.* (And the very first step will be to start a set of TOWLE Sterling . . . My Christmas money is going right into solid silver)."[103]

The "smart" girls of the sterling silver ads never put their brain power to use figuring out how to earn their sterling-buying money. Instead, they spent much of their time sweetly scheming to get into the pocketbooks of their affluent friends and relatives. Ads for Reed & Barton, Gorham, Towle, and International Sterling all advised the reader to just "drop a hint" to their friends and relatives, and then expect the gifts to come pouring in. Towle even devised an ingenious strategy that allowed girls to subtly communicate their sterling heart's desires to potential gift-givers, in the guise of a "pattern pin" to be worn as jewelry: "When you pick a TOWLE pattern you're entitled to wear one of the wonderful little TOWLE pattern pins—a miniature teaspoon that is a perfect reproduction of the pattern of your choice!"[104]

Towle marketed its pattern pin as a way for entitled girls to get what they wanted while maintaining their feminine façade of passive desire. The May 1950 Towle girl explains the genteel subterfuge: "A couple of months ago I picked my pattern—TOWLE's French Provencial—and I've been wearing my little pattern pin around. It's much more ladylike than hinting! And what a way to build a set of TOWLE Sterling—the easy way, through gifts."[105] Thus, Towle's pattern pin allowed girls to signal their silverware design preferences, sidestepping the need to ask. The pin also allowed the wearer to signal her domestic aspirations (for marriage and homemaking) to the boys in her life.

Still, advertisers needed girls to get the word out about their love of sterling and encouraged them to speak up with their close relatives and, most particularly, with each other. International Sterling sponsored gatherings where small groups of "real" girls of high school and college age got together to choose their silver patterns. These sessions showcased the social class element of sterling collecting. The ads featured a changing array of girls clad in sweater sets and pearls meeting in rarefied social settings, from "Dallas coeds" at "Southern Methodist University"[106] to "Louisville Belles" at "Louisville's famous Pendennis Club"[107] to "Birmingham teen-agers" at "the fashionable Birmingham County Club."[108]

Although these International Sterling girls appeared to share a common social class status and interest in sterling silver, the ads also divided the young women into personality types—which just happened to match the company's range of silver patterns. In one ad, each young woman wears a different pastel-hued dress (reflecting her "individuality") and selects a different sterling silver pattern. In another, International Sterling published a key for the reader to use to match her personality with her perfect sterling choice, which included these examples:

> Perhaps you're idealistic, love tradition. You'll like French-inspired Joan of Arc [. . .]
>
> You may be an individualist, with a flair for the unusual. For you—magnificent, massive Northern Light [. . .]
>
> There's a bit of the minx about you, a glint in your eye. Choose Enchantress—half blossomy, half suave—all beautiful [. . .]
>
> You've a fresh, sparkling, alive quality. Pick Spring Glory, springlike, bridelike, with a perfect unfolding flower [. . .][109]

Although advertisers appeared to be promoting silver collecting as a communal bonding experience among middle- and upper-class girl consumers, they also relied on a divide-and-conquer strategy with silver acquisition as a competitive sport. Once girls selected the patterns that best expressed their "unique" personalities, they were positioned (by the advertiser) for rivalry. The May 1950 Towle ad provides an example of the competition brought to the silver-collecting table. The teen narrator sets the stage:

> I thought I was the only one with a bright idea—"I want TOWLE Sterling for graduation," I told my family. And then I found out most of the senior class said the same thing! We compare notes every noon—Sue's ahead, with six whole place settings of Rambler Rose—but my Uncle Joe hasn't been heard from yet, so I have hopes![110]

The Fairy Tale

Like this teenager, *Seventeen*'s advertisers had hopes: to sell their products to a consumer force that would march into the future branded and ready to buy. To that end, they worked to court, counsel, and—ultimately—create a postwar teen girl consumer. Together they composed a narrative that echoed the age-old fairy tale in which the princess begins her journey armed with beauty, finds her prince, marries him, and lives happily ever after in his castle on the hill (in this case, with a full set of sterling silver). *Seventeen*'s postwar advertisers provided variations of this fairy tale and offered the reader strategies for achieving its happy ending. They advised her not just on the products of body wear, body care, and domestic work, but also on romance and homemaking—how to capture the prince and run the castle.

Seventeen's wartime and postwar advertisers understood that "Teena Mean[t] Business." But in order to sell her their products, they first had to sell her a dream and a vision of the future. The vision they created with their pictures and stories was one bounded by gender, race, sexuality, and social class. To some extent, this was moderated by the war, which created a temporary opportunity for the blurring of boundaries. Overall, however, *Seventeen*'s advertisers constructed and counseled a teen girl who possessed ideal 1940s femininity: white, unblemished skin, delicate facial features, slender figure, able body, upper/middle social class, a two-parent home with siblings, and disciplined heterosexual desires.

Although the advertisers' Teenas mirrored the "model" Teenas of *Seventeen*'s editorial pages, the world reflected in the advertising pages was much less diverse than the world as represented by *Seventeen*. For example, while *Seventeen* included articles and pictures of people of color and from different nations, the advertisers' pages were largely populated by white Teenas. When people of color did (rarely) appear, it was as ethnic caricatures or counter-ideals. This contrast is best illustrated by a March 1945 Nan

Figure 4.4. Nan Scott Advertisement, March 1945 *Seventeen*

Scott ad (Figure 4.4), which featured two white teenage models sporting lovely frocks who, while on a leisurely stroll, encounter and literally look down upon a young African American boy, asleep in a cotton pile that he had apparently picked.[111] While the inclusion of a person of color offered a semblance of ethnic "diversity" to *Seventeen*'s advertising pages, the depiction harked back to the days of slavery, thereby serving to shore up—not tear down—racial boundaries.

After the war, the advertisers' tales became more specific and less open to interpretation. During the war period, the advertisers who talked to teen girls generally ended their stories at the princess finding love with the prince (product + girl = romance). The reader could envision her own version of the future—perhaps the princess married the prince but continued to work outside the castle. In the postwar period, however, the tale told by the domestic advertisers always ended in marriage and homemaking.

It is ironic that as time went by, *Seventeen*'s advertisers began presenting Teena as a fully autonomous individual, unique in her consumer desires, while simultaneously selling her a dream that allowed for almost no variation in real-life desires. But as a marketing strategy, it has its logic, however counterintuitive. In the early 2000s, a similar concept emerged in the U.S. Army's advertising slogan "An Army of One." *Seventeen*'s advertisers were building a similar "army"—an army of individual female consumers.

CHAPTER 5

Seventeen Magazine at Peace

Teena Leaves the World, Enters the Home, and Loses Her Mind

It's five whole years

This is our birthday—we're five years old. And, as we blow out the candles on the cake, we have that special birthday feeling which combines a lot of pleasure with a little private stocktaking. How did I use this past year, what will I do with the new one which is about to be born? Magazines, like people, have their birthday thoughts.

We can't help wondering whether you were a reader of our first issue. If you were, you may possibly remember that we promised you a magazine that would try to reflect what you do, what you think, what you are. We said we would report on "everything that concerns, excites, annoys, pleases and perplexes you."

Sensing your own deep sincerity, we talked about the kind of human being you are. Not just about your clothes and your face, or even your talents and tastes . . . but also about your relation to your family and your friends, your interest in the world and all the people in it.

You have proved yourself thoughtful, practical, attractive. You have shown skill and talent and an enormous amount of sense. All in all, we'd say you have been most satisfactory—and a very good friend. We'd like to feel that you can say as much for us. We hope that this is the magazine you really want—that it gives you plenty of help and fun and something to think about. Many things have happened in five years. We know how greatly you have grown, we hope we've done a bit of growing too. But one thing remains constant. That squiggle below still says, as it did in our first issue, love to you from all of us on SEVENTEEN.

[Helen Valentine, "It's Five Whole Years," *Seventeen*, September 1949, 103]

Five years after her letter of introduction, Helen Valentine again spoke directly to the reader in a birthday greeting. Although the two letters have similar elements and address similar topics, they differ in tone. Valentine's first letter brimmed with an excitement that came from looking to the future; her letter marking *Seventeen*'s fifth birthday looks back and assesses the past. Valentine mentions the magazine's "private stocktaking": *Seventeen* magazine was her baby, the reader her concern, the magazine staff her responsibility, the intersection of the three her project. Whether she knew it yet or not, this letter was her last—a farewell to the project and the people to which she had devoted the past five years of her life.

As Valentine noted in her letter, "Many things [had] happened in five years." Changes had occurred in the global and national arenas, in the magazine industry, and at *Seventeen.* In the five years following *Seventeen*'s first birthday, a world war had ended and a cold war begun. The United Nations—an organization mentioned frequently in the pages of the magazine—became a reality, as did the Central Intelligence Agency (CIA) and the North Atlantic Treaty Organization (NATO). In the United States, Benjamin Spock published his childcare manifesto, *Dr. Spock's Baby and Child Care,* while Alfred Kinsey shocked (and titillated) the reading public by detailing the *Sexual Behavior in the American Male.* Racial boundaries were being challenged: Jackie Robinson became the first African American major league baseball player, and President Truman signed legislation ending racial segregation in the military.[1]

In the magazine industry, *Seventeen*'s success had been noticed and competitors began to appear on newsstands. In April 1946, William M. Cotton, Philadelphia publisher of pulp magazines *Movie Stars, Movie Life, Personal Romances,* and *Intimate Romances,* tried to join his competitor Walter Annenberg in reaching out to a younger, more "wholesome" audience.[2] *Deb* magazine, Cotton's contribution to the teen magazine genre, followed *Seventeen* in both format and content, with articles covering fashion, fun, food, and future choices. *Deb* differed from *Seventeen,* however, in its smaller size, its advertiser support and, ultimately, its longevity.

The February 23, 1946 issue of *Business Week* announced *Deb*'s entry into the teen magazine market, noting that it would "[a]dd to the growing list of magazines directed at the younger strata of feminine society."[3] Among that growing list was *Junior Bazaar,* the progeny of fashion magazine *Harper's Bazaar. Junior Bazaar*'s "coming out"—both figurative and literal, as it initially appeared as a several-page subsection of *Harper's Bazaar*—was publicized in a four-page

Life article, as well as in a full-page advertisement in the fashion industry's bible, *Women's Wear Daily*. The ad introduced not just the magazine but the magazine's readership to the business community:

> The new young monthly magazine READY WITH the young leaders of America—Young Americans, living, learning, earning—all listening in through the fresh young pages of *Junior Bazaar*, every month beginning November, 1945. Of course you won't meet all of them to start, but you will meet the leaders—the girls that all other girls follow in fashion, accessories and beauty. Already alert advertisers are filling the advance pages of *Junior Bazaar* to contact these influential young leaders in the big three markets—the high school girl—the college girl—the girl on the job. For the first time—under one cover, the complete Junior Fashion Market.[4]

The accompanying illustration featured a representative of each of its three target reader markets: teenage girl, college coed, and young working woman. Although this attempt to merge the interests of three different age ranges into one magazine set *Junior Bazaar* apart from *Seventeen,* they had many similarities. *Junior Bazaar* was the brainchild of *Harper's Bazaar*'s powerful editor-in-chief, Carmel Snow, who, like Helen Valentine, received her training at Condé Nast, under *Vogue* editor-in-chief Edna Woolman Chase.[5] Snow drew inspiration from *Seventeen*'s success, recognizing the potential of the teenage market.[6] Much like Valentine at *Seventeen,* Snow surrounded herself with staffers who strove for excellence in all facets of *Junior Bazaar*'s publication, from writing to art to photography.[7]

Junior Bazaar, also following *Seventeen,* celebrated its birthdays; however, unlike *Seventeen,* it would not live to see its fifth. In June 1948, *Junior Bazaar* was reintegrated into *Harper's Bazaar,* ostensibly because it diverted too much of Snow's attention away from its more profitable progenitor.[8] While *Seventeen* originally inspired *Junior Bazaar, Junior Bazaar* may have served as inspiration for Walter Annenberg, who insisted in 1948 that Valentine—against her editorial preference—integrate features and advertising targeting the more mature, junior-size college-age crowd.[9]

Publishers of adolescent girl magazines became aware of the economic benefits of "growing up" and appealing to a more mature—and pocketbook-carrying—readership. Beginning in 1948, *Calling All Girls* shifted its attention from its original preteen reader to *Seventeen*'s market, the high school girl.[10] In 1949, the editors made this growth spurt official, renaming the magazine *Senior Prom . . . for Teens, Debs, and Co-eds.* Despite *Senior*

Prom's inclusion of articles about college and career, columns on shopping and romantic advice, and fiction by well-known authors such as Phyllis Whitney and Madeleine L'Engle, it continued to differ from *Seventeen* in terms of aesthetics. *Senior Prom* may have jettisoned its "Girls," but it retained its middle-class "real girl" look and feel. From an artistic standpoint, *Seventeen* remained the more sophisticated girl on the block, especially after the demise of *Junior Bazaar*.

Seventeen had done some growing and changing of its own in the five-year period between its birth and fifth birthday. Many of the original "family" members were gone, including fashion editor Eleanore Hillebrand and beauty editor Irma Phorylles. Alice Thompson had risen from writer to executive editor to publisher. Graphic designer Cipe Pineles had been hired as art director, changing the magazine's style with her award-winning designs. There were additional changes brought about not only by the end of the war but also by Walter Annenberg's increased supervision over the magazine's content—including his mandates to include the interests of older "juniors" and to limit pictures of "negros."[11]

The pied pipers of *Seventeen* had been busy in the intervening years, spreading their message beyond the magazine's New York City offices. In 1948 and 1949, *Seventeen* published and sold a series of thirteen "Reader Service Booklets" that advised teen girls on issues addressed in the magazine's editorial pages: appearance and fashion ("Fashion and You" and "Young Beauty"); domestic endeavors ("Food for Your Crowd," "Successful Parties," "Your Home and You," "Favorite Handknits," and "Make Your Own Gifts"); relationships ("Your Parents and You," "Everybody's Shy," "Popular Girl," and "Your New Emotions"); and vocational and avocational interests ("Choosing a Career," and "Club Notes"). These booklets set the parameters of the "ideal" teen girl—then followed through with how-to advice.[12]

Beginning in 1946, *Seventeen* staffers took their educational message to the schoolhouse, creating monthly home economics supplements called "*Seventeen* in the Classroom" which they distributed to schools for classroom use. Each month's edition offered a curriculum plan that linked specific articles in *Seventeen* to topics and exercises geared toward the needs of teachers of home economics, foods and nutrition, clothing, household management, home planning, and personality development, as well as guidance advisors and home economics club advisors.[13]

Also in 1946, *Seventeen* developed a radio show called *It's Up to Youth* that introduced both *Seventeen* and the "Seventeener" to a national audience. In promoting the show to the readership, *Seventeen* described it as a forum for giving both the magazine and teenagers (both girls and boys) a "voice":

> Your favorite magazine has found its voice . . . .Every Wednesday evening SEVENTEEN will broadcast "IT'S UP TO YOUTH"—a program about your problems—a program that will give you and your friends a chance to say what you think. Each week a teen-age problem will be dramatized; then a panel of high school girls and boys will talk it over. Be sure to listen to your local Mutual station for "IT'S UP TO YOUTH"—the program that talks about SEVENTEENERS and gives SEVENTEENERS a chance to talk about themselves.[14]

Five years had passed since Baby's first birthday. As Valentine concluded at the end of her letter to the reader: "Many things have happened in five years. We know how greatly you have grown, we hope we've done a bit of growing too." Just how much and in what ways had the magazine "grown" since birth? The answers lie in the magazine itself: the thirteen issues published from *Seventeen*'s fifth birthday to sixth birthday (September 1949 through September 1950).

These postwar issues are of particular interest for several reasons. First, they offer a look at the early developmental period for both *Seventeen* (as a teen magazine genre) and the teen girl ideal. Second, during this time period, Annenberg and Valentine found themselves at odds over editorial and business issues, with Annenberg (and publisher Alice Thompson) exerting more control over the creative direction of the magazine. Finally, these issues were created during and shaped by a period of significant sociocultural change, as America (and Americans) shifted from world war labor to cold war domesticity.

Postwar *Seventeen* Magaziine

War's end brought about a shift in the cultural messages about women's roles. As American soldiers (the majority of them male) returned from war, the U.S. government sought to return them to their "rightful place" as breadwinners. Making a 180-degree turnabout from its wartime stance, the government, again with the assistance of the advertising industry, began a campaign encouraging women to leave the workforce for the home front, and to serve their family and nation through consumption (rather than production).[15] Despite the fact that many women did not want to leave their paid employment,[16] the government's efforts were apparently not in vain, as women's employment rates dropped and their fertility rates rose.[17] These societal shifts were reflected in the pages of postwar *Seventeen* magazine.

Seventeen's covers and editorial coverage changed, as did its advertising (see Chapter 4) in the postwar period. Postwar issues mirrored the transformations taking place in society and in the magazine's staffing, but also retained many of their former stylistic elements. For example, the magazine maintained its larger-than-average dimensions and its simple cover look—a look that also continued for other women's magazines of the period. In February 1948, *Seventeen*'s cover price increased from fifteen cents to twenty-five cents, and in March 1950, the cover signaled the magazine's expansion beyond the borders of the United States, noting, in fine print, a purchase price of thirty cents in Canada.

With the end of World War II came the end of *Seventeen*'s war-themed covers. Gone were the signs of American patriotism and appeals to global citizenship; fashion now commanded center stage. In addition, the postwar covers reflected *Seventeen*'s ever-increasing variety of "special issues." During its first year, the magazine designated three special issues: April's "Girl Meets Boy," July's "Your America," and September's "Birthday." In the time between September 1949 and September 1950, more than half of the magazine's issues had special themes: September 1949's "Birthday"; October 1949's "Your Home and You"; November 1949's "Your Parents and You"; January 1950's "Your School and You"; April 1950's "Girl Meets Boy"; May 1950's "It's All Yours"; June 1950's "How-To-Be-Pretty"; and August 1950's "High School Fashions." The covers used illustrations as well as captions to signal the special issue subjects, such as a locket with a picture of a mother and father for "Your Parents and You," a model lounging in a long robe for "Your Home and You," and a model carrying department store packages for "High School Fashions."

Seventeen introduced its special issues over the five years between its first and fifth birthdays. "Girl Meets Boy," "Birthday," and "Your Parents and You" debuted in 1945; "It's All Yours" (an annual teen-reader-created issue) and "Back to School Fashions" in 1947; "Young Beauty" and "Your School and You" in 1948; and "Your Home and You" in 1949. The focus of the special issues reflected changes in society. After World War II, *Seventeen*'s attention shifted from global and national to more individual concerns such as school, appearance, and—increasingly, as the 1950s unfolded—home and domesticity.

"Careerists" were phased out of both society and *Seventeen* after the war, with one exception: modeling, a job that took place outside the home but epitomized ideal feminine beauty. The magazine began to identify not just the photographer but also the model in its inside cover acknowledgment in June 1950. That model, fourteen-year-old Gay Scott, was the first *Seventeen* model mentioned by name elsewhere in the magazine, when she was spotlighted in the December 1949 "They Worked with Us This Month" column.[18]

Seventeen's cover models changed their clothing style slightly from 1945 to 1949, but their ideal beauty not at all. Hairstyles changed the most, as long tresses were cut; ten of the thirteen covers between *Seventeen*'s fifth and sixth birthdays featured models with bobbed hair. The bob functioned as a symbol of America's postwar fascination with "modernity." The January 1950 "Your School and You" cover featured two girls engaged in conversation at the bottom of a set of concrete school steps, using the length of their hair and dresses to contrast tradition (1900) and modernity (1950) (Figure 5.1). The representative of the turn of the century has long dark hair controlled by a braid, a bow, *and* a hat, wears a floor-length dress, and carries her large textbooks in a bookstrap. With a short bob and a knee-length jumper, her modern companion carries a notebook and small textbook in the crook of her arm. Everything about the "modern" girl's appearance signals freedom from encumbrances—especially in relation to her archaic counterpart. Still, some feminine "encumbrances" remain constant despite the era.[19] The inside cover acknowledgment makes this clear, reminding girls that "To look pretty for school is still as much in style as it was in 1900!"[20]

Seventeen Magazine Grows and Changes

Seventeen's size, measured by number of pages, more than doubled—and for some issues, tripled—between birth and sixth birthday. The first issue had 88 pages, whereas the "First Birthday" had 168. The "Fifth Birthday" issue was 244 pages, and the August 1950 "High School Fashions" issue held a whopping 296 pages.[21] This growth can be attributed to the increase in advertising that followed the end of the war, which increased the number of advertisements but also paid for the expansion of the editorial pages.

The magazine's most dramatic growth spurt occurred in 1946 when the U.S. government lifted its wartime paper restrictions, permitting *Seventeen* to fill as many pages as it could. *Seventeen*'s largest issues were those that were most advertiser-friendly; thus, the August "Back to School" issues, with their focus on clothing and shopping, had the most pages and the highest ratio of advertising to editorial copy. Conversely, the smallest issues

Figure 5.1. Cover, January 1950 *Seventeen*, photographer Richard Litwin

were the summer issues, which focused on leisure pursuits and featured fewer fashion spreads and much lower advertising ratios. The differences in issue content and issue size throughout a year's run were noticeable, provoking at least one reader to write a letter of complaint about the dearth of fashion coverage in the July 1950 issue. The editors used that opportunity to educate the reader(ship) on the business basics of women's magazine publishing:

> We hope most of you had fun with our "summer fun" issue. Perhaps we should explain how the fashion business works. The July issue of any magazine is low in fashion pages, simply because there are very few clothes made to sell in July. The manufacturers are busy working on their fall lines; stores push "sale" merchandise in July. But, as you can see from our August and September issues, we've rounded up big back-to-school fashion wardrobes for you.[22]

Directives from both the business and editorial sides of *Seventeen* led to changes in the magazine's fashion pages. At odds with Helen Valentine's original vision, owner Walter Annenberg decided that extending *Seventeen*'s readership to include college-age women would increase the magazine's profitability. He ordered Valentine to expand the magazine's editorial fashion pages, previously reserved for teen-size wear, to include junior-size clothing. Valentine balked, but Annenberg prevailed, and *Seventeen*'s fashion pages began to include junior attire in 1948.[23] "Chubbie" sized clothing, on the other hand, remained an anomaly in *Seventeen*, receiving coverage in only two fashion features out of 175 during that time period. The titles—"On the Slimming Side"[24] and "To Slim You Down"[25]—reveal the magazine's attitude toward the "chubbie" body type.

Creating an aesthetically sophisticated magazine remained important to Helen Valentine; while she edited *Seventeen*, the all-important birthday covers were entrusted to Francesco Scavullo, who also photographed many of the inside fashion spreads and most of the covers for the magazine during Valentine's tenure (forty-two covers between November 1944 and September 1949). The sumptuous September 1949 "Fifth Birthday" cover exemplified the early look of Scavullo's work and of *Seventeen*'s covers/cover girls (Figure 5.2). Two young women, a brunette and a blonde, lean forward to blow out the seventeen candles on a birthday cake, their red bow mouths puckered in preparation. The pale ecru background sets off their porcelain complexions, and the varying shades of pink, from tablecloth to cake to sweetly bowed party frocks, create a visual cotton candy confection. The gauzy, dreamy feel of the picture—typical of Scavullo—is at the same time youthful and elegant.

Art director Cipe Pineles also made her mark on *Seventeen*'s postwar pages. In the magazine's first year of publication, art director Jan Balet relied upon Francesco Scavullo and a handful of other male photographers for the magazine's photographic layouts. Pineles, on the other hand, enlisted the assistance of a wide array of photographers and illustrators, both up-

Figure 5.2. Cover, September 1949 *Seventeen*, photographer Francesco Scavullo

and-coming and established, some of them women and people of color. In the year between the fifth and sixth birthdays, Scavullo photographed only three covers, his last in March 1950; the remaining ten were photographed by five other photographers, including one woman, Tana Hoban. The result: fashion pages that often broke the mold of convention, diverse in look but united in their creativity, artistry, and quality.[26]

Readers, editors, and advertisers all recognized *Seventeen* as a fashion magazine, but Helen Valentine never forgot that it was a service magazine, too. As Valentine had stressed in her September 1944 introductory letter to the reader, *Seventeen* would cover fashion—but also beauty and health, self in relation to others, the life of the mind, and leisure activities in a rather equitable way.[27] Valentine's purposes matched *Seventeen*'s early reality, as measured by its first year editorial content. After World War II, however, this aspect of *Seventeen* became less pronounced. Home became a major theme, together with the romance that would lead to a home of one's own. Boys, clothes, and bodies became much more important for the American teen girl.

Consuming Fashion

At the same time that American women were being called upon to control their bodies in 1950s America, they were also being asked to loosen up their spending and become "purchaser citizens," a term coined by historian Lizbeth Cohen to describe the postwar model of (female) consumption as the means to both personal and societal prosperity.[28] As the United States moved into the postwar era, the gender freedom of the war years was redefined as the freedom to spend.[29] One fashion trend in the pages of postwar *Seventeen*—the accessory—was directly related to this new consumer mandate and Americans' rising disposable incomes. Barely mentioned in 1944–1945 *Seventeen*, accessories became an important part of the fashion landscape in 1949–1950, covered in multiple features in every issue during the period. Adorning the body with "Those Little Touches"—everything from socks, stockings, shoes, slippers, hats, gloves, watches, jewelry, and even luggage—became the norm; plain garments would no longer suffice.[30] In particular, *Seventeen* considered the buying of jewelry an important enough endeavor to devote an entire article—"Your First Piece of Real Jewelry"—to the how-to's of assessing and collecting wearable metals and gems.[31]

With all this attention to accessories and other accoutrements, it would be easy to get the impression that *Seventeen* was encouraging a new era of conspicuous consumption, but the magazine continued to include features stressing frugality and thoughtful buying. The September 1950 feature "DAY out . . . NIGHT out" suggested accessorizing as a way to *extend* the usefulness for certain pieces of a wardrobe:

> The dresses above go all around the clock; come up looking fresh and, what's more, different for evening. We call them dual-life dresses because they can

> look casual by day, yet in the twinkling of a rhinestone, shed a jacket, retie a shawl, toss on a bib and go to dinner in high style.[32]

Changes in the American culture translated into changes in the fashion pages of *Seventeen*; the two words that best describe the fashion trend in women's clothing of the postwar period are *domesticity* and *romance.* In *Seventeen*'s fashion spreads, home and hearth often served as the backdrop for the young models, many of whom sported pajamas. Indeed, although bedtime wear was rarely featured in *Seventeen*'s war-period fashion pages, it became a postwar fashion staple. Appearing in fashion features in more than half of the magazine issues of this time period, models wearing jammies even graced the covers of two issues: June 1950's "How to Be Pretty" and October 1949's "Your Home and You" (Figure 5.3). Among all the fashion photos taken in home settings, those featuring fleece robes, frilly nighties, and flannel pj's best signified the cozy warmth of the 1950s domestic ideal.

In addition, the fashion transition from relaxed, informal, and menswear-inspired clothing of the war period to the form-fitting, formal, and feminine attire of the postwar period, beginning in the August 1945 issue, was complete by 1949. At the same time (and not coincidentally), boys moved from background to foreground in the magazine's fashion pages; by 1949–1950, the driving fashion question in *Seventeen* had become "What do boys like?" The answer—found in the feature "Boys Like Floaty Party Sheers"—was "Dresses like these [that] make a girl look so much like a girl."[33] Another feature, "The Boys Speak Up," queried young men on their views "about graduation dresses and their fabrics." In case the reader didn't fully appreciate the significance of male approval, *Seventeen* laid it on the line:

> All the clothes on these and the following six pages were put up for inspection before perhaps the most discriminating, and certainly one of the most important, audiences in the world: boys. Our all-male audience was made up of the teen-age lower classmen at the U.S. Merchant Marine Academy at King's Point, Long Island. Their smiling faces, and the comments they made, tip off the happy ending to our story.[34]

Although *Seventeen* still featured school wear, especially in the August and September issues, clothing for *after*-school activities dominated the postwar fashion spreads. Particularly popular were dresses for dates, dances, and parties—venues and events where boys were present and, for the most part, *the point.*[35] In fact, teen life in 1950, as seen through the lens of *Seventeen*'s fashion

Figure 5.3. Cover, October 1949 *Seventeen*, photographer Francesco Scavullo

pages, was one fun-filled party, populated by boys in suits and girls in tea dresses with tiny cinched waists that showed off their hourglass figures (Figure 5.4).

Body Projects

Of course, not all feminine figures follow the form of an hourglass, which created an opening for another fashion trend of the 1950s: foundation

Figure 5.4. "Wearing a New Shade of Blue," September 1949 *Seventeen*, photographer Francesco Scavullo

wear (bras and girdles). Meriting only a couple of mentions in 1944–1945 *Seventeen*, discussions and images of undergarments became *de rigueur* in 1949–1950, featured in every issue of the magazine. Often, the relationship between the form-fitting fashions of the period and the need for proper undergarments was only inferred, but sometimes it was spelled out, as in the feature "A Better Figure for You," which described its garments as "Three long-wearing cotton bras, three light nylon girdles to make your clothes look nicer."[36] Bodily control was the ultimate goal of these figure-formers and the girls who wore them. As the feature "Get Into Shape" simply stated: "Everything's under control—figuratively speaking—when you wear any of these girdles and bras."[37] In ways both metaphorical and material, the 1950s body modeled the broader cultural ideal of corporal control (or the illusion of control) as a "good thing."[38]

While articles in 1944–1945 *Seventeen* referred on occasion to diet and exercise, it was always in the context of health and vitality, suggesting that girls eat nutritious meals and get lots of exercise through sports and general activity in order to feel well. By 1949–1950, however, the emphasis was on body aesthetics—that is, improving the look of the body in order to best show off the clothes that adorned it. For example, the article "Scale That Figure Down" described dieting as "what you have to do to get thin," the result of which would be you "look[ing] slim and pretty in your new spring clothes!"[39] "Posture Perfect?" addressed the relationship of fashion to body control, warning that "even the prettiest clothes won't help if you stand in a slump, walk in a slouch, sit in a heap."[40] In addition, what constituted "exercise" changed from generalized activity (including sports) to the specific activity of calisthenics and stretching, as set out in the article "Figure on These."[41]

Apparently, some girls got the slim-and-trim message only too well. Although *Seventeen's* beauty editor Jean Campbell wrote about eating to *gain* weight in "Pad That Frame,"[42] her article was accompanied by a fashion spread with a caption that read that a "skin-and-bones girl can look wonderful."[43] This prompted reader "Sorry-too-late Sue" to write in and ask:

> But can she *feel* wonderful? Last year I became obsessed with the idea of looking like a fashion model. I got to normal measurements by exercise, to model's measurements by sheer starvation—I fasted for days at a time. I was often sick, found it hard to breathe, now believe I wasted a whole year of my life. I hope other girls who read this won't ruin their health as I did mine![44]

Seventeen answered Sue, stating:

> We, too, found it hard to breathe when we read your letter! We sincerely hope that your suicidal starvation did no permanent damage; that you've fully recovered from your wish to look like someone else (see "Who's a Dummy?" on page 50). Although a "skin-and-bones" girl can improve her

> looks temporarily with the right clothes, she should, of course, work to "Pad That Frame."[45]

"Who's a Dummy?," the article to which *Seventeen*'s response referred, was also written by Campbell. Questioning teen girls' criticism of their own bodies, "Dummy" asked them to consider their physical uniqueness and to reject attempts to become "anonymous copycats."[46] However, Campbell opined that the desire "to be prettier than we are at the moment, both to please ourselves and the men (eventually the man) in our lives" was a "natural female desire" and advised girls to "make ourselves prettier, but [. . .] within the boundaries of our own given frames."[47]

The bulk of *Seventeen*'s advice on body maintenance continued to be about its care and grooming. Every issue contained detailed how-to advice on grooming, covering such topics as applying makeup,[48] giving a home permanent,[49] caring for feet,[50] and the necessity of wearing deodorant.[51] In *Seventeen,* grooming as a whole body regimen involved piecing out individual body regions, assessing every facet, and then applying some sort of solution—usually through the use of a product. *Seventeen*'s 1950 special issue, "How to Be Pretty," answered the question "What Makes a Pretty Girl?" by identifying the body's grooming areas. The resulting seven articles—"Your Face... Its Care, Its Trimming," "Your Hair," "Your Fragrance," "Your Hands," "Your Feet," "You Can't Be Almost Clean," and "These [products] Make a Pretty Girl"—offer an illustration of grooming as a system of related tasks.[52]

In February 1949, *Seventeen* introduced the column "Dear Beauty Editor," opening up a dialogue between readers and editors on the topic of beauty. Readers sent in questions about their health and beauty "problems" (covering a vast area of concerns, including hair, skin, makeup, and menstruation) and the editors answered with advice, which generally fell into three categories: accept it, ask your doctor, or use this (fill-in-the-blank) product. The "conversation," however, left one reader dissatisfied; her letter of complaint revealed one unspoken characteristic of *Seventeen*'s body ideal:

> Dear Beauty Editor:
>
> I read your magazine every month and think it's wonderful. I am sixteen and a junior in high school. I want to know why you never give Negro girls suggestions on cosmetics, how to care for hair, colors we should use, etc. We teenagers want to look our best, too.[53]

Seventeen's editor responded weakly (by contemporary standards):

> Your concern that Negro teenagers do not receive sufficient guidance in beauty, health and grooming problems is understandable. However, SEVENTEEN doesn't like to think that Negro girls feel neglected or overlooked when it carries articles on these subjects. These articles contain, for the most part, information on cleanliness and appearance that apply to all our readers. We have tried to touch on the universal (or more accurately, the usual) problems that are likely to affect all teen-agers. We had hoped that our general features contained enough specific information so that girls, whether blonde, brunette, redhead or Negro, might find help for their own individual problems.[54]

Although the editor went on to provide beauty care suggestions particularly suited to African American women, her response illuminated what was likely invisible to any reader not of color: the "universal" body, according to and addressed by *Seventeen,* was white.

Love and Marriage

The postwar articles about "How You Feel and Look" were the least affected by either staffing changes or cultural shifts. Apparently, beauty was (and is) an American girl's duty, regardless of her time period.[55] On the other hand, an interesting change occurred to "the world" in the postwar pages of *Seventeen*: it shrunk—at least as measured by the magazine's coverage. In addition, "Getting Along in the World" became getting along with boys. This shift toward love and marriage took place in the magazine's content as a whole, but the articles in "Getting Along in the World" are of particular interest because of how "the world" came to be redefined as the world of boys next door—and the point of getting along with boys was getting married. While wartime issues asked young women readers to consider a "careerist" future in the work world, postwar issues often assumed a future of labor in the home.. In November 1948, *Seventeen* published an article by anthropologist Margaret Mead entitled "Can Homemaking Really Be a Career?" Mead, somewhat ironically as a working woman, answered her question with a resounding "Yes!"[56]

While the pro-work position didn't completely disappear from *Seventeen*'s postwar issues, the number of articles promoting careers declined, the "world" of illustrated employment choices became smaller, and the types of jobs covered toed the (high-heeled) line of standard feminine fare. For example, four of the seven articles about future work options detailed careers in typical female arenas, including home decorating ("Wizardry in Four Walls"[57]), retail sales ("Rising in Retailing"[58]), the beauty industry ("Beauty is BIG BUSINESS"[59]), and clerical work ("On Minding Your KEYS and Cues"[60]). Only three articles on work were less gender stereotypical, detailing the work of humanitarian nonprofit agencies ("You, Too, Can Work for Something"[61]), the banking industry ("Finance: Feminine Gender"[62]), and medical laboratory technicians ("Labs and Lassies"[63]). But even within the less stereotypical career articles of the postwar period, there were signs of the traditionalist model. For example, "Labs and Lassies" lamented the low pay of an otherwise challenging science career, and then quoted a male hospital administrator, who rationalized the economic disparity: "'There's an attraction to working in modern laboratories with modern methods, moving ahead the barriers that block so much of our understanding. And then, too,' he adds with a grin, 'there's an attraction to the medical students—must be, or the girls wouldn't date and marry them the way they do.'"[64]

Indeed, *Seventeen,* as it ventured further and further into the postwar era, increasingly promoted male approval and marriage, cornerstones of the traditional model of gender relations. Thus, 1945's "If He Could Only Cook,"[65] in which boys cooked for girls, was replaced in 1950 with the directive to "Bake Him a Pie."[66] In 1945, "Jobs Have No Gender"[67] argued that the division of household labor should be equitably distributed among a home's "citizens," but five years later "Who Does Your Laundry?" seemed to *expect* a gendered division of labor, stating: "When daughters get to be teen-age, they should be of some help. If your mother does all her own laundry, you've probably assumed your rightful position as her helper long since."[68]

Wartime advice on "What's a girl to do/wear/say" was filtered through a citizenship paradigm, but by 1950, it was filtered through the perspective of "what a boy likes." A new column that debuted in the April 1950 "Girl Meets Boy" issue, entitled "From a Boy's Point of View" and written by twenty-one-year-old Peter Leavy, exemplifies this shift. Writing in an authoritarian tone, sometimes with sarcasm, Leavy delivered monthly lectures on male-female relations to *Seventeen*'s readership. His address to *Seventeen*'s predominantly young women readers in his very first column set the stage for columns to come:

> You girls, I'm convinced, must all belong to the same club. And your meetings must consist largely of sitting around and standardizing your plans for entangling us unwary males. I know it's true, because as soon as a fellow shows any

> affection toward you, to the last girl, you jump, or rather leap, to the conclusion that you must be *the* woman in his life.[69]

In a couple of columns, captioned "Somebody Would Like to Meet You"[70] and "Just the Way You Look Tonight,"[71] Leavy schooled *Seventeen*'s readership on the physical attributes and body adornment that boys found attractive in girls. Face it, he told them:

> Whether you like it or not, it's a fact of life. When a fellow takes a girl out, the better she looks, the more he'll enjoy himself. Naturally, it's nicer to be able to look across the table at someone pleasing to the eye. And, if his date elicits admiring glances from the surrounding gentry, a guy feels flattered in the bargain.[72]

Leavy's column—and the gender relations shift that it represented—did not go unchallenged by *Seventeen*'s readers. Young women and men alike wrote to complain, including L.F., a male reader who referred to Leavy as "the critic [who] raises his ugly head."[73] *Seventeen* even followed Leavy's August 1950 column with a disclaimer of sorts, noting "The Editors of *SEVENTEEN* believe we can all afford to listen to a boy's point of view, but we hope you realize that it isn't always our point of view."[74] The important point, however, was that even if "A Boy's Point of View" didn't represent the viewpoint of some, most, or all of *Seventeen*'s editors, they chose to continue it, keeping Leavy as a columnist. On the other hand, the magazine discontinued "For Seniors Only," the column that had historically promoted and disseminated some of *Seventeen*'s least traditional messages about gender relations.

While the postwar era brought about significant change in *Seventeen*'s advice to the reader on "Getting Along in the World," the greatest transformation occurred in the magazine's (in)attention to her mind. During its first year, *Seventeen* had filled the "Your Mind" section with articles on world politics, geography, and history, often advocating social ideals such as universal equality. By 1949, however, "Your Mind" had been reduced to a skeleton of monthly columns. This and similar changes can be linked to the end of the war and the shift in national attention from the world stage to the domestic front. In *Seventeen*'s pages, (female) citizens and workers were out, homemakers and hostesses were in. Almost immediately after war's end, *Seventeen* moved the column "Teens in the News" from "Your Mind" to "Having Fun"—in effect, signaling a shift in what the magazine (and perhaps society in general) deemed newsworthy in regard to exemplary teen behavior.

Table 5.1 Editorial Content in *Seventeen* Magazine

	September 1949 to March 1950						
	9/49	10/49	11/49	12/49	1/50	2/50	3/50
Issue Size–	247 pp	179 pp	195 pp	123 pp	123 pp	171 pp	227 pp
Special Issue	5th Bday	Home	Parents	Xmas	School		
What You Wear	**28%**	**22%**	22%	22%	18%	**26%**	**24%**
How You Feel/Look	4%	5%	4%	6%	5%	5%	4%
Fiction	17%	17%	13%	18%	16%	23%	16%
Getting Along/World	9%	9%	11%	8%	**21%**	6%	12%
Your Mind	13%	11%	15%	6%	11%	7%	9%
Food & Home	10%	17%	8%	15%	14%	14%	13%
Having Fun	19%	19%	**27%**	**25%**	15%	19%	22%
Percent of total copy	36%	43%	39%	54%	57%	41%	40%

Note: Issue size equals actual page count plus ad space on covers (inside front, inside back, and back cover). Categories receiving the greatest editorial coverage appear in boldface type.

In addition, the war-period column "Science and Medicine" was discontinued, replaced by an intermittently occurring column called "Science . . . and You." Although the titles of the two columns sound similar, their foci differed. While the monthly installments of "Science and Medicine" suggested job possibilities in those fields, "Science . . . and You" (penned by Barbara Hertz, Helen Valentine's daughter) highlighted new products made available through modern science and technology (e.g., Dramamine, canned milk, Pantastic, electric hairbrushes, neomycin, vitamin B12, etc.). Thus, the former offered the reader a world of occupational opportunities while the latter offered her "new and improved!" buying opportunities. Just as the U.S. government was asking of adult women, *Seventeen* was asking its readers to revision themselves as consumers (rather than workers/producers).

Seventeen didn't completely abandon the more cerebral content of "Your Mind," continuing to publish readers' letters, monthly book reviews, the reader-produced writing and artwork of "It's All Yours," and occasional educational articles about science and art. For the most part,

Table 5.1 *(continued)*

	April 1950 to September 1950						
	4/50	5/50	6/50	7/50	8/50	9/50	Avg
Issue Size–	211 pp	211 pp	131 pp	115 pp	299 pp	227 pp	
Special Issue	Girl/Boy	Yours	Pretty		School	6th Bday	
What You Wear	**25%**	20%	**24%**	22%	**30%**	**27%**	24%
How You Feel/Look	5%	6%	21%	3%	9%	4%	6%
Fiction	15%	18%	19%	19%	12%	13%	17%
Getting Along/World	13%	15%	6%	10%	4%	11%	10%
Your Mind	10%	9%	3%	2%	6%	10%	9%
Food & Home	11%	7%	9%	9%	16%	12%	12%
Having Fun	22%	**25%**	18%	**35%**	22%	22%	22%
Percent of total copy	39%	38%	45%	73%	35%	41%	45%

however, "Your Mind" in the postwar period lost much of its status, ceding space and significance to the magazine's new postwar section, "Food and Home Doings."

Hearth and Home

Almost immediately upon war's end, *Seventeen* moved "the home" from backdrop to forefront, according domesticity its own table of contents category. Debuting in November 1946, "Home Doings" expanded to "Food and Home Doings" in January 1947. During the period from fifth to sixth birthday, *Seventeen* devoted more editorial space to "Food and Home Doings" than to "Getting Along in the World," "Your Mind," or "How You Look and Feel," but less than to "Having Fun," "What You Wear," or "Fiction" (Table 5.1).

In several ways, the articles of "Food and Home Doings" had much in common with those of "How You Look and Feel" and "What You Wear." Features in each of these sections gave pointed advice to "you" on the "how-to" of certain tasks (how you should groom, how you should dress, how you should home-make). In addition, the underlying foundation of each of these sections, whether subtle or overt, was romance, either in the present (dating) or in the future (marriage). Finally, the subjects of each of these sections (fashion, grooming, homemaking) were consumption-oriented, with success in each of these areas achieved by buying something.

Seventeen's special October 1949 "Your Home and You" issue, not surprisingly, contained the highest percentage of editorial copy on "Food and Home Doings." The frontispiece essay set out the parameters for what *Seventeen* considered a "home," and the accompanying portrait created the ambience for the essay (Figure 5.5).[75] It pictured a young blond woman sitting cross-legged in a living room, reading the newspaper comics and surrounded by the comforts of home: a cozy overstuffed chair to her right, a coffee table topped with flowers and books to her left, and behind her a stone fireplace, crackling fire warming the room. The essay begins: "You probably don't think about it much. Your home, we mean. You probably take it for granted. It's there—it's comfortable—it's familiar. It's just home [. . . but] home is a lot more than a roof over your head."

Text and photo establish that home is "comfortable"—and that comfort is made up of several elements. For instance, the reader is reminded that home means *family*—which includes "you" (a daughter), a mom, a dad, and at least one sibling:

> Home is the chair dad sat on too hard three Thanksgivings ago. It's the masterpiece you painted at the age of four which *still* hangs in mother's room [. . .] It's your Prom-date calling for you with a corsage. And your brother giving you both the clammy eye.

Home is where women cook (for men):

> It's dashing back from school into the warm, spicy kitchen and telling mother you've been elected to the student council [. . .] It's dad valiantly swallowing down your first (hard-as-rock) angel cake and exclaiming, "it's delicious!"

Home is where "you" entertain friends:

> It's Polly coming over to spend the night and do homework and try out hair-dos [. . .] Home is the gang dropping in, rolling up the rugs and dancing.

And finally, home is for "Things" (with a capital "T"):

Sunday is the best of all

Figure 5.5. Frontispiece, (Your Home) November 1949 *Seventeen*, photographer Carmen Sciavone

> Home is your collection of books and records and Things [. . .] Your home and you? Well, when you come to think of it, home is many things . . . and all pretty wonderful at that.

The features of "Food and Home Doings" addressed every facet of home-making, from dining to decorating to domesticating. And in postwar *Seventeen*, home was definitely a woman's (separate) sphere, its tasks the exclusive work of women. Judging from the amount of space allotted to it, *Seventeen* apparently considered food preparation the preeminent homemaking task. Articles such as "To Market, To Market"[76] taught the rudimentary basics of properly choosing food; tutorials on recipe terms,[77] herbs and spices,[78] and beginning cooking tips[79] helped the novice with culinary basics, readying her to enter the kitchen and cook—for herself, her family, her beau, and her friends.

Seventeen often presented breakfast and lunch as meals that young women should prepare for themselves, associating these two meals with health and beauty. For instance, "Why Breakfast?"[80] answered its query with an argument about the beauty benefits of the morning meal, while "Bring It in a Basket"[81] suggested some lunch menus, including one for "weight-watchers." Most of the time, however, *Seventeen* highlighted dishes that teen girls could make for others. Cooking features encouraged girls to "Practice on the Family,"[82] raising the question, practice for what? (Answer: to perfect your domestic skills for your *future* family.)

According to the magazine, cooking for other people required divining their desires, and *Seventeen* offered itself as the voice of experience, confidently advising on just what to make for whom. "Family Favorites,"[83] for example, suggested specific recipes for each member of the family (mom, dad, brother, sister), while another feature asserted that "Every Family Likes . . . Pancakes."[84] *Seventeen*'s culinary clairvoyance extended to the preferences of teen boys, about whom they advised "Bake Him a Pie,"[85] sharing their knowledge that "Whether he's six or sixty, 'most any man will pick a pie as his favorite dessert." Presentation mattered too, so "A Box Social"[86] offered hints on creating a "beau-catching" box to hold his lunch.

Seventeen also devoted a significant amount of advice to the art and science of party giving. Every issue of the magazine during the 1949–1950 period included multiple articles about hostessing successful parties. Parties could be related to holidays or birthdays, but more often than not, *Seventeen* presented them as an opportunity to get "the gang" together for some fun. The monthly feature "Every Crowd Likes . . . " suggested party foods and recipes for every month of the year, from frozen custard in August to hot cross buns in April to fried chicken in July. *Seventeen* advised on every facet of the party-giving experience, from themes to menus to recipes to party games; one article, "Party Lifesavers,"[87] even included suggestions on (and buying information for) appropriate party attire (Figure 5.5).

Cooking articles, like clothing features, were almost always accompanied by buying information, including brand names. For example, in the feature "Simple but Super," the recipe for butternut cream pie called for "Amazo Instant Dessert Mix," the peanut butter cookies included "Bisquick," and the icebox roll required "Baker's Cocoa Mix."[88] At the ends of articles on party desserts[89] and a rodeo theme party,[90] the magazine even encouraged readers to shop at their local IGA grocery store.

The magazine often promoted convenience foods, which it equated with modernity. Gelatin, canned soup, and frozen juice concentrate all found favor as valuable time savers in many of the magazine's recipes. However, *Seventeen* lavished its highest praise on luncheon meat, including Spam, that now-disparaged meat product that apparently epitomized culinary modernity in the 1950s. In "Plan a Picnic," the magazine extolled Spam's virtues:

> [M]ake the shish-kabab of luncheon meat (as we did). Why? Because it's all done up in its own hermetically sealed can (ready and willing to keep until you say the word and wind the key or use the can opener). Which means it travels better than any other food item of its sort, keeps its pristine freshness no matter how hot the weather is, comes out of its tin jacket firm and easy to handle.[91]

Another article in the same issue urged the reader to "Open a Can" of this miracle meat and its various relatives:

> Luncheon meat they call it . . . we call it convenient food [. . .] Whether you want a party snack or a man-sized meal, you can make it with canned meats. There are dozens of varieties to choose from . . . frankfurters, Vienna sausages, tongue, sandwich spreads [. . .] Take luncheon meats (those pressed loaves made of chopped pork, ham, beef and/or veal): see on our make-believe store across the page some of the variations you can ring up and dish out when you *open a can*![92]

While *Seventeen* presented cooking and hostessing as important domestic labors, it also addressed other tasks, including decorating and furnishing a home. As with cooking, the advice that *Seventeen* shared on decorating had a "now and later" quality. *Now* you can decorate your bedroom to match your age ("Your Room Comes of Age"[93]) or your favorite painting ("Plan from a Picture"[94]). *Now* you can make your small bedroom feel bigger ("small rooms and how they GROW"[95]) or more private—despite having to share it with your sister ("Bird's-eye View of Two to a Room"[96]). Always visible in the distance, however, was the vision of your own future home. Thus, your bedroom could suffice as "Your OWN Living Room"[97] while waiting for a future abode.

Although some decorating articles suggested an attention to frugality by reusing or renovating existing objects, they were not the norm.[98] Instead, most highlighted the "must have" accoutrements of a modern home, giving specific decor suggestions, example pictures, and buyer information for every product either listed or pictured, from rugs to mattresses to linens to clocks. In the feature "A Good Night's Rest," *Seventeen* explained this service as the result of reader demand, saying: "When you saw this bedroom for the first time in our July 1949 issue, you wrote to us, in droves, that *you'd* bounce up and down, too, if it were only yours."[99]

Achieving the modern home evidently required buying the most recent advances in household products. New tools and gadgets were the technological equivalent of Spam. In February 1947, *Seventeen* introduced an intermittently occurring column devoted to the consumer education of their readership, entitled "Does Your House Need This?" This column suggested household "necessities" such as an alarm clock, Dritz lampshade kit, Mouli rotary steel grater, egg poacher, and Pyrex ware. *Seventeen*'s promotional literature advised advertisers that "Teenas" could influence their parents' product consumption,[100] and this appears to be the strategy of this column, which suggested in its Christmas version that "Mom would love one [toaster, radio, waffle iron, vacuum, coffee percolator] for Christmas, from all of you."[101]

At times, *Seventeen* suggested that the reader buy certain products in preparation for her assumed future life as a homemaker. This was the theme of the monthly column "Your Treasure Chest" which debuted in August 1949. The column's title referred to a hope chest, the popular feminine furniture necessity of the period, meant to store a young woman's "hope" (i.e., domestic tools and furnishings) for the future. The first installment of "Your Treasure Chest" pinpoints that ultimate hope as a home, which could then be filled with innumerable commodities:

> Although it's too soon to do any more than dream of the day you'll march down the Orange Blossom aisle that leads to a home of your own, it's not too soon to begin to plan your hope chest and get a head start on your future. Then when the great day arrives, you'll be ready with the essentials. And since you'll have had plenty of time to collect them, they'll be exactly what you want instead of last-minute pick-ups.[102]

The most essential item for purchase was, of course, the hope chest itself, and the column suggested a particular brand (Lane) that could be found at a particular department store (Gimbels). Later "Treasure Chest" columns advised readers to use their holiday and graduation money to buy the essentials of future marital entertaining: sterling silver, china, glassware, and dinnerware. The discourse of hope chests and the dream of future marital bliss runs counter to the discourse of the independent working woman from *Seventeen*'s war period issues, which warned the reader not to put all her hopes in the expectation of a long-lasting marriage and homemaking as a career. But in a span of five years, transformation had taken place in the culture and at *Seventeen*. In the postwar years, young women were being encouraged to marry (up) and settle down into lives as mothers and consumers—and this was reflected in the pages of *Seventeen*. Girls were given a new "study" mandate: intellectualism and classic literature were out, homemaking and domestic guides were in. The advice of the July 1950 "Your Treasure Chest" expresses this change:

> Talk about a hope chest and the first things you think of are satin and lace, linen and silver. But how about a few practical thoughts in another direction? . . . You study French, math and chemistry out of books, why not homemaking? Granted, experience may be the best teacher, but it can be cushioned with a bit of insight into the realms of sewing, cooking and housekeeping. And before you balk at dull book larnin' [*sic*], look again. All of these books are pretty-to-look-at, easy-to-read and will probably turn out to be your most constant reference companions.[103]

Shopping as Fun (and) Work

The postwar period brought changes to the lives of young American women and the pages of *Seventeen*, but "Having Fun" remained a constant, and this section saw the least change across time. Examined through the lens of *Seventeen*, the activities and pursuits that constituted "teen fun" were somewhat timeless. "Having Fun" continued to include features on hobbies and sports, as well as the entertainment industry and celebrities (one change: jazz musicians were out, actors and actresses were in). In addition, the backbone of this section continued to be its monthly features of brain teasers, record and movie reviews, and the monthly "how not to act" comic—now illustrated by Annette Hagyard with poetry penned by a number of *Seventeen*'s writers.[104] In addition, new monthly features were added, including a crossword puzzle and a club column ("Next on the Agenda"), as well as "Teens in the News" and "Let's Go Shopping," original monthly features that *Seventeen* shifted from other table of contents categories to "Having Fun."

By moving "Let's Go Shopping" from "What You Wear" to "Having Fun," *Seventeen* expanded the shopping opportunities far beyond fashion. Unrestricted by apparel boundaries, the "Let's Go Shopping" buyers were freed to explore a broader variety of stores, shopping for items for every room of the house and for every member of the family. Indeed, buying gifts—a pursuit that *Seventeen* also encouraged during the war period—became even more a part of the magazine's interpretation of "Having Fun" during the postwar period, particularly around holiday time.

But an interesting thing happened on the way to the postwar store—*Seventeen* couldn't seem to decide if shopping was fun or work. Moving "Let's Go Shopping" to "Having Fun" seemed to signal the opinion of shopping as an enjoyable leisure pursuit. However, "Shopping Takes More Than Money," written by former fashion editor Betty Gulesian, read like an instruction manual, complete with scripts (e.g., what to say to a pushy saleswoman) and guidelines to follow at all stages of shopping, from preparation to perusal to purchase. Gulesian concluded her article by pointing out the laborious aspects of the "fun" enterprise of shopping: "We hope you have begun to see why shopping demands more of you than money-in-the-purse. You also need patience, self-discipline, taste, an intelligent standard of values, a sense of proportion, a sense of responsibility [. . .] And, of course we needn't tell *you* that shopping can be a lot of fun!"[105]

Sixth Birthday

Seventeen's sixth birthday lacked the trappings and hoopla of years past. No special birthday cover announced the occasion, no birthday letter from Helen Valentine mused about "Baby's" growth—in fact, Helen Valentine had left the magazine she founded several months earlier.[106] *Seventeen* entered the 1950s with new leadership and a new attitude, in a "modern" postwar America that once again promoted traditional gender roles for its women.

Like sand through an hourglass, the world of *Seventeen* shifted inversely in five years' time. Wartime *Seventeen* had balanced the lighter fare of fashion, beauty, and fun with serious subject matter on service, citizenship, and intellectual growth. The magazine's early articles and features reflected an ideal teen girl whose life/work focused on four different parameters: her body ("What You Wear" and "How You Feel and Look"), her world ("Getting Along in the World"), her mind ("Your Mind"), and her leisure ("Having Fun"). By concentrating on these four areas, *Seventeen* communicated to teen girls that these were *their* areas—areas that they could claim as their own, work sites worthy of their attention and labor. The ideal teen girl, as constructed by the magazine during the first year, groomed and clothed her body, shopped responsibly, excelled in school, volunteered in her community, planned for college, aspired to a "careerist" future, fought inequality, learned about "others," expanded her mind—and had a little fun on the side. Postwar *Seventeen,* on the other hand, metamorphosed into a magazine about fashion, fun, and home—sprinkled with a little bit of citizenship, intellectualism, and culture. In comparison to the magazine's earlier representations, the teen girl's world shrank, while the importance of her home (present and future) grew.

The turning point in *Seventeen*'s changing worldview occurred after war's end, when it added the new topical category of "Food and Home Doings." In doing so, the magazine positioned "home" at the center of a young woman's life, adding it to her body, mind, and world (redefined as the world just outside her doors). Cooking and decorating, which the magazine previously presented as "having fun" or just another activity in "getting along in the world," became women's domestic work—that is, home work. Its inclusion diminished *Seventeen*'s attention to the teen girl's outside world ("Getting Along in the World") and her mind ("Your Mind").

The postwar teen girl ideal followed the shift in the table of contents categories. The "modern" teen girl still needed to groom and properly clothe herself, do well in school, and plan for college, but the motivation for her "work" changed. As homemaking supplanted career as her future goal, boys and men became the measures (and measurers) of her success. Thus, "Getting Along in the World" now meant getting along with boys, "What You Wear" became a boy's business, and Peter Leavy was hired to dispense "A Boy's Point of View." The role of an ideal teen girl as a world citizen (and future leader) lessened, while her role as a consumer increased. The call to consumption, previously confined to body work, expanded to include home work; modern Teena had to decorate not only her body but also her house.

Ironically, following a trend in the magazine more generally, the features of the "Food and Home Doings" section often referred to the wonders of modern life. This consumerist version (or vision) of modernity, however, was a far cry from the global wonders preached in "Your Mind" and "Getting Along in the World" of wartime *Seventeen* magazine. Thus, as the 1950s would prove, "progress" does not always follow a linear vertical path. Indeed, in marching "ahead" into the 1950s, Teena, *Seventeen*'s teen girl ideal, left the world, entered the home, and lost her mind.

CHAPTER 6

Divorce in the Family

Seventeen Magazine Loses Its Matriarch—and Its Way

With her we play in harmony—
The Maestro, Mrs. V.
You think her teen-ideas are keen?
Well, frankly, so do we!

[From "The Editors Serenade You," *Seventeen*, September 1948]

Seventeen's "Fourth Birthday" issue featured a "family portrait" and descriptive poem that profiled the magazine's most important staffers, entitled "The Editors Serenade You" (Figure 6.1). The illustration, by artist Joe Kaufman, depicted each of the editors as a musician performing on a stage, with Helen Valentine as the "major" conductor and Alice Thompson as the "minor" conductor. The picture and poem were at once affectionate and humorous, but the most surprising and amusing detail of Kaufman's picture appeared upon close inspection. Holding back the curtains that framed the stage and the featured players were owner Walter Annenberg and general manager Kenneth Friede—in the guise of two smiling cupids![1]

Kaufman's illustration presented the perfect picture of a harmonious workplace family. But the same family that appeared to make beautiful music together in their fourth-birthday portrait experienced a painful separation little more than a year later. Walter Annenberg and Helen Valentine had begun to differ on editorial policy; two issues, in particular, created problems between them. The first came to a head in 1946, when pictures from two articles in the magazine's November issue resulted in a debate between publisher and editor. The articles, "They Do Unto Others," about a racially integrated Quaker work camp, and "Swing Your Partner," about a barn dance sponsored by Pepsi-Cola, were both accompanied by pictures of white and

Figure 6.1. "The Editors Serenade You," 1948 *Seventeen*, illustrator Joe Kaufman

black teenagers socializing together.[2] In particular, "They Do Unto Others" led with an almost full-page picture of white and black teens bowing their heads in prayer at a dinner table (Figure 6.2). Expressing concern that such portrayals of racial integration could offend advertisers, Annenberg sent general manager Ken Friede to deliver a message to Helen Valentine: limit

you've been our inspiration for four happy years

Ed Miller is our only man.
A set-up not so bad;
And if he seems a bit *distrait*,
Poor boy, he's movie-mad

Cheery Beryl Walter pounds
The Home and Food percussion
Which even booms out loudly in a
Drink-more-milk discussion

"All teens and stores, meet SEVENTEEN."
Is Barker Ellis' shout.
She sometimes uses microphones—
You'd hear her though, without

Art Director C. P. claims,
In laying out the book,
The writing is irrelevant,
But pictures make you look!

We feature fashions fit for teens
And Ro McM. makes sure
That if you like a dress, then you
Can buy it from a store

From bright idea to closet rack,
A dress's path is rough.
To charm it down the fashion-ways,
Betty G. does her stuff

109

the number of pictures of Negroes in the magazine. Valentine immediately sent a letter of reply to Annenberg, balking and expressing disappointment that he hadn't contacted her directly. Speaking about the feature on the Quaker camp, Valentine wrote: "Surely the presence of colored children in <u>that</u> story should delight any kindly human being. Anyone who is offended

The young famine fighters of the Friends' summer work camp in the mountains of Kentucky observe silent grace before their own meal

THEY DO UNTO OTHERS

Here is a handful of young Americans whose Thanksgiving really began last July high in the blue mountains of Kentucky.

Like many of you teens, they came out of busy cities to spend their summer on a farm work camp. But these boys and girls put no wages into their banks; instead, each paid his share of camp expenses out-of-pocket. The aim which they put above vacationing or earning last summer was to harvest five thousand quarts of food for Europe. Thankfully, they reached that goal in two months of backbreaking work. The boys and girls were the members of the Friends' Work Camp at Hazel Green Academy, Hazel Green, Kentucky.

Although the camp is operated by the Society of Friends and the food canned there taken overseas by them, only one of the ten campers and five volunteer adult advisers was a Quaker. The others, both white and Negro, representing half a dozen other faiths and coming from a dozen *(Continued on Page 215)*

158

Figure 6.2. "They Do Unto Others," November 1946 *Seventeen*, photographer Dickey Meyer

by it should not be holding a copy of SEVENTEEN."[3] Continuing, she also questioned the logic of Annenberg's argument, pointing to its irony:

> Amongst national advertisers we are trying to attract, I suspect there are many more people with anti-Semitic feelings than there are with anti-negro.

> Yet we are not concerned about the Jewish names on our masthead. Moreover, I think it's rather unbecoming for members of one minority group to show any lack of sympathy for another.

Annenberg's rebuttal arrived by mail several days later. In it, he challenged Valentine's liberalism, lecturing her on his own version of democracy:

> I happen to believe that ordinarily ethnic groups have significant contributions to make and should be preserved. I suspect you think it would be good for the world for negroes to marry whites. I don't. That's not the democratic way. Democracy implies the right, nay, the duty, of minority groups, to make their contributions as living and ardent minorities.[4]

Annenberg went on to disparage Valentine's educational approach in the magazine, which he likened to "a nurse strap[ping] the child in a highchair and stuff[ing] the food down his throat." Annenberg, fifteen years Valentine's junior, asserted his authority by concluding with the question, "Do I make myself clear?" and signing the letter "Old Dad." Valentine heard his message (she had no choice); fewer pictures of black teens appeared in later issues, and pictures of black and white teens together disappeared.

The other issue about which Annenberg and Valentine disagreed was the age range of the magazine's target audience. Annenberg had become convinced that he could increase *Seventeen*'s profits by expanding its target audience to include young women up to the age of twenty-four—women who had more money to spend than those aged thirteen to seventeen. Annenberg insisted that Valentine add editorial and fashion content for this older constituency, and once again, Valentine found herself losing the battle of control over her creation.[5]

There were other signs of discord. In April 1949, the *New York Times* ran an announcement that executive editor Alice Thompson had been promoted to publisher—a position above her former boss, editor-in-chief Helen Valentine.[6] Two weeks later, *Time* magazine printed a longer article about Thompson's promotion, explaining that Annenberg thought the magazine needed someone to oversee its promotion, advertising, and editorial departments.[7]

In retrospect, Thompson's promotion to a position over Valentine and Annenberg's public explanation represented minor rumblings that should have put the employees at *Seventeen* on the alert. Editorial assistant Ingrid Loewenstein remembers sensing a growing tension between Valentine and Thompson, but most staffers were too busy taking care of the daily tasks of running a successful magazine to notice. And successful it was. In celebration of its fifth birthday in September of 1949, the magazine held a luncheon, and *Newsweek* ran an article lauding Valentine's role in *Seventeen*'s origins:

> But looking back last week on her strapping brain child's first five years, Helen Valentine liked something better than her magazine's prospering business. She was as pleased as a teen-ager with a sleek new dress that Teena—as *Seventeen* staffers like to call the prototype of their readers—turned out to be the kind of girl she had foreseen.[8]

That last paragraph hinted at the changes to come: Helen Valentine did indeed like "something better than her magazine's prospering business"—she liked and respected her staff and her millions of readers. Owner Walter Annenberg, however, approached the magazine as a business with profit as the bottom line. This disjuncture between editorial and business goals became increasingly problematic. According to Estelle Ellis:

> Into the fifth year, there were rumblings that were going on, the business side of the magazine was not happy with the progress that she [Valentine] was making . . . Who knows! [*Voice elevates.*] I don't know what their argument was because the magazine was so damn successful. But whatever it was, they were looking to have someone who was more amenable to whatever the business side—the business interests of the magazine was all about, and Alice filled the bill. She was, um, *amenable* to whatever sweet words were being whispered in her ear.[9]

Unbeknownst to most of the staffers, Annenberg and Thompson were on their way to becoming *Seventeen*'s new power couple, and significant change at the magazine was only a matter of time.[10] Even for Estelle Ellis—good friend of Helen Valentine and high up in the workplace hierarchy—the impending events would still shock. Asked if she saw it coming, Ellis responded:

> No, we were, you know, *we were not even aware of it* [. . .] I mean we didn't think of it! I mean she [Thompson] was part of what was making this magazine *go* and, you know, I was busy doing what I was doing. I was certainly . . . *not* tuned into anything like this. I mean, I mean—we were all Girl Scouts here! We were really beating tambourines, we were doing our job—and who was thinking about anything like this. And suddenly . . . "[11]

Helen Leaves Her Baby

And suddenly... everything changed. And those changes were cataclysmic. On February 15, 1950, Helen Valentine sent a letter of resignation to Walter Annenberg, writing:

> Dear Walter:
>
> Because you refused to speak to me on the telephone or see me when I came to Philadelphia, I feel that my direct approach to you must be through this letter. What I have to say is so important that I prefer not to reach you through Joe.
>
> You sent me a message suggesting "a cooling off period" and then further discussion of the "details and terms of our future relations." I have used the former to think this through from every angle. The latter will not be necessary because I have decided not to renew my contract.
>
> [...] As you must know this was a most difficult decision, not only because of the many good years of our association, but also because I know that few people are granted the happy privilege of seeing their idea so beautifully realized. For this I am and shall always be grateful.
>
> Sincerely,
>
> Helen Valentine[12]

Although nominally voluntary, Valentine's resignation appears at least prodded—if not pushed. Annenberg refused to discuss the matter with her, either by phone or in person. Only Annenberg, Thompson, and Valentine knew what was going on behind the scenes. But according to her friends, Valentine was ever the well-bred lady (this was, after all, the woman who wrote *A Guide to Charm*), one who frowned upon gossip, being loud, and making a fuss. Annenberg accepted her resignation, and much to the shock of most of the staff, Valentine announced her departure from the magazine she had created. In an article published on March 6, 1950, *Time* reported on the events of that day. The article began by highlighting Valentine's nurturing relationship with the magazine and her staff: "She liked to call it 'my baby' and mothered not only the money-making teenagers' monthly [...] but the 50 girls and lone man on its editorial staff." As further evidence of this familial relationship, the article quoted Valentine's resignation speech to her "brood": "*Seventeen* has grown up [...] It's a big girl now." *Time* continued the maternal metaphor by stating: "Like a mother who has watched her daughter growing away from her, 'Mrs. V' was reluctantly ready to say goodbye."[13]

The magazine reported that staffers wept at Valentine's announcement—an account that was not media hyperbole. Former staffer Alberta Eiseman remembers the day of Helen's resignation:

> All of us who were the editorial assistants in the various departments—each department had at least one and some departments had more—we were very unsophisticated, very young so there was all this crying as though it had been a college dorm. Crying is the way I remember it [. . .] Because Helen was leaving, because she was sort of the mother of us all.[14]

The *Time* article went on to describe the fissure that had developed between Valentine and Thompson, the woman who had been both friend and nemesis. Calling Valentine's resignation "dignified," the article quoted Thompson as responding: "Helen thinks that *Seventeen* is not only her baby—and, true, it was her idea—but also her property." It ended by noting that the two former friends were no longer talking to one another and that Thompson would now take over as editor-in-chief—as well as "Lady High Everything Else" since four *Seventeen* editors and directors were voluntarily leaving with Valentine.[15]

The April 1950 issue of *Seventeen* was Valentine's final issue as editor-in-chief. Several months later, her name appeared as editor-in-chief on the masthead of *Charm,* another magazine that she would transform for a second constituency of American women—"women who work." Four *Seventeen* staffers accompanied Valentine to *Charm*: promotion director Estelle Ellis, art director Cipe Pineles, managing editor Andrée Vilas, and fashion editor Carolyn Saks; they were joined there by former *Seventeen* fashion editor Eleanore Hillebrand.[16]

Staffers who remained at *Seventeen* struggled with the aftermath; Ingrid Loewenstein remembers that "it came as a shock. I don't really recall whether, you know you always sense things, I guess, you know I never thought it would happen, she [Valentine] would not be there."[17] Lowenstein's friend and fellow editorial assistant Alberta Eiseman describes the effect of Valentine's absence on herself and the other young staffers: "She was extremely nice, you know, very kind to the younger staff members so it was a big blow, it was a big blow for the magazine and everything."[18]

Loewenstein remained at *Seventeen* throughout Thompson's tenure and into that of her successor, Enid Haupt—Walter Annenberg's sister—enabling Ingrid to compare the magazine under its different editors. In contrasting the leadership styles of Valentine and Thompson, she explains: "I think Helen was more relaxed and more warm in person. Alice was very businesslike and, you know, she wasn't too interested in dealing with people like me who had no position at that time."[19]

Thompson's "businesslike" leadership style, however, would be the wave of the future at the magazine, a stance that Enid Haupt would also take. Loewenstein further observes:

> You know they [Alice Thompson and Enid Haupt] were running a magazine, Helen was more hands on and more sensitive to young people, I think, and she really felt caringly about the magazine and about young girls, you know she wanted to be of service to them. The others, I think, were just eager to have a good job and a career. This is, you know, after years of hindsight I suppose, too.[20]

Loewenstein also reports that, over time, the professional business model slowly altered the magazine's editorial focus:

> I think it was a little less casual than what I had felt before. More things that were revolving around advertising and, you know, it was getting to be less about—how can I put it—I mean we all felt that we were doing a service, that it was a service magazine and we were really giving information to kids that they valued and were important to them, but I think after a time, and it wasn't necessarily right after Helen left, but through the years the emphasis became much more on the commercial side. Advertising was really the important section of the magazine rather than the service end.[21]

For Estelle Ellis, the story of Helen Valentine and her Baby, while bittersweet in many ways, is ultimately a tragedy, particularly in regard to Alice Thompson's role in it:

> Alice—that's a tragic story . . . 'cause. . . Alice was one of Helen's good friends. Walter Annenberg was *besotted* with her and she [*sigh*]. . . was very happy to take over. I mean, we don't have to go beyond there. I feel as if it was very tragic, but, you know, if you have any kind of realistic understanding of what happens in the world of business, she [Helen] was being displaced. But the terrible part was that he [Walter] . . . picked her [Alice] as the successor and

Table 6.1. Editorial Content in Seventeen: Percent Change Between 1944-45 and 1949-50

	September 1949-50 Compared to September 1944-45						
	Sept	Oct	Nov	Dec	Jan	Feb	Mar
What You Wear	+5%	+2%	0%	+3%	−6%	+7%	+4%
How You Feel/Look	−8%	−4%	−5%	−4%	−2%	−5%	−3%
Fiction	+17%	+17%	+13%	+18%	+6%	+14%	+4%
Getting/World	−6%	−14%	−8%	−12%	+1%	−15%	−15%
Your Mind	−12%	−5%	−4%	−18%	−5%	−15%	−8%
Food & Home	+10%	+17%	+8%	+15%	+14%	+14%	+13%
Having Fun	−7%	−10%	−4%	−2%	−7%	0%	+5%

that she was in a sense buying into it. Whereas the three of us [Helen, Estelle, and Cipe] pulled out.[22]

Considered retrospectively, Alice Thompson's comments on women in business, in a 1945 "Girl Meets Boy" *Seventeen* column, are ironic given her conflicts with Helen Valentine:

> Today a woman in business need seldom fear another woman. We've learned in a few decades of being allowed to work, how to help each other. There are still a few of the early business women pioneers who are pitiless and jealous of their bitterly-earned positions. But very few. And there's no more devoted fraternity than a group of women working together on a job they like.[23]

Seventeen Magazine's Metamorphosis

Events between the magazine's first and sixth birthdays worked to shift the editorial balance from the whole person to the domestic woman. The consumer-friendly content of "What You Wear" and "Food and Home" increased, while the citizenship-focused content of "Getting Along in the World" and "Your Mind" declined (Table 6.1). *Seventeen*'s focus moved away from Valentine's original model of service and citizenship and toward

Table 6.1. *(continued)*

	September 1949-50 Compared to September 1944-45						
	Apr	May	June	July	Aug	Sept	Avg
What You Wear	+10%	+4%	+5%	+7%	+4%	+2%	+4%
How You Feel/Look	−2%	+1%	+12%	−5%	+1%	−2%	−2%
Fiction	−1%	+8%	+12%	+7%	+1%	0%	+9%
Getting/World	−18%	0%	−15%	−2%	−6%	−2%	−9%
Your Mind	−8%	−12%	−15%	−33%	−20%	−7%	−12%
Food & Home	+11%	+7%	+9%	+9%	+16%	+12%	+12%
Having Fun	+8%	−7%	−7%	+14%	+2%	−4%	−2%

the more familiar traditional/feminine model of fashion, romance, and homemaking. Articles on boy-girl parties replaced articles on political parties. Eventually, Annenberg forced Valentine out of her position as editor-in-chief, essentially severing the relationship between creator and creation—or, as Valentine and others would often frame it, between mother and "baby." How and why did this all happen in just six years' time?

These changes can be explained, at least in part, by examining the forces that exerted pressure on Valentine and *Seventeen* almost from the beginning. They include the historical context, particularly in the transition from war to postwar period; the economic structure of the magazine industry; the preferences and desires of the readership; and power relations at the magazine itself.

The Culture

Of these forces, the cultural changes that took place as America moved from war to postwar period provide the most easily identifiable explanation for the changes in *Seventeen*'s content between 1944 and 1950. The America of World War II was somewhat anomalous in the nation's history. The war created opportunities that, for its duration, made gender and racial boundaries more permeable, certainly in regard to occupational opportunities.[24] Government and the advertising and media industries operated in tandem to recruit American women as war workers. American women's and girls' magazines, *Seventeen* among them, were asked to help advance the war cause. As a result, women's magazines of the war period sung the praises of women in the workforce, creating a harmonious "pro-work" chorus.[25]

Seventeen's early careerist content was also driven by editor Helen Valentine's belief—embodied in her own experience—that women could work *and* raise a family. Rather than limiting the magazine's editorial content to coverage of government-sanctioned jobs such as nursing and war factory work, Valentine and company encouraged *Seventeen*'s early readers to consider careers in media production, advertising, and promotions, and in male-dominated fields such as medicine, law, and science.

Once the war ended, government and advertising again joined forces to effect change in the U.S. economy, this time asking women to leave their jobs in order to make way for returning male soldiers.[26] The patriotic feminine ideal transformed from working-woman poster girl Rosie the Riveter to televised homemakers such as June Cleaver.[27] Media, in particular, were showing and telling women that their work was in the home—as (beautiful) companions, homemakers, mothers, and consumers.[28]

Naomi Wolf theorizes that the "beauty myth"—the cultural narrative that asserts that women's value is based in their beauty—"flourishes after constraints on women are loosened," as a kind of corrective backlash.[29] World War II presented just such a "loose" environment, and Betty Friedan was among the first to identify the backlash that followed war's end. She pinpoints the early postwar period as the source of the "feminine mystique"—the consumer/homemaker/sex- object model represented in the pages of postwar women's magazines and internalized by many American women.[30] Friedan contends that although many American men and women entered the postwar period with a longing for stability and the shelter of home, advertisers (with the tacit blessing of the government) exploited this idealized image of home and homemaking by playing on men's and women's insecurities in order to sell products. Certainly, these kinds of images became more common in both the editorial and advertising pages of postwar *Seventeen* magazine.

The Magazine Industry

While the cultural transformation in postwar America—driven in part by the efforts of government and advertising—offers the most obvious explanation for the shift in the magazine's editorial content, other forces exerted pressure on *Seventeen* from its inception. Chief among these was the economic structure of the magazine publishing industry, whose financial house is built upon the foundation of advertising revenue.[31] Mainstream magazines cannot subsist without the economic support of advertisers, who wield a significant amount of power over the editorial content of a magazine.[32] At *Seventeen,* this advertiser effect was visible from the beginning in the construction of the promotional campaign Teena—especially when contrasted with the magazine's original editorial teenage girl ideal.

Helen Valentine knew firsthand the importance of selling her infant magazine and its readership to advertisers and business, having held the position of promotion director at *Mademoiselle,* another magazine that faced the challenge of selling itself and a previously unidentified market group (college-age women) to the business world. Valentine knew that no matter how successful *Seventeen* could or would become with a devoted teenage readership, its economic viability was predicated upon its acceptance and adoption by adult businesspeople (mostly men). Thus, promotion director Estelle Ellis's task—perhaps the most important task at the fledgling magazine—was to craft a campaign that would sell teen girls as a consumer market niche to business. To do this she created "Teena, the prototypical teen-age girl" and introduced her to manufacturers and advertisers as the embodiment/representative of *Seventeen*'s (idealized) readership. Although Ellis imbued Teena with many of the characteristics and virtues espoused in the magazine's editorial pages, Teena's main selling points were: (1) her financial ability to shop and buy, (2) her vulnerability and openness to buying suggestions and incentives (as a "blank slate" yet to be "branded"), and (3) her dialectical copycat/leadership consumer roles. The Teena who "went to market" was the type of consumer that advertisers and businesspeople were in the market for—thus, the market joined the magazine in constructing the promotional Teena ideal.

The economic mandate to attract and hold advertisers also explains why the editorial Teena ideal became more like the promotional Teena over time and, similarly, why *Seventeen*'s editorial content—originally balanced between citizenship and consumption—shifted toward consumption. Although the magazine's promotion campaign was intended to educate advertisers about *Seventeen* and its readership, the advertisers turned the tables, becoming primary educators in the magazine, creating and visually communicating an idealized lifestyle that went far beyond soap or soup or sanitary napkins.[33]

Teen Readers

The government and advertisers were not the only forces pushing *Seventeen* toward the more traditional model. *Seventeen*'s readers also voiced their opinions on the magazine's content, both through their often impassioned letters to the editor and through *Seventeen*'s two commissioned market surveys, published as *Life with Teena I* and *II*.[35] Young letter writers pleaded for more articles on beauty-related topics such as makeovers and modeling; similarly, a majority of surveyed girls reported a preference for content about fashion and beauty, with only a minority of girls preferring content about careers and citizenship.[36] A majority of the teen girl respondents also revealed that they enjoyed learning about and practicing the arts of domesticity. They reported that they participated in these kinds of endeavors in the present, taking cooking classes at school and giving parties at home, but perhaps more importantly, they aspired to a life of domesticity in the future. Indeed, a majority of girls in both surveys responded that they did not want to work after marriage, preferring instead to "keep house."[37]

One can only imagine the dilemma—both ideological and practical—that this disconnect between editorial vision and reader aspiration created for Helen Valentine, who had spent her entire adult life working *and* raising a family, and who had promoted both in her magazine. The 1949 promotional document "The Dummy That Made Sense" offers some insight into her views. Billed as "An Editor Thinks on Paper" and written in Helen Valentine's hand, the "Dummy" presented a prototype of a *Seventeen* magazine issue. Words in black pencil represented Valentine's vision for the magazine in 1944; words in red pencil represented her thoughts on the magazine's reality in 1949 (its fifth birthday). Under the heading "Career Department," Valentine "envisioned" (in black pencil) a magazine in which it was "Our job to discuss" a balanced agenda of options, including:

Job horizons for women

Work—a stop-gap before marriage?

Job training

Preparation for marriage

Marriage as a career

Marriage *plus* a career—

pros and cons

Her red pencil words of 1949, however, testified to the dominant reader sentiment on this issue, lamenting: "Poor pros didn't stand a chance! Our surveys proved Teena wants to be a full-time homemaker."[38]

Meet—Again—Walter Annenberg

The final explanation for the transformations at *Seventeen* between birth and sixth birthday relates to the power structure and struggles at the magazine itself. Helen Valentine's position as editor-in-chief and her unique vision for the magazine came to an end because of her business partner and Baby's cocreator, *Seventeen*'s owner, Walter Annenberg. Annenberg documented Valentine's important role in the origins of *Seventeen* in his letter of October 2, 1944, detailed in Chapter 1, which established Valentine as *Seventeen*'s creator, responsible for the magazine's concept and name.[39] Annenberg also stated that Valentine had been assured that she would be allowed to edit *Seventeen* "with an absolutely free hand." While true for her first few years at the magazine, this did not last, as Annenberg began to exert more pressure on the magazine's direction, first nudging and then shackling Valentine's "free hand." Over time, Annenberg and Valentine diverged more and more over the magazine's ideology and direction, creating a divide that eventually culminated in Valentine's exit as editor.

More than a century before *Seventeen* magazine, philosopher Karl Marx noted that the pursuit of profit necessitates the exploitation of laborers by owners, and that although a contract made between owner and laborer may appear both "fair" and freely given, it *is not*.[40]

Valentine made a contract with Annenberg that set out their relations as an *apparent* partnership. However, the day that Valentine entered Annenberg's employ, she ceded ownership of her own cultural creation (the magazine as a concept) to him. She sold not just her labor to Annenberg but her idea, too. Years later, Estelle Ellis described her own frustration in watching Valentine lose ownership of her intellectual property, not just at *Seventeen*, but also at *Charm*, the magazine she edited and re-created as a magazine for working women during the 1950's:

> *[T]wice* in Helen's career lifetime she had created two incredible documents, historical documents, about women, and the importance of women, and the changes in women, and the significance of teenagers and then working women. She had translated them into two successful magazines

> and if she had done that, if she had developed it, like a zipper or a safety pin, she would have been credited with her legacy, but because it was a magazine, and because these were times where women didn't behave the way Martha Stewart did to go buy back her title from Time/Life, women didn't know that they had that kind of power. She just . . . allowed it to happen. And so nobody other than the publisher benefited from the creation of these two historical publication documents.[41]

The unequal business relationship between female editors and male owners was and is not unique to *Seventeen,* but rather the model for almost all women's magazines. Although a magazine's editor-in-chief appears to wield substantial power in a magazine workplace, that power is superficial. In reality, the editor is vulnerable to the whims of the owner.

Alice Thompson, Annenberg's replacement for Valentine, learned this lesson too. Thompson, who had worked her way to the top in a familiar gendered way (by ingratiating herself with her male boss), eventually found herself on the wrong end of Annenberg's good graces. Annenberg's biographer, Christopher Ogden, explained the turn in relations from Annenberg's perspective: "Walter and Thompson got along well [. . .] until the editor one day made the same mistake as her predecessor [Valentine] and forgot who was actually in charge."[42]

Annenberg replaced Thompson with his sister, Enid Annenberg Haupt. Years later, in a *New York Times* interview, Haupt described the events that led up to Thompson's dismissal and her own hire. Haupt's version illustrates yet another aspect of inequality in the hierarchy of relations between staff and owner, and editor and reader—that of cultural elitism: "Walter foisted the editorship on me when he was terminating a lady [Thompson] who had become a great nuisance. I knew nothing about running a magazine, but my brother said, 'You can bring culture to the average working person who has not had your advantages.'"[43]

Apparently, at least for Annenberg, a socially "advantaged" editor without experience or a college degree but with a clear understanding of "who was actually in charge" was a superior choice over an editor with experience, but without said understanding. In this case, nepotism established a marriage made in heaven (albeit somewhat incestuous), and Haupt served as *Seventeen*'s publisher, editor, and editor-in-chief until 1970. Together, Haupt and Annenberg controlled both the business and editorial sides of *Seventeen*—as well as its institutional history—for almost two decades.

Annenberg's Triangle Publications owned and published *Seventeen* until 1989, when it sold the magazine to Murdoch Magazines.[44] Annenberg died at the age of ninety-four in 2002, having been named in that year's *Fortune* magazine as the thirty-ninth wealthiest American, with an estimated net worth of $4 billion. Obituaries lavished praise on him for his contributions to charities, including the endowment of two prestigious journalism schools, the Annenberg School for Communication at the University of Southern California and the Annenberg School for Communication at the University of Pennsylvania. They remembered his appointment as U.S. Ambassador to Great Britain by his good friend President Richard Nixon, and his "creation" of *Seventeen.*

The Associated Press obituary, picked up by many U.S. newspapers, reported that Annenberg "founded" *Seventeen* and that his sister, Enid Haupt, was its editor; Helen Valentine's role as conceptual creator and first editor received no mention.[45] In the *Independent,* a London newspaper, Annenberg's obituary also highlighted his "launching" of *Seventeen* and Haupt's position as editor.[46] Although the *New York Times* obituary did refer to Helen Valentine as Annenberg's "collaborator" at *Seventeen,* the authors attributed the idea for the magazine to Annenberg, repeating the story told in his biographies, in which he received his initial revelation of teen girls as an untapped magazine market while walking down Fifth Avenue.[47]

For those people either present in the early days of *Seventeen*'s creation or familiar with the documentation (media accounts and correspondence) from the time of its origins, Annenberg's obituaries fifty-eight years later raise a disturbing question: Why did Annenberg's role in the public narrative of the magazine's history grow more important over time, while Valentine's role diminished, sometimes to the point of oblivion? The answer to this question also lies in power, particularly in power as a privileged position for storytelling.

Friedrich Nietzsche (and later Michel Foucault) turned the adage "knowledge is power" on its head, noting instead that "power is knowledge."[48] Across time, the stories of history have been told by the people in power, their versions bound into books and magazines and newspapers and the public consciousness, becoming "knowledge" or "the truth" or just "the way it was." Lost in these tellings, however, are the "truths," lives, or actions of the people without power—usually women, people of color, the poor and working class, the young and the old, the illiterate, and the disadvantaged. Although Helen Valentine maintained some influence in her six years as *Seventeen*'s editor-in-chief, her exit severed her relationship with her "baby," not just as a business and magazine but as a historical narrative. From that point on, Annenberg didn't just control the magazine as a business; he also controlled the magazine's institutional history. Estelle Ellis contends that Annenberg began rewriting *Seventeen*'s history when his sister Enid Haupt entered the picture:

> You have to understand that one of the things that happened was Helen Valentine's name was off the radar. And the reason for it—that when Walter got tired of Alice Thompson, he put his sister in charge, and from that point on, he wanted the memory of where this began *erased*. And he wanted the memory of it to begin with Enid Haupt.[49]

The retelling of *Seventeen*'s origins happened in the magazine, in media reports about the magazine and Walter Annenberg, and in Annenberg's biographies.[50] The erasure of Helen Valentine from the narrative of *Seventeen*'s origins began almost immediately in the magazine, through the omission of any references to her founding role in the magazine's birthday/anniversary issues. The tenth anniversary "Happy Birthday" essay in the September 1954 issue noted the magazine's "birth" but without mention of Valentine. Departing altogether from the celebratory tradition established by Valentine, *Seventeen* ignored its own twentieth and twenty-fifth birthdays.

In September 1974, *Seventeen* returned to the tradition of birthday recognition, noting its thirtieth birthday—but again, without any mention of Valentine. A decade later, the magazine's fortieth anniversary issue included a birthday message from Annenberg, in which he reflected back on the magazine's origins. Although he quoted from Valentine's original "credo" letter to the reader, he spoke of it using the editorial "we" (as in "'We are interested in the kind of human being you are,' *we* said in that inaugural issue") without citing the essay's author.[51] In fact, just once in the fifty years after Valentine left *Seventeen* did the magazine make reference to its creator, and only after it was no longer owned by Triangle Publications. Carolyn Miller, the magazine's editor-in-chief in 1994, wrote in the fiftieth anniversary issue that "Helen Valentine, *Seventeen*'s founding editor-in-chief [. . .] was ahead of her time."[52] Miller was an acquaintance of Estelle Ellis and possibly knew of Valentine's role in the magazine's origins through her association with Ellis. In October 2004, however, *Seventeen*—under the editorship of Atoosa Rubenstein—published a sixtieth anniversary collector's edition that once again lacked any mention of Helen Valentine.

Valentine's omission from *Seventeen*'s institutional history occurred not only in the magazine but also in the public discussion of the magazine. While media reports during Valentine's tenure at *Seventeen* documented her role as the magazine's creator, articles following her exit ignored or forgot her role. In some instances, Valentine and others tried to correct the inaccurate media accounts. For example, in September 1967, *Women's Wear Daily*'s "Inside Fashion" column quoted Nancy White, then editor-in-chief of *Harper's Bazaar,* as saying that Enid Haupt had created her "own" magazine—*Seventeen.*[54] Valentine immediately sent a letter requesting a correction. White wrote back, saying, "Helen dear: Of course I know you started *Seventeen* . . . I am so sorry—I will try and reach Eugenia [the columnist] but I don't know how she feels about retractions."[55] Valentine also contacted Annenberg, who still owned *Seventeen,* asking for his support in correcting the account. Annenberg, dismissive of Valentine's personal concerns and of women in general, replied in a letter dated September 26, 1967:

> I note the photostat you sent me from *Women's Wear Daily,* embodying the quote of Nancy White's in relation to my sister.
>
> Mrs. White's ignorance of the facts, of course, has nothing to do with the unpredictability of women in general, and, therefore, I think it would be diplomatic for us to view this with some sympathy and understanding.

Annenberg ended his letter, "Helen, let us continue not to take ourselves seriously," and then signed off, "Warmly, Walter."[56]

Easy for him to say—he wasn't the person being written out of history. In fact, Annenberg was being taken very seriously by government and by media, and his public stature as *Seventeen*'s creator increased with the passage of time. In June 1970, *Fortune* magazine did a long feature article on Annenberg's appointment as the U.S. Ambassador to Great Britain.[57] The article, written by journalist A. James Reichley, detailed Annenberg's myriad business accomplishments and represented *Seventeen* as Annenberg's creation and Enid Haupt as its most influential editor. This time, *Fortune* reader and *Seventeen*'s first advertising director, William Rosen, wrote a letter of correction to *Fortune*'s managing editor, Louis Banks, with a copy to Valentine. In his letter, Rosen set out the origins of *Seventeen* in no uncertain terms:

> [. . .] Mr. Reichley infers that the idea for *Seventeen* was Mr. Annenberg's. Actually, this is not entirely true and I believe that the person who conceived and edited *Seventeen* for the first six years of its existence should be given full credit

> for having had the vision to recognize the potential of the teenage girl market at a time when none of the readership surveys even measured teenage readers.
>
> In 1944, I was Advertising Director of the Annenberg magazines which included several movie magazines. Mr. Annenberg suggested to me that it might be a good plan to have a Hollywood fashion section in the movie publications in an effort to secure some of the fashion advertising which could not find space in the overloaded fashion magazines during the period of paper shortages.
>
> In interviewing possible editors for the fashion section, Mr. Annenberg met with Mrs. Helen Valentine who was, at that time, Merchandising Director of *Mademoiselle* Magazine. It was she who sold him on the need for a teenage girl's magazine and *Stardom* was immediately converted to *Seventeen*. The publication was an instantaneous success under Mrs. Valentine's direction and in a short time, it became a teenage girl's bible.
>
> Mrs. Valentine left in 1950, as I did, and up until that time Mrs. Enid Haupt played absolutely no role in *Seventeen*'s growth.[58]

Cultural studies theorist Stuart Hall sees popular culture as a battlefield, a site where different forces—of varying strength and influence—struggle for dominance.[59] *Seventeen*'s morphing institutional history offers an illustration of this process at work. Because Annenberg wielded control over the magazine after Valentine left, and because he was an influential public figure, his version of *Seventeen*'s origins became the predominant narrative over time. Valentine and others, at least in the beginning, attempted to challenge the dominant version—but they were ultimately unsuccessful.

Today, most of the people who were present at *Seventeen*'s birth are gone: Helen Valentine died in 1986. Estelle Ellis, one of the few surviving staffers, continues to promote Valentine's prominent role in *Seventeen*'s origins to anyone who will listen. Unfortunately, one voice cannot shout over the cacophony of a dominant discourse. After a while, a dominant discourse takes on a life of its own, is written down as history, and becomes part of the culture. Thus, it is not surprising that in 1993, a *New York Times* article about teen magazines reported that *Seventeen*—the first teen magazine—was "started by Walter Annenberg in 1944 and edited by Enid Haupt."[60] Helen Valentine eventually seemed to tire of fighting the system and reliving the injustices of the past. In an oral history interview that she gave in 1982 for the American Jewish Committee, the interviewer asked her why she left *Seventeen*. Valentine answered: "Well, that's a long and complicated story and really not necessary to tell."[61]

But that "long and complicated story" was and is necessary to tell, because it allows us a rare view into the realities of magazine-making. Joy Leman describes the disconnect between magazine image and business reality, and the problem of accepting the first without recognizing the second:

> The image of the magazine is as the work of a group of friends—mainly women—bringing together their individual skills and pooling these in a co-operative venture as informal and friendly as if the paste-up had been done on someone's scrub-top kitchen table. This image has maintained the seamless garment of the ideology of women's magazines—with no production processes, ownership battles and takeovers, sackings of personnel, advertising pressures, self-censorship by journalists, political attitudes, government advice, etc. . . . only the voice of "one of those friends we specially value, the ones who are always the same and always different."[62]

The story of *Seventeen*'s origins helps us understand the magazine as a cultural product within a sociohistorical context, as the result of the labor of people working in a hierarchy, and as the battleground for competing discourses. It fleshes out and gives human form to the inequalities of gender, race, and social class that underlie the structure and relations of the magazine industry. *Seventeen*'s story also helps explain how a smart woman armed with ideas and ideals can be forced out of power by circumstances beyond her control. And how a single magazine created to educate girls as "whole human beings" and responsible global and community citizens became a magazine genre that primes girls to be discontented about their bodies and their lives—and therefore eager consumers of the promises of advertising.

For all that, and perhaps most especially, to return Helen Valentine to her rightful place in *Seventeen*'s institutional history—that's why it's an important story to tell.

Seventeen Magazine and Teena in the Twenty-First Century

> Well, we made history, we made publishing history. [*Seventeen*] identified the youth market long before anyone understood where this behemoth of a market was going or before everybody knew that we would create euphoria and a youth culture that would shape the world for decades to come, and we're still studying that generation as they mature. [Estelle Ellis, Ellis Oral History]

When last we saw *Seventeen* and Teena, Walter Annenberg had appointed Alice Thompson as editor-in-chief, replacing her four years later—for being a "nuisance"[1]—with his sister, Enid Annenberg Haupt, who edited *Seventeen* from 1954 through 1970. Four editors followed Haupt in quick succession, until Midge Turk Richardson took over in 1976. Turk, a former nun, ran *Seventeen* magazine for the next seventeen years.[2] Following Turk's departure from *Seventeen,* another five editors came and went, one (Annemarie Iverson, 2001–2002) in less than a year's time.

The magazine also changed ownership during this same time period. Triangle Publications, Annenberg's company, sold *Seventeen* to Murdoch Magazines in 1989; Murdoch sold it just two years later to K-III Magazines, later known as Primedia Magazines. In 2003, Primedia sold *Seventeen* to the Hearst Corporation, which owned the magazine at the time of this writing. There is, of course, some irony in *Seventeen* ending up in the hands of the Hearst Corporation, which for years had been the other side of an Annenberg business rivalry that began with William Randolph Hearst and M. L. Annenberg.

In 2003, Hearst executives persuaded *CosmoGirl!* founding editor Atoosa Rubenstein to leave *her* baby for an opportunity to revitalize *Seventeen.* Rubenstein became one of the most influential—or at least the most covered—of recent women's magazine editors. As the daughter of Iranian Muslim immigrant parents, her much-discussed ethnic and religious background reflected cultural changes in the United States and the U.S. media. Rubenstein approached *Seventeen* with a vision and a mission to make the magazine more relevant, more sophisticated, and more "young woman" (versus girl) oriented, with a view toward reclaiming its status as the premier teen magazine. Rubenstein took *Seventeen* back to its roots, restoring the original italicized logo to the cover and reducing the number of cover lines for a simpler, more elegant look—an ornate version of the early magazine. Inside the magazine, she brought back columns and articles about etiquette, decorating, cooking, and entertaining.[3]

Rubenstein left *Seventeen* at the end of 2006, having made her mark but also having received considerable public vilification, much of it by her staff who reportedly referred to her as "Atoosa the Hun."[4] Hearst Corporation replaced her with Ann Shoket, who had also succeeded Rubenstein at *CosmoGirl!* Shoket was *Seventeen*'s fifth editor in the first six years of the twenty-first century, a sign of the magazine's inability to establish a stable identity in the shifting markets of contemporary youth culture. Shoket told *Mediaweek* magazine that she wanted *Seventeen* to communicate teenage "energy" and that she intended to "lighten" the editorial content.[5] The reference to "energy" echoes *Seventeen*'s early promotional documents, seeking to sell advertisers on the idea of Teena, the prototypical teenager, as a tireless consumer.

By the first decade of the twenty-first century, Teena had entered a whole new world, both figuratively and literally. In 2009, *Seventeen* published thirteen international editions in the following countries: Argentina, Chile, Colombia/Venezuela, Ecuador, India, Indonesia, Malaysia, Mexico, Philippines, Singapore, South Africa, Thailand, and Turkey.[6] In the U.S., *Seventeen* ranked ninth in circulation rates (with a circulation of two million[7]) among women's magazines in the last six months of 2008.[8] According to Hearst's corporate website, *Seventeen* "reaches over thirteen million total readers per month."[9] But *Seventeen* was not the only teen magazine seeking girl readers.

For the second half of the twentieth century, three giants dominated the teen magazine industry: *Seventeen*, *YM* (the modern iteration of *Calling All Girls*), and *Teen*, which began publication in 1954. In 1988, Jane Pratt introduced *Sassy*, the teen magazine genre's cheeky cousin, as a challenger to the ruling triad. Then, starting in the late 1990s and early 2000s, adult women's magazines began to spin off younger "little sister" counterparts to compete for the teen magazine reader. *Teen People*, published by Time, Inc., and *CosmoGirl!* published by Hearst, both began in 1998; *Elle Girl*, published by Hachette

Filipacchi Media, entered the market in 2001, followed by *Teen Vogue*, published by Condé Nast, in 2003. *Men's Health* even spun off a "little brother" magazine called *MH-18* in 2000.

Almost as quickly as the market expanded, however, it began to implode. *Sassy* was folded into *Teen* in 1996. *MH-18* died in 2001, after less than a year's run. *YM* shut down in 2004 when publisher Gruner + Jahr sold its circulation list to Condé Nast's *Teen Vogue*.[10] *Elle Girl* and *Teen People* ceased publication in 2006 (the latter's readership receiving substitute subscriptions to *Seventeen*). Hearst folded *CosmoGirl!* into *Seventeen* in 2008. *Teen*, the last of *Seventeen*'s most enduring competitors, ended publication in 2009, shortly after Hearst, its final owner, scaled it back to a quarterly. At the end of 2009, only *Teen Vogue* existed as a paper competitor to *Seventeen*.

Seventeen Magazine at Sixty-Five

Ann Shoket was editor of *Seventeen* in September 2009 when the magazine celebrated a major anniversary milestone: its sixty-fifth birthday. In recognition, *Seventeen* gifted its subscribers with a special-edition issue that sported three different covers, each featuring Hispanic tween/teen Disney actress Selena Gomez. Gomez, a Latina Teena, represents a changing American ethnic landscape, one in which one out of three teenagers is *not* white.[11] The choice of Gomez as cover girl also represents a nod to the future and to *Seventeen*'s readership, 14 percent of whom are of Hispanic descent.[12] Judging by the special edition's fluorescent-hued cover lines that vie for attention in shades of hot pink, yellow, orange, and green, *Seventeen* imagines a future that is—at the least—very bright.

A comparison of these contemporary covers with *Seventeen*'s first cover provides a striking contrast. The debut cover featured an unknown model on a spare pastel background with the singular cover line "Young fashions & beauty, movies and music, ideas and people"; in contrast, the modern version features a well-known celebrity surrounded by a colorful cacophony of words, visually shouting: "936 Fashion and Beauty Ideas!"; "The Best Clothes for Your Body and Budget"; "Selena Gomez (Who's She Crushing on Now?)"; "AMAZING HAIR Every Day"; "Pretty!"; "Flirty!"; "Fun!"; "Find the Perfect First-Day Outfit for YOUR Style"; "BACK-TO-SCHOOL BLOWOUT!"; and "FLAT ABS!" Finally, after taking in the almost psychedelic landscape, the eye is drawn to the unusually (in context) reserved black type in the right-hand corner, reading: "My Coach Secretly Filmed Me Naked! Could This Happen to You?"

The cover lines "advertise" specific stories, but what do readers encounter inside the magazine generally? According to "independent research" cited in *Seventeen*'s 2009 Media Kit, the editorial content reflects a mix of: Fashion—36 percent; Beauty—21 percent; Self-Help/Relationships—14 percent; Health & Fitness—9 percent; Culture & Humanities—7 percent; Entertainment—6 percent; and Miscellaneous—7 percent.[13] In comparison to the 1940s magazine, the content of contemporary *Seventeen* places significantly more emphasis on a young woman's body. In 2009, fashion, beauty, and health coverage makes up 66 percent of the magazine's content, while in *Seventeen*'s first year, body-related articles made up only 28 percent of the total content, and in its sixth year, 30 percent. Stated proportionally, contemporary *Seventeen* places twice as much emphasis on a young woman's body than did Helen Valentine's *Seventeen.*

Seventeen's only paper competitor in its sixty-fifth birthday year, *Teen Vogue,* has a different look and a somewhat different focus. The most obvious way in which *Teen Vogue* diverges from *Seventeen* is in its diminutive size. Measuring about one-third smaller than the average magazine, this "Euro-size" competitor emulates the smaller-size versions of *Glamour* magazine that Condé Nast sells in Europe.[14] *Teen Vogue* has more fashion and entertainment content than *Seventeen* and less beauty and "other" content.[15] As a spinoff of *Vogue,* this makes sense: *Teen Vogue* is first and foremost a fashion magazine—which limits its readership to some degree. With a circulation rate of just over one million, *Teen Vogue* draws about half the readership of *Seventeen.*[16]

According to some media forecasters, the future of teen magazines lies in the internet, in a web presence rather than a paper presence.[17] In fact, most of the teen magazines that died a material death live on in cyberspace. *Teen People* continues at People.com; *Elle Girl* continues at Ellegirl.Elle.com; *Teen* and *CosmoGirl!* both exist as websites (Teenmag.com and Cosmogirl.com) under the "Hearst[Teen]Network," along with MisQuinceMag.com (celebrating the Hispanic tradition of the quinceañera), MyPromStyle.com, and Seventeen.com. *Seventeen*'s website debuted in the fall of 1998 and targets girls and women between the ages of thirteen and twenty-two—the same constituency as its paper version.[18] Of all the defunct paper magazines, only *YM* did not receive a cyber incarnation; instead, visitors to YM.com find themselves directed to teenvogue.com.

Under Ann Shoket's leadership, *Seventeen* has become more internet-savvy; Shoket writes a daily blog, and the magazine's pages often include directives that send readers to the website.[19] According to published reports, *Seventeen*'s website receives somewhere between 216,000 and 1.3 million visitors a month.[20] Besides the website, *Seventeen* has a presence on social networking sites MySpace, Facebook, Twitter, and YouTube.[21] Produced by and for generations raised on *Sesame Street* and rapid-fire cartoons, all of these websites tend toward short snippets of content and bright flashy imagery.

From Teena to Actionista

Despite the availability of online teen magazine content, a substantial number of teenage girls and young women continue to read paper magazines. According to market researchers, 77 percent of teenage girls read a magazine for pleasure on a weekly basis, spending an average of 2.6 hours in magazine reading per week.[22] Although magazine reading among fifteen to seventeen-year-old girls has declined from a high of 85.6 percent in 2002, it remained at almost 80 percent in 2007. The rates are even higher for women ages eighteen to twenty-four—an age group that *Seventeen* claims as a significant readership—92 percent of whom report reading magazines on a regular basis.[23]

Although the ascendancy of the internet is often used as an explanation for the near demise of a once thriving teen magazine market, the survey numbers suggest that young women have not given up reading paper magazines. Another possible explanation points to the changing nature of the teen girl herself. As E. L. Konigsburg, author of many young adult novels, remarked on the *Today* show in 2004, if Booth Tarkington's novel *Seventeen* were written today, it would have to be entitled *Twelve*.[24] Some industry insiders call this trend "girls getting older younger," and argue that contemporary teen girls prefer to read their big sisters' magazines, including *Cosmopolitan, Elle,* or *Vogue*.[25] This conventional wisdom, however, is belied by research, which suggests that teen girls tend to read teen magazines.[26] *Seventeen*'s research finds that its average reader is a sixteen-year-old girl—close to the magazine's "age" of seventeen.[27] Instead of focusing on reader preferences or behaviors, a more plausible explanation might be found by looking at the economics of the contemporary media industry, in which a handful of conglomerates now own the majority of the media holdings. From this perspective, integration of magazines, while reducing the diversity of consumer choices, results in more efficiency and larger profits for the parent corporation.[28]

And what about Teena, *Seventeen*'s original prototypical teenager? What has happened to Helen Valentine's ideal teen girl in the twenty-first century? *Seventeen* has replaced her with a new contemporary counterpart named "Actionista." Actionista has her own Facebook and MySpace pages. The MySpace site details her demographics as an eighteen-year-old girl from Everywhere, New York, U.S., and includes a paragraph called "About Me," which describes her as a "trendspreader," a "constant" shopper, and a "fabulous" looker.[29] Although the introduction cites Actionista's other qualities, including confidence, good grades, and leadership, it's clear that her consumer characteristics are her most important, as they receive first mention. Of course, the same could have been said for Teena—at least for the Promotional Teena that *Seventeen* introduced to advertisers so many years ago. In fact, contemporary *Seventeen*'s Actionista campaign mirrors the Teena campaign, in that it markets two variations of Actionista: one to the readership and one to the advertisers.

Readers meet their Actionista on social networking sites like Facebook, MySpace, and YouTube, and discover a young woman—perhaps much like themselves—who engages in consuming but also in volunteer activities and educational pursuits. For example, a YouTube video called "*Seventeen*'s Actionistas" features "real girl" Actionistas expressing sentiments like "I love helping underprivileged kids—and I take fashion risks," and "I always recycle—and I love getting manicures every week."[30]

On the other hand, the Actionistas that *Seventeen*'s advertisers meet through the magazine's 2009 Media Kit are portrayed just as consumers—valued for their clothing and cosmetic expenditures, their shopping behaviors, and their (and their parents') income. In comparing the readership of similar magazines to their own, *Seventeen* claims that frequent mall shoppers are more likely to read *Seventeen* than *Teen Vogue, Glamour, Cosmo,* or *Allure,*[31] and that the magazine's Actionistas are more apt to spend money on clothing and perfume than readers of *Glamour, Teen Vogue, Lucky, Marie Claire,* and *Allure.*[32]

Consuming Teens

As *Seventeen* celebrates its sixty-fifth birthday, the teenage girl (both real and ideal) and business are going strong, their relationship closer then ever. According to Harris Interactive, a marketing firm owned by Harris Poll, teenagers have become an important consumer entity in the U.S. economy, spending $94.7 billion annually.[33] Teenage Research Unlimited (yes, teens are now so important that an entire business industry has risen to track their preferences and behaviors) reports that 76 percent of American teenagers go shopping in any given week, spending an average of 4.4 hours a week at the mall. Those figures increase for teenage girls, 83 percent of whom shop an average of 5.3 hours per week. And, much like their older sisters and mothers, they report that they shop for leisure and social bonding, and not just for material acquisition.[34]

Unlike their adult counterparts, teenagers' spending has historically been less vulnerable to economic factors than adults'; in 2009, *Seventeen* editor Ann Shoket described teens as "recession-proof."[35] This means that they tend to spend more consistently than adults—a characteristic that makes them particularly valuable to the business community. Just as *Seventeen* discovered through its own early research in the 1940s, contemporary researchers report that teenagers help their parents make spending decisions, including for family vacations, cars, and electronics. In addition, many parents—strapped for time—ask their teens to research and shop for certain products.[36] Still, as the recession of 2009 taught youth retailers, teen spending could be slowed, if not stopped, and young consumers could—and would—learn to love a bargain.[37]

Shopping also continues to be a particularly feminine endeavor. Nationwide, teen girls spend more money than teen boys in all consumer categories except video games.[38] So what exactly are girls buying? Lots of goods and services, but especially apparel; girls spend most of their money on clothes and shoes.[39] Although young women's propensity to spend hasn't changed much since the 1940s, the brand names of their clothing lines have—somewhat dramatically. Names that simply signified the teen age, such as American Debuteen, Teen-Set, York Teen, and Teentimers, have been replaced with brand names selling much more provocative fare, such as sexuality and sex appeal (Teeze Me, Dzzire, Hot Kiss, LoveTease, Torrid), transgression and urban hipness (Rampage, Rubbish, h.i.p., Baby Phat), and—probably for some market-researched reason—X's (Trixxi, Roxy, Ruby Rox, XOXO, BCX). These brands come in "junior" sizes 5 to 13; the "teen" sizing category promoted in the pages of 1940s *Seventeen* no longer exists.

Another consumer change can be found in the clothes-shopping destination. Back in the 1940s and '50s, teen girls bought their clothes in the teen shops of major department stores. Again, as with clothing manufacturers, the names of these shops all signified the teenager, as in Teen Shop, Teen-Age Shop, and High School Shop. Today, comparable shops in department stores sport names that reflect a broader constituency—or are completely open to interpretation. For example, J. C. Penney, Dillard's, and Macy's each have a Juniors section; Saks Fifth Avenue's youthful wear can be found in the Contemporary section; Nordstrom has the BP (the Brass Plum) and Marshalls, The Cube. Modern teens, however, are more likely to shop in malls, at stores that are completely devoted to youth wear, such as Abercrombie & Fitch, Aeropostale, American Eagle Outfitters, Buckle, Deb, Delia's, Hollister, Hot Topic, PacSun (formerly Pacific Sunwear), and Victoria's Secret Pink.[40] Online sites, such as Alloy.com, are also popular—and most of the brick-and-mortar stores offer online shopping, too.

These changes in shopping habits and shopping habitats reflect broader cultural shifts. The teen shops and the teen brand names of the 1940s and '50s were focused on a particular age range—the teen age (or, similarly, the high school age). They represented an emerging social acknowledgment of this age as a particular time of life on the way to becoming an adult; adult women of the 1940s would not buy their clothes in a teen shop. On the other hand, the Juniors or even more open significations of the contemporary shops, as well as the youth stores, allow entrée for more mature shoppers. The distinction among female shoppers today is not youth as an age, but youth as expressed through hipness (and thinness). In this new shopping world, all women—given the proper body type and *joie de vivre*—can be youthful consumers.

Teen magazines, as with women's magazines, offer pages and pages of shopping information and direction. A 2003 research report by the Magazine Publishers of America found that teens who read magazines make more purchases than nonreaders—and heavy magazine readers buy the most products.[41] For young women, this translates into increased consumption of health and beauty products. Much like her 1940s and 1950s counterpart, today's teenage girl buys cosmetics and related body products made by major manufacturers rather than teen-specialized manufacturers. Maybelline, Revlon, and Tampax remain major *Seventeen* advertisers, but they've been joined by many more recent additions, including Clinique, Cover Girl, L'Oréal, MAC, Neutrogena, Rimmel, and Wet 'n Wild.

A new teen merchandise area, which harks back to *Seventeen*'s earliest days, is home décor. Pottery Barn, for example, debuted Pottery Barn Teen in 2003, along with its corresponding website, pbteen.com.[42] Pottery Barn

Teen markets to youthful consumers between the ages of twelve and eighteen, who treat their bedrooms as their first apartments—not a new concept, as *Seventeen*'s editors recognized and encouraged this idea more than sixty years earlier. Target (pronounced *Tar-zhay* by the hippest fashionistas) has also begun marketing to youthful decorators, through website links to dorm-related accessories and an annual fall distribution of glossy "college prep" catalogs.[43] J.C. Penney carries youth-oriented linen lines, including Dorm Life and Seventeen—an affiliated brand of *Seventeen* magazine. The linens and decorating accessories sold as teen-related often reflect the bright and wild colors found on the covers of teen magazines.

Beyond clothes, cosmetics, and home décor, modern teenage girls are also consuming services, including spas and salon treatments. New York City hotels such as the Regency, the Ritz-Carlton Central Park, and the Peninsula have all recently offered get-away packages for teen girls.[44]

Teena's Legacy: Popular Culture as Teen Culture

At the beginning of the twenty-first century, the *New York Times* described the role of the teenager in contemporary popular culture as a powerful dialectic of market and marketing tool:

> America is obsessed with youth, awash in the largest generation of young people since the baby boomers themselves passed through. […] Teenage tastes set the tone for mass culture from hip-hop to South Park, and teenage bodies are used to sell cars, clothes and the promise of perpetual youth to people old enough to be the models' parents.[45]

As the article suggests, contemporary American culture is steeped in youth. Unlike earlier eras when teen culture made up just one segment of the larger culture, some media industry insiders argue that teen culture is becoming more and more inescapable as the dominant culture.[46] *Entertainment Weekly* declared the summer of 2008 as the summer of "teen-tertainment," citing impending movies such as *Nick and Norah's Infinite Playlist*, the *Sisterhood of the Traveling Pants* sequel, and *High School Musical 3*.[47] The fifteen top-grossing movies of 2009 were *Avatar, Transformers: Revenge of the Fallen, Harry Potter and the Half-Blood Prince, The Twilight Saga: New Moon, Up, The Hangover, Star Trek, The Blind Side, Alvin and the Chipmunks: The Squeakquel, Sherlock Holmes, Monsters vs. Aliens, Ice Age: Dawn of the Dinosaurs, X-Men Origins:*

Wolverine, Night at the Museum: Battle of the Smithsonian, and *2012*—every one of them arguably targeting a youthful (toddler through young adult) audience.[48] It is difficult to find mass-produced television shows, magazines, or music that feature many main characters beyond the age of 30. And consider the plight of twentieth century teen icon Britney Spears. Next to her twenty-first century counterparts—pop culture music-makers such as Miley Cyrus, Taylor Swift, and the Jonas Brothers—Spears, age twenty-seven at the time of this writing, seems quite old in contrast.

Like it or not, teens have become our cultural milieu and our cultural tastemakers. The creators of *Seventeen* could never have predicted this long-term outcome of their attempts to bring some cultural and consumer credibility to the teen girl. But Estelle Ellis is dismayed. Contrasting their Teena to her modern-day progeny, Ellis says:

> She wasn't the girl that you see on the cover of teenage magazines today, who is only interested in sex and boys and face and ass. You know, I mean the whole—the point is, Teena was a whole human being! With a head, a brain, a heart, and a sense of responsibility to not only her age group, but to the world in general.[49]

As an indicator of the further decline (and ascendancy) of teen culture, Ellis points to the July 2003 issue of *Vanity Fair*, an *adult* women's fashion magazine. This issue, with a cover caption declaring "It's Totally Raining Teens," featured a cover photo featuring nine young and nubile "teen and tween stars." Ellis describes the cover as a "Lolita orgasm" meant for adult consumption, and identifies a cultural shift in which teens have expanded their influence from a market segment to an ideal that is marketed to adults.[50] To that end, they are no longer just consumers, but also the consumed.

Helen Valentine is not alive to assess the contemporary state of the teenager, but—ever foresightful— she seemed to see it coming, as reflected in an undated essay entitled "What Are We Doing to Our Teenagers?" Although she wrote it some time around 1960, her message remains remarkably relevant—and worthy of our consideration. Because the story of *Seventeen* and Teena began in the mind of Helen Valentine, I think it's only right to let her have the last words of this book:

> Isn't it about time we stopped thinking of teenagers as commercial gold mines and remembered that they will soon be running the world? Instead of filling them full of vital information on seductive perfumes and nail polishes

which are "jewels for fingers and toes," why don't we try to make it fashionable to have something to say and the right words to say it with? [...] Let's examine our own split-level, gadget-laden lives and see what we are doing to our offspring. Let's shift a little emphasis from permanent waves to brain waves; from the color of hair to the caliber of thinking; from buying for the future to building for it.[...] And let's see teens for what they are—the product of our past, the reflection of our present, and, if we will help them, the hope of our future.[51]

NOTES

PREFACE

1. See Charmaz 2004 for more on the method of grounded theory.
2. Although I collected data on the stories that made up the fiction category, I eventually chose to focus exclusively on the magazine's nonfiction editorial ideology.
3. Goffman 1979; Barthes 1972.
4. Portelli 1981, 100.
5. Portelli 1981.
6. Ellis, personal interview, June 19, 2003.
7. See, for example, Shafer 2002, 2006.
8. Scotford 1999, 98.
9. Marzolf 1978, 13.

INTRODUCTION

1. Media scholar Douglas Kellner coined the term "media culture" as a preferable alternative to the term "popular culture." See Kellner 1995a, 35. Before Kellner, other theorists found the term problematic, including Jameson 1979, and Horkheimer and Adorno 1944.
2. Croteau and Hoynes 2003, 3.
3. Kellner 1995a, 1995b; Ritzer, Goodman, and Wiedenhoft 2001; Schor 1998.
4. Laqueur 1990; see also Shahar 1994; Warren 1998; Wolf 1991, 13.
5. Bordo 1993; Kilbourne 1999; McCracken 1993; Schor 1998; Wolf 1991.
6. Bordo 1993; Kilbourne 1999; McCracken 1993; Wolf 1991.
7. Cohen 2003, 75; see also Zukin 2004, 33.
8. Schor 1998, 76.
9. Kilbourne 1999, 35, 44; see also Cohen 2003, 319.
10. See Bartky 1988; Featherstone 2001; Friedan 1963; Hesse-Biber 1996; Kilbourne 1999; Scanlon 1995; Wolf 1991.

11. Cortese 1999.
12. Cortese 1999; Dinnerstein and Weitz 1998. Gender scholar R. W. Connell calls this "hegemonic masculinity" (1987, 183–88). For more on aging, see Bazzini, McIntosh, Smith, Cook, and Harris 1997. For more on the mandate of thinness and its repercussions, see Bordo 1993; Brumberg 1997; Chernin 1981; Garner, Garfinkel, Schwartz, and Thompson 1980; Glassner 1992; Hesse-Biber 1989, 1996; Malkin, Wornian, and Chrisler 1999; Mazur 1986; Morgan 1998; Owen and Laurel-Seller 2000; Rothblum 1994; Seid 1989, 1994; Silverstein, Perdue, Peterson, and Kelly 1986; Silverstein, Peterson, and Perdue 1986; Striegel-Moore, Silberstein, and Rodin 1986.
13. Bartky 1988; Bordo 1993; Brumberg 1997.
14. Brumberg 1997.
15. Bartky 1988; Brumberg 1997; Tiggemann and Kenyon 1998.
16. Bartky 1988.
17. Bartky 1988.
18. Bordo 1993.
19. Bordo 1993; Dellinger and Williams 1997; Hamermesh and Biddle 1994; Jackson 1992; Schor 1998, 38; Zukin and Maguire 2004, 182.
20. Average circulations for the first six months of 2006: *Good Housekeeping,* 4,609,209; *Cosmopolitan,* 2,908,861; *Glamour,* 2,248,961; *Seventeen,* 2,013,357 (Magazine Publishers of America 2007).
21. Currie 1997, 1999; Duffy and Gotcher 1996; Durham 1996, 1998; Friedan 1963; Massoni 2004; McCracken 1993; Peirce 1990, 1993; Ruggiero and Weston 1985; Smith 1987, 1990; Wolf 1991.
22. Johnson and Prijatel 1999, 120.
23. See, for example, Steinem 1995.
24. For example, McCracken 1993; Peirce 1997.
25. Johnson and Prijatel 1999, 188. "Piffle" was period jargon for "trivial nonsense"; "No passion" was a reference to service magazines' exclusion of "sentimental short stories."
26. Johnson and Prijatel 1999, 190. For example, neither *Good Housekeeping* nor *Ladies' Home Journal* originally included features on beauty, health, and diet, but both do today.
27. According to http://thesaurus.reference.com/browse/model (accessed May 6, 2007).
28. Bordo 1993; Crane 1999; Kilbourne 1995, 1999.
29. Kilbourne 1999.
30. Brumberg 1997; Gilligan 1982; Orenstein 1994; Pipher 1994.
31. Currie 1997, 1999.
32. Crane 1999.
33. Currie 1997, 1999; Peirce 1993.
34. McCracken 1993.

35. Budgeon and Currie 1995; Currie 1999; Duffy and Gotcher 1996; Evans, Rutberg, Sather, and Turner 1991; Signorielli 1997.
36. Budgeon and Currie 1995; Currie 1999; Duffy and Gotcher 1996; Evans, Rutberg, Sather, and Turner 1991; McCracken 1993; Peirce 1990; Signorielli 1997.
37. Budgeon and Currie 1995; Duffy and Gotcher 1996; McCracken 1993.
38. Durham 1996, 1998.
39. Durham 1998.
40. McCracken 1993.
41. Durham 1996, 1998.
42. *Standard Rate and Data Service* 1996 (emphasis added).
43. Peirce 1993.
44. Massoni 2004.
45. Duffy and Gotcher 1996; Massoni 2004.
46. Croteau and Hoynes 2003; Currie 1997; Gerbner 1998; Kellner 1995a; Smith 1987, 1999; Steeves 1993.
47. Bielby and Bielby 1996; Croteau and Hoynes 2003; Gist 1993; Lafky 1993; Steeves 1993.
48. Smith 1987.
49. Johnson 1993; Zuckerman 1998.
50. Joliffe and Catlett 1994.
51. Milkie 2002.
52. Currie 1999; McCracken 1993.
53. Steinem 1995.
54. Friedan 1963.

Chapter 1

1. Cook 2004, 91; Palladino 1996, 4–5; Schrum 2004, 11–12.
2. Schrum 2004, 18–19.
3. "'Tricks' Bring Crowd to Buy War Stamps," *New York Times,* October 18, 1942, 5. Ascertained through a keyword search for "teen" using the *New York Times* archival database (covering the years 1857 to present). Also, I base my spelling of the word "teenage" on current preferred usage. In quotations, however, spelling follows the the original quote as determined by the time period.
4. Ascertained through a word search using the *New York Times* archival database (covering the years 1857 to present).
5. Lord & Taylor advertisement, *New York Times,* October 4, 1934, 5.
6. See Schrum 2004; also Cook 2004.
7. Peirce 1995a.
8. Mathieu and Jones 1943/44.

9. Mathieu and Jones 1943/44.
10. Many of the youth magazines of the day, in fact, catered to a religious constituency, including *The Catholic Boy, Catholic Student, The Challenge* (for Presbyterian youth), *Children's Friend, The Christian Youth, The Friend, Girls Today* (Methodist), *The High Trail, Junior Catholic Messenger,* and *Teens* (for "Christian youth between 13 and 19").
11. See Reynolds 1955 and Peck 1995 for thorough coverage of the history of *Mademoiselle.*
12. Reynolds 1955.
13. "Teen-Age Market: It's 'Terrif,'" *Business Week,* June 8, 1946, 72.
14. Peck 1995; Reynolds 1955; Zuckerman 1998.
15. Blum 1976; Covert 2003; Foner 1998, Chapter 10, "Fighting for Freedom"; Fox 1975; Honey 1984.
16. *Magazine War Guide* 1944–1945.
17. *War Jobs for Women* 1942.
18. *War Jobs for Women* 1942, 45.
19. Cited in Honey 1984, 224–25, N29.
20. Blum 1976; Cohen 2003; Foner 1998.
21. Reskin and Padavic 1994.
22. Ellis telephone interview, July 13, 2004.
23. Blum 1976; Covert 2003.
24. "Teen-Age Market: It's 'Terrif,'" *Business Week,* June 8, 1946, 72.
25. Valentine Oral History, 1. American Jewish Committee Archives.
26. Valentine Oral History, 9. American Jewish Committee Archives.
27. Valentine Oral History, 9. American Jewish Committee Archives.
28. Valentine Oral History, 2. American Jewish Committee Archives.
29. Valentine Oral History, 2. American Jewish Committee Archives.
30. Valentine Oral History, 14. American Jewish Committee Archives.
31. Valentine Oral History, 15. American Jewish Committee Archives.
32. Valentine Oral History, 14–15. American Jewish Committee Archives.
33. Reynolds 1955, 230; also telephone interview with Barbara Valentine Hertz, February 27, 2006.
34. *Better than Beauty* was reprinted in 2002 by Chronicle Books.
35. In retrospect, one is left to wonder whether Alice Thompson should have taken her own etiquette advice, as stealing the job of one's best friend and mentor certainly seems the height of rudeness.
36. Peck 1995; Zuckerman 1998.
37. The first of these daughters died soon after birth. See Cooney 1982; Ogden 1999.
38. Cooney 1982; Ogden 1999. The affectionate sibling relationship between the Annenberg sisters and their brother would be challenged and eventually critically damaged after Walter became the primary beneficiary of his father's estate.

39. Cooney 1982; Ogden 1999.
40. Cooney 1982; Ogden 1999.
41. Cooney 1982; Ogden 1999.
42. Cooney 1982; Ogden 1999.
43. Cooney 1982, 18.
44. Cooney 1982, 18, 52.
45. Cooney 1982; Ogden 1999. Later in Annenberg's life, Peddie's second-rate status would become a sore spot of sorts, and he donated millions of dollars to the school to improve its standing. The school's website documents the importance of Annenberg's contribution in its history; see http://www.peddie.org/podium/default.aspx?t=16400 (accessed March 5, 2010).
46. Cooney 1982; Ogden 1999.
47. Cooney 1982, 182.
48. See Gaines 1985.
49. Cooney 1982; Ogden 1999.
50. Cooney 1982; Ogden 1999.
51. Cooney 1982; Ogden 1999.
52. Cooney 1982; Ogden 1999. Krancer quoted in Ogden 1999, 247.
53. Cooney 1982; Ogden 1999.
54. Cooney 1982; Ogden 1999.
55. Gaines 1985.
56. Beinhoff and Bekken 1995; Seebohm 1982. See also Zuckerman 1998.
57. Scotford 1999; Zuckerman, 1998. Also see "Seventeen: A Unique Case Study," *Tide*, April 15, 1945, Estelle Ellis Collection, Archives Center, National Museum of American History, Behring Center, Smithsonian Institution, Box 18, File 5.
58. Cooney 1982; Ogden 1999.
59. Valentine Oral History, 5–6. American Jewish Committee Archives.
60. "*Seventeen* Is Five," *Newsweek*, August 29, 1949, 47.
61. Cooney 1982; Ogden 1999; Reynolds 1955; Scotford 1999; Valentine Oral History. American Jewish Committee Archives.
62. Valentine Oral History, 6. American Jewish Committee Archives.
63. Cooney 1982, 183; Ogden 1999, 284.
64. Cooney 1982, 184.
65. "*Seventeen:* A Unique Case Study," *Tide*, April 15, 1945. Estelle Ellis Collection, Archives Center, National Museum of American History, Behring Center, Smithsonian Institution, Box 18, File 5.
66. "The Women," *Time*, March 6, 1950, 56–57.
67. For example, "Two Years Before the Masthead," an article from *Seventeen*'s "Second Birthday" issue, explained to the reader that "*SEVENTEEN* was, and is, Helen Valentine's baby."

68. The magazine's promotional literature, directed at advertisers and retailers, often referred to *Seventeen* as "baby." For example, an advertisement that ran in industry publications on the one-year anniversary of *Seventeen*'s "birth" read: "Although the baby is only one year old, she certainly is big for her age!" (referring to the average size of the issues). Estelle Ellis Collection, Archives Center, National Museum of American History, Behring Center, Smithsonian Institution, Box 25, File 6. This advertisement also reveals—if there was any question left—baby's gender: it's a girl!
69. Personal correspondence from Walter Annenberg to Helen Valentine, dated October 2, 1944, copy of which is in author's possession; original in the possession of Valentine Hertz Kass, Helen Valentine's granddaughter. This letter is covered in full later in this chapter. The story of Valentine selecting the name for *Seventeen* is also recounted in Cooney 1982, 183.
70. Cooney 1982, 183.
71. Cooney 1982; Ogden 1999.
72. Ogden 1999, 287.
73. Cooney 1982, 182.
74. Cooney 1982, 183; Ogden 1999, 285, 287. In an email communication on July 24, 2007, on this topic, former promotion director Estelle Ellis questions Annenberg's version, stating that any kind of decision about advertising "would have been Helen's."
75. Ogden 1999, 287.
76. Ellis personal interview, New York City, June 19, 2003.
77. Reynolds 1955, 231
78. *Tide*, April 15, 1945; Estelle Ellis Collection, Archives Center, National Museum of American History, Behring Center, Smithsonian Institution, Box 18, File 5.
79. Ellis telephone interview, July 6, 2004.
80. Ellis personal interview, New York City, June 19, 2003.
81. Ellis telephone interview, July 6, 2004.
82. See Martha Scotford's 1999 book, *Cipe Pineles: A Life of Design.*
83. Reynolds 1955, 237.
84. "The Women," *Time*, March 6, 1950, 56–57.
85. Ellis Oral History, 10–11. American Jewish Committee Archives.
86. Personal correspondence from Walter Annenberg to Helen Valentine, dated October 19, 1946, copy of which is in the author's possession; original in the possession of Valentine Hertz Kass.
87. Barbara Valentine Hertz, telephone interview, February 27, 2006; Hertz vividly remembers her mother, Helen Valentine, describing these luncheon meetings, made memorable by Annenberg's predilection for using "clean" money to pay his tab: "Mom used to go down to Philadelphia periodically to have lunch with him. And the only thing I [*small giggle*]—I was still pretty damn young then—remember her telling when she came back from these meetings was that at the end of

lunch the . . . one of his valets or somebody like that, would come in with new or carefully laundered money because he would only handle *clean* money. Which you know his father died in jail and Walter was always trying to live down this reputation. And I remember that always so absolutely impressed mom—she was always both amused and impressed by it. We used to hear about the *new money* that was brought in after lunch."

88. Barbara Valentine Hertz, telephone interview, February 27, 2006; Estelle Ellis, personal interview, New York City, June 19, 2003; Alberta Eiseman, telephone interview, March 27, 2006; Ingrid Lowenstein Sladkus, telephone interview, April 20, 2006.
89. See Johnson and Prijatel 1999, 164–68, for more about the editor-in-chief position generally.
90. Johnson and Prijatel 1999, 168. Authors refer to this position as a magazine's "sergeant."
91. Johnson and Prijatel 1999, 168–69, for more about the positions of managing editor and executive editor generally.
92. Ellis's upbringing, her chance meeting with Valentine, and her work as *Seventeen*'s promotion director are detailed at length in Chapter 4, "Teena Goes to Market."
93. Ellis personal interview, June 19, 2003.
94. *Seventeen,* November 1947, 40.
95. Scavullo 1984, 3.
96. According to Social Security Death Index Records (available online), Alice Dickey Thompson Beaton's birthday was October 31, 1905; however, Alice sometimes gave her birthdate as October 31, 1910, representing herself as five years younger than she actually was (see, for example, *Who's Who of American Women* 1958–1959).
97. Barbara Valentine Hertz, telephone interview, February 18, 2006.
98. "Backstage with *Seventeen,*" September 1945, 24.
99. Judging by pictures, names, and other reports, some of the illustrators were women of color—Mary Suzuki, for instance—and several of the contributing artists were people of color. Estelle Ellis reports that a young Puerto Rican woman named Rosalind Santori briefly worked in the fashion department (Ellis email, July 11, 2006).
100. Eiseman telephone interview, March 27, 2006.
101. Sladkus telephone interview, April 20, 2006.
102. Sladkus telephone interview, April 20, 2006.
103. *Women's Wear Daily,* August 9, 1944, 17.
104. "New Teen-Age Magazine," *Business Week,* August 26, 1944, 94–95.
105. "Bobby Sox Forum," *Newsweek,* November 30, 1944, 89–90.
106. A copy of this letter is in the author's possession; original in the possession of Valentine Hertz Kass.

Chapter 2

1. According to Johnson and Prijatel 1999, 109, a magazine's tone is made up of four different facets: verbal style, overall appearance, business operations (this includes promotion), and attitude. Editorial philosophy entails "what the magazine is intended to do, what areas of interest it covers, how it will approach those interests, and the voice it will use to express itself." See also Mann 1989.
2. See Mann 1989.
3. Gender scholars find this "tone of intimacy" to be a continuing, pervasive, and particularly gendered feature of women's and teen (girl) magazines, historically; far more common a discursive strategy in magazines produced for girls and women than for boys and men. Joy Leman (1980) and Cristanne Miller (1987) both consider it to be a part of a larger system of gender oppression. Leman, critiquing it from a Marxist feminist position, argues that it is a way to distract the reader from existing political and economic inequalities (particularly in employment and consumption). Miller focuses on the power hierarchy that it seems to construct between producer and reader (as tutor and student) while magazines for men and boys address the reader more equitably, as a comrade or pal. See Kramarae 1981 and Willemsen 1998 for more on the differences between teen boy magazines and teen girl magazines.
4. *Seventeen,* September 1944, 33.
5. The author thanks Marissa Massoni for this observation.
6. Scavullo, 1984, 4. Writing in his autobiography, Scavullo reminisces about his work at *Seventeen*: "I did everything during those *Seventeen* days—the makeup, the hair, I even helped with the fashions. I'd tell Eleanore Hillebrand to have Claire McCardell's dresses copied, and when I worked with Betty Gulesian and Ray Crespin at the magazine, we sparked up the teenage look away from those terrible Vicki Vaughn dresses and those awful Toni permanents. I nearly lost *Seventeen* their Toni advertising account. I was doing so much straight hair in rebellion. When Toni finally threatened to pull out their advertising, I capitulated, and used a model called Anne Hemingway who had a mass of curly hair—and features like Katharine Hepburn." Vicki Vaughn, an early advertiser in *Seventeen,* manufactured affordable dresses with price tags that wouldn't break an average family's budget.
7. *Seventeen,* June 1945, 2.
8. *Seventeen,* February 1945, 2.
9. Valentine Kass, quoted in Scotford 1999. The first black model did not appear in the pages of *Seventeen* until 1963 (see Palladino 1996). *Glamour* was the first mainstream women's magazine to feature a black model on the cover, when Katiti Kironde II appeared on its August 1968 cover (See Gross 1995, 238).
10. Scavullo 1984. Francesco Scavullo tells an interesting story in his biography that seems to reflect his eagerness to integrate *Seventeen*'s pages: "I remember one trip to Africa I took with Rosemary [McMurtry, *Seventeen* assistant fashion editor]—she got a telegram and came to me white-faced: 'My God, they've changed the

issue to 'See America First'! We're supposed to make this look like America!' All those beautiful blacks walking around in colorful turbans and I was supposed to make it look like the Grand Canyon or Oshkosh, Wisconsin? I was learning about the magazine business." (Scavullo 1984, 3–4).

11. Estelle Ellis Collection, Archives Center, National Museum of American History, Behring Center, Smithsonian Institution, Series 1, Box 25, File 6.
12. The percentage given for fiction represents the average across all thirteen issues published during this time period. Because *Seventeen* didn't include fiction until January 1945, however, this average slightly underrepresents the ratio of space devoted to fiction after its inclusion. From January 1945 to September 1945, the magazine devoted an average of 11 percent of editorial space to fiction. I do not include a discussion of fiction in my analysis, as I am focusing on the magazine's nonfiction editorial ideology.
13. *Seventeen,* March 1945, 148.
14. *Seventeen,* April 1945, 58–59.
15. *Seventeen,* January 1945, 9.
16. *Seventeen,* July 1945, 45. During the war years, "bulky" suits and coats with menswear detailing were a fashion trend for women of all ages. Teen girls also wore denim jeans and untucked shirts. See Gordon and Gordon 1987, 228.
17. See Gordon and Gordon 1987, 245–46.
18. *Seventeen,* August 1945, 16.
19. *Seventeen,* September 1945, 81.
20. See McCracken 1995, 4. McCracken defines covert advertising as "the promotion of products, disguised as editorial material or hidden in some other form so that they appear to be non-advertising material."
21. "We Go Shopping," *Seventeen,* September 1944, 8.
22. See Zukin 2004, 41. According to Zukin, fashion magazines (and other media arenas) offer everyone, regardless of economic status, the opportunity to "gain cultural capital by vicarious consumption."
23. "Pattern Wardrobe," *Seventeen,* July 1945, 70.
24. See Cohen 2003 on the Citizen Consumer.
25. See "Ideas for Teen-Agers," *New York Times,* April 21, 1945, 16, and "600 Teen-Age Girls See Sewing Exhibition," *New York Times,* April 22, 1945, 36.
26. *Seventeen,* March 1945, 76–77.
27. *Seventeen,* April 1945, 100.
28. *Seventeen,* August 1945, 96–97.
29. *Seventeen,* September 1945, 80–1, 144–45.
30. *Seventeen,* February 1945, 67.
31. *Seventeen,* April 1945, 100.
32. *Seventeen,* February 1945, 78–79, 128.

33. *Seventeen,* November 1944, 44–45.
34. *Seventeen,* September 1944, 66–67.
35. *Seventeen,* December 1944, 88–89, 101.
36. *Seventeen,* June 1945, 64–65, 161.
37. *Seventeen,* July 1945, 22–3.
38. *Seventeen,* September 1945, 63.
39. See Brumberg 1997; Bartky 1988.
40. *Seventeen,* September 1945, 63.
41. *Seventeen,* January 1945, 54.
42. This is another instance of what McCracken 1995 refers to as "covert advertising."
43. *Seventeen,* September 1944, 4; October 1944, 4.
44. *Seventeen,* December 1944, 112–13, 116.
45. *Seventeen,* July 1945, 114.
46. *Seventeen,* April 1945, 18.
47. *Seventeen,* May 1945, 79.
48. See Aronson 2002, 5. Amy Aronson asserts that these kinds of competing discourses have long been a characteristic of women's magazines; using Bakhtin's concept of the dialogic, Aronson envisions competing discourses within a magazine as conversing, or talking back to one another.
49. *Seventeen,* May 1945, 162.
50. *Seventeen,* October 1944, 26, 28.
51. "Send Yourself to College," *Seventeen,* June 1945, 114–15; Eleanor Hiteshew, "State College B.A.," *Seventeen,* June 1945, 86–89, 122, 123, 148–152.
52. Alice Beaton, "For Seniors Only," "With Chance for Advancement," *Seventeen,* January 1945, 81, 107.
53. *Seventeen,* May 1945, 90–91, 145, 148–49.
54. *Seventeen,* January 1945, 68–69, 103.
55. *Seventeen,* September 1945, 74–75, 122, 161.
56. *Seventeen,* December 1944, 80–81, 102.
57. *Seventeen,* September 1944, 60.
58. *Seventeen,* March 1945, 16–17, 146.
59. This was a characteristic of the "citizen consumer" ideology, as previously addressed (see Cohen 2003).
60. *Seventeen,* August 1945, 24, 158.
61. *Seventeen,* August 1945, 96, 97.
62. Palladino 1996.
63. *Seventeen,* December 1944, 70–71, 86–87.
64. *Seventeen,* March 1945, 26, 159.
65. *Seventeen,* May 1945, 34–35, 128.

66. *Seventeen,* May 1945, 35.
67. *Seventeen,* May 1945, 128.
68. "British Girls Are Busy," *Seventeen,* September 1944, 38–39; "Chinese Girls Are Fighters," *Seventeen,* October 1944, 44, 45, 74, 75; "This Is Russia," *Seventeen,* November 1944, 46, 47, 90, 91; "Girls of India," *Seventeen,* December 1944, 68, 69, 115, 117; "Les Enfants de la Patrie," *Seventeen,* January 1945, 58, 59, 97, 99, 118; "Our Good Neighbors," *Seventeen,* February 1945, 84, 85, 114, 115, 122; "Girls of Canada," *Seventeen,* March 1945, 82, 83, 145, 147, 155; "Turkish Girls, New Era," *Seventeen,* April 1945, 72, 73; "He Mau Kaikamahine O Hawaii," *Seventeen,* May 1945, 86, 87; "At the Konditeri," *Seventeen,* June 1945, 96, 97.
69. *Seventeen,* May 1945, 87.
70. In a letter dated October 19, 1946 (cited more extensively in Chapter 6), Annenberg decried Valentine's progressive agenda in the magazine, stating at one point: "I suspect you think it would be good for the world for negros to marry whites. I don't."
71. "Bravo! The Ballet," *Seventeen,* March 1945, 127.
72. "Teens in the News," *Seventeen,* June 1945, 168.
73. "Can All You Can," *Seventeen,* June 1945, 101.
74. "Letters to the Editor," *Seventeen,* April 1945, 7.
75. *Seventeen,* December 1944, 49.
76. *Seventeen,* September 1944, 54, 56, 84.
77. *Seventeen,* April 1945, 20; and August 1945, 35.
78. "Straw Vote," *Seventeen,* October 1944, 10–11.
79. "News Breaks into the News," *Seventeen,* July 1945, 56–57.
80. "Around the Cracker Barrel," *Seventeen,* July 1945, 66–67, 98 99.
81. "The Dumbarton Oaks Plan for World Organization," *Seventeen,* March 1945, 80–81, 139.
82. *Seventeen,* April 1945, 11–12.
83. *Seventeen,* May 1945, 94–95, 121, 136.
84. *Seventeen,* August 1945, 94–95, 124, 127, 150.
85. *Seventeen,* September 1945, 88–89, 162, 164–65.
86. *Seventeen,* September 1945, 24.
89. *Magazine War Guide* 1944–1945.
90. "The Unkindest Cut of All," *Seventeen,* August 1945, 61, 120, 162.
91. "Can All You Can," *Seventeen,* June 1945, 101, 142–44, 162.
92. "The Fight Against Inflation," *Seventeen,* August 1945, 94–95, 124, 127, 150.
93. "You—A Safety Engineer," *Seventeen,* July 1945, 28, 113.
94. "Christmas Weighs Five Pounds," *Seventeen,* October 1944, 22, 140.
95. "Join the Junior Red Cross," *Seventeen,* May 1945, 140.
96. "Serving the U.S. #1: Hospital Aides" *Seventeen,* July 1945, 81.

97. "Gone Are the Days," *Seventeen,* August 1945, 82–83, 148.
98. "The Dumbarton Oaks Plan," *Seventeen,* March 1945, 80–81, 139.
99. "Be a Volunteer Farmer," *Seventeen,* April 1945, 86–87, 117, 138, 146–47; and "From My Own Garden," *Seventeen,* May 1945, 64, 65, 122, 127.
100. *Seventeen,* April 1945, 14.
101. Betz and Clark, "This Couldn't Possibly Be You," August 1945, 84, 85.
102. *Seventeen* articles by Dixon Gayer: "Xavier Cugat was a Brat," October 1944, 54-5, 85; "His Hi-di-highness," November 1944, 58-9, 92-3, 95; "3X Plus 2Y Equals Woody Herman," December 1944, 76-7, 103-4; "A Trumpet in the Sugar Bowl," January 1945, 78-9, 108; "One Night Stand," February 1945, 98-9, 142, 159; "Swing's Doctor of Philosophy," April 1945, 92-3, 158; "Happy with Prima," June 1945, 92-3, 124.
103. The focus on entertainment industry jobs continues today; see Massoni 2004.
104. "What a Way to Earn a Living!" *Seventeen,* May 1945, 68–69.
105. "Editors Are Frequently People," *Seventeen,* September 1945, 68–69. *Seventeen* continues to represent work in the entertainment industry as fun and glamorous. See Massoni 2004 on this point.
106. "If He Could Only Cook," *Seventeen,* March 1945, 76.
107. "Advertising News and Notes," *New York Times,* August 23, 1945, 27.
108. Helen Valentine, "Happy Birthday," *Seventeen,* September 1945, 61.
109. In letters dated October 16 and October 18, Annenberg and Valentine debated the merit of including pictures of "negros" in *Seventeen,* Valentine arguing for and Annenberg against. This correspondence is described in more detail in Chapter 6.

Chapter 3

1. A version of this chapter was published as an article in a special "teen" issue of the *Journal of American Culture*; see Massoni 2006.
2. Estelle Ellis, personal interview, June 19, 2003.
3. Estelle Ellis, private correspondence, n.d.
4. Ellis Oral History. American Jewish Committee Archives.
5. See Isaacs 1999; Friedan 1963.
6. Ellis Oral History, 1. American Jewish Committee Archives.
7. Ellis Oral History, 12. American Jewish Committee Archives.
8. Ellis Oral History, 5. American Jewish Committee Archives.
9. According to Fredric Jameson (1979, 136), artistic genres existed pre-capitalism as "signs of something like an aesthetic 'contract' between a cultural producer and a certain homogeneous class or group public," but under capitalism have come to represent a market relationship.
10. Ellis Oral History, 6. American Jewish Committee Archives.

11. Ellis Oral History, 6. American Jewish Committee Archives.
12. Ellis Oral History, 6. American Jewish Committee Archives.
13. Ellis Oral History, 7. American Jewish Committee Archives.
14. Ellis Oral History, 7. American Jewish Committee Archives.
15. The author thanks Carol Holstead, University of Kansas Associate Professor of Journalism and former magazine editor, for this information.
16. Ellis Oral History, 13. American Jewish Committee Archives.
17. Estelle Ellis, personal interview, New York City, June 19, 2003.
18. Ellis Oral History, 19. American Jewish Committee Archives.
19. Ellis personal interview, New York City, June 19, 2003.
20. Ellis Oral History, 43. American Jewish Committee Archives.
21. Ellis Oral History, 43. American Jewish Committee Archives.
22. Ellis Oral History, 43. American Jewish Committee Archives.
23. Ellis personal interview, New York City, June 19, 2003.
24. Ogden 1999, 287. Again, as detailed in footnote 81 of Chapter 3, Estelle Ellis disputes Annenberg's memory of the amount of influence he exerted on *Seventeen's* advertising policy.
25. Ellis, personal interview, New York City, June 19, 2003.
26. Ellis, personal interview, New York City, June 19, 2003.
27. Ellis, telephone interview, July 13, 2004.
28. Ellis, telephone interview, July 13, 2004; Ellis Oral History, 42. American Jewish Committee Archives.
29. See Benson & Benson, Inc., 1945; Opinion Research Corp., 1947. Estelle Ellis Collection, Archives Center, National Museum of American History, Behring Center, Smithsonian Institution. Box 18, Files 1–4.
30. Ellis, telephone interview, July 13, 2004.
31. Ellis, telephone interview, July 13, 2004.
32. Ellis, personal collection, n.d.
33. Estelle Ellis, personal collection, n.d.
34. Estelle Ellis Collection, Archives Center, National Museum of American History, Behring Center, Smithsonian Institution, Box 18, Files 1–4.
35. Estelle Ellis Collection, Archives Center, National Museum of American History, Behring Center, Smithsonian Institution, Box 18, Files 1–2. According to the Consumer Price Indicator on the Federal Reserve Bank of Minneapolis website, $13.48 in 1944 translates to $163.00 in 2009 and $2.13 translates to $25.80; http://www.minneapolisfed.org/index.cfm (accessed September 16, 2009).
36. Estelle Ellis Collection, Archives Center, National Museum of American History, Behring Center, Smithsonian Institution, Box 18, Files 1–4.
37. Estelle Ellis Collection, Archives Center, National Museum of American History, Behring Center, Smithsonian Institution, Box 18, Files 3–4.

38. Estelle Ellis Collection, Archives Center, National Museum of American History, Behring Center, Smithsonian Institution, Box 18, Files 3–4.
39. Estelle Ellis Collection, Archives Center, National Museum of American History, Behring Center, Smithsonian Institution, Box 38, File 5.
40. C.f., Kellner 1995a; Smith 1987.
41. Estelle Ellis Collection, Archives Center, National Museum of American History, Behring Center, Smithsonian Institution, Box 38, File 5.
42. Estelle Ellis Collection, Archives Center, National Museum of American History, Behring Center, Smithsonian Institution, Box 38, File 5.
43. Estelle Ellis Collection, Archives Center, National Museum of American History, Behring Center, Smithsonian Institution, Box 38, File 5.
44. Estelle Ellis Collection, Archives Center, National Museum of American History, Behring Center, Smithsonian Institution, Box 17, File 10.
45. Estelle Ellis Collection, Archives Center, National Museum of American History, Behring Center, Smithsonian Institution, Box 17, File 11.
46. Estelle Ellis Collection, Archives Center, National Museum of American History, Behring Center, Smithsonian Institution, Box 17, File 11.
47. Estelle Ellis Collection, Archives Center, National Museum of American History, Behring Center, Smithsonian Institution, Box 25, File 6.
48. "Seventeen: A Unique Case Study," *Tide,* April 15, 1945. Estelle Ellis Collection, Archives Center, National Museum of American History, Behring Center, Smithsonian Institution, Box 18, File 5.
49. Estelle Ellis Collection, Archives Center, National Museum of American History, Behring Center, Smithsonian Institution, Box 32, File 8.
50. Estelle Ellis Collection, Archives Center, National Museum of American History, Behring Center, Smithsonian Institution, Box 38, File 5.
51. Estelle Ellis Collection, Archives Center, National Museum of American History, Behring Center, Smithsonian Institution, Box 38, File 5.
52. Estelle Ellis Collection, Archives Center, National Museum of American History, Behring Center, Smithsonian Institution, Box 26, File 1.
53. Estelle Ellis Collection, Archives Center, National Museum of American History, Behring Center, Smithsonian Institution, Box 38, File 5.
54. Estelle Ellis Collection, Archives Center, National Museum of American History, Behring Center, Smithsonian Institution, Box 25, File 6.
55. Estelle Ellis Collection, Archives Center, National Museum of American History, Behring Center, Smithsonian Institution, Box 38, File 5.
56. Estelle Ellis Collection, Archives Center, National Museum of American History, Behring Center, Smithsonian Institution, Box 25, File 6.
57. Estelle Ellis Collection, Archives Center, National Museum of American History, Behring Center, Smithsonian Institution, Box 38, File 5.

58. "Teen-Age Market: It's 'Terrif,'" *Business Week*, June 8, 1946, 72.
59. Estelle Ellis Collection, Archives Center, National Museum of American History, Behring Center, Smithsonian Institution, Box 38, File 5.
60. Estelle Ellis Collection, Archives Center, National Museum of American History, Behring Center, Smithsonian Institution, Box 38, File 5.
61. Estelle Ellis Collection, Archives Center, National Museum of American History, Behring Center, Smithsonian Institution, Box 38, File 5.
62. Estelle Ellis Collection, Archives Center, National Museum of American History, Behring Center, Smithsonian Institution, Box 38, File 5.
63. For example, Kellner 1995b; McCracken 1993; Schor 1998.
64. Cf. McCracken 1993.
65. Estelle Ellis Collection, Archives Center, National Museum of American History, Behring Center, Smithsonian Institution, Box 38, File 5.
66. Cf. Joliffe and Catlett 1994.

Chapter 4

1. Estelle Ellis Collection, Archives Center, National Museum of American History, Behring Center, Smithsonian Institution, Box 38, File 5.
2. Kilbourne 1995; McCracken 1993; Steinem 1995; Tuchman 1978.
3. Lux ad, *Seventeen*, November 1944, 63.
4. Flame-Glo ad, *Seventeen*, September 1944, 70.
5. Fox 1975.
6. Sickles 2004.
7. Featherknit ad, *Seventeen*, March 1945, 141.
8. Jantzen ad, *Seventeen*, June 1945, 49.
9. *Seventeen*, February 1945, 49.
10. Dr. Pepper ad, *Seventeen*, June 1945, 109; Judy Kent ad, *Seventeen*, May 1945, 52.
11. See Connell 1987, 183–88, on hegemonic masculinity/emphasized femininity; see Mulvey 1975 on the male gaze.
12. Joan Lord ad, *Seventeen*, May 1945, 2.
13. Heart Throb Fashions ad, *Seventeen*, January 1945, 19.
14. Keepsake Diamond Rings ad, *Seventeen*, April 1945, 104. The fact that *Seventeen* accepted ads for engagement rings seems to contradict Annenberg's later assertion in his biographies that he forbade all ads that encouraged early marriage.
15. That "daintiness" became a salable quality during the war years may have represented a reaction (or backlash) to women's movement into areas previously the bastions of men—for instance, as factory workers and heads of households. Once the war ended and servicemen returned to take back their positions at work and

home, the daintiness focus disappeared. It is also possible that it was in response to a continuing concern with the hygiene habits of immigrants, particularly women, who might not shave or wash their underarms, use deodorant, or change their underwear in ways pleasing to the American nose.

16. Companies using the "daintiness" discourse were: Jr First Fashions (teen), Jane Love Teen Frocks (teen), Teen-Set Dresses (teen), Diana Corset Company, Gossards Foundations (teen), Kleinert's Foundations (teen), Tampax, Kotex (teen), Rand Dress Shields (teen), Kleinert's Dress Shields, Lux Lingerie Soap, Lux Clothing Soap, Odorono Deodorant, Nonspi Deodorant (teen), DuraGloss Nail Polish, Prim New Spice Deodorant (teen), Mavis Talcum.
17. Nonspi ad, *Seventeen,* April 1945, 143.
18. Lux ad, *Seventeen,* April 1945, 108.
19. Mavis Talcum ad, *Seventeen,* June 1945, 158.
20. While *Seventeen* didn't formally organize advertisements in the same way it organized its editorial content, advertisements were *informally* organized in a spacial and chronological hierarchical order. Magazines, as a whole, generally structure their material (both editorial and advertising) using "wells," which are blocks or sections of content. In *Seventeen*'s case, the magazine used a modified "monowell" structure, in which a large uninterrupted block of editorial material in the middle of the magazine was flanked on either side with wells made up of a mix of (mostly) advertising and (some) editorial content. The most important and influential advertisements appeared in the first section, usually as full-page ads. In addition, full-page ads could also be found on the inside of the front cover and on either side of the back cover. Smaller, less expensive, and less noticeable ads appeared in the third section of the magazine. This section usually included partial-page ads (some very small) for clothing and accessories, girdles and bras, off-brand grooming supplies, feminine hygiene products, medicines, vocational training opportunities, and other miscellaneous products. See Johnson and Prijatel 1998 for more on different magazine structures.
21. Yardley ad, *Seventeen,* April 1945, 120.
22. Yardley ad, *Seventeen,* April 1945, 120.
23. Rose Laird ad, *Seventeen,* May 1945, 16.
24. Elizabeth Arden ad, *Seventeen,* September 1945, 3.
25. As evidenced in Chapter 3, "branding" teen girls while they were young and impressionable was a major tenet of *Seventeen*'s promotional campaign.
26. Kotex ads, *Seventeen,* October 1944, 16 (body type); November 1944, 16 (junior hostess); March 1945, 110 (care for your hands and brows); May 1945, 32 (keep jewelry from tarnishing); June 1945, 32 (get exercise); July 1945, 23; (catch the attention of a boy); August 1945, 33 (play tennis); September 1945, 33 (end a date).
27. Kotex ad, July 1945, 23.
28. Tone ad, *Seventeen,* January 1945, 5.
29. Nonspi ad, *Seventeen,* December 1944, 98.

30. Nonspi ad, *Seventeen,* April 1945, 143.
31. Ex-Lax ad, *Seventeen,* June 1945, 119.
32. Emphasis of "too strong" and "too mild" is mine and meant to accentuate the gender stereotypes of relating strength to men and passivity (mildness) to women.
33. Ex-Lax ad, *Seventeen,* September 1945, 143.
34. Ellis, personal collection, n.d.
35. Swan ad, *Seventeen,* August 1945, 60.
36. Swan ad, *Seventeen,* September 1945, 60.
37. Revlon ad, *Seventeen,* June 1945, 104–5.
38. Revlon ad, *Seventeen,* September 1945, 108–9.
39. See Cook 2004 on the emergence of the teen clothing industry. Although Estelle Ellis's narrative of *Seventeen*'s origins includes their "creation" of the teen clothing industry, the reality is that while *Seventeen* promoted and significantly contributed to the industry's growth, it already existed prior to the magazine's debut.
40. Interestingly, representation of Western department stores seemed to stop short at Ogden, Utah (L. R. Samuel's); except for Saks Fifth Avenue's Beverly Hills outpost, no regional department stores from the West Coast, and in particular, California, advertised in the magazine during the first year.
41. Schrum 2004.
42. Jaunty Junior, Peggy Paige for Juniors, Juniorite, Jonathan Logan Junior Casuals.
43. Junior Firsts, Minx Modes Juniors, Doris Dodson Junior.
44. Unidentified brand from a Hecht Co. Department Store ad.
45. Topsey Originals.
46. Cook 2004; see also *Business Week,* "Teen-Age Market," June 8, 1946, 72.
47. Emily Wilkens ad, *Seventeen,* December 1944, 32.
48. J. P. Allen in Atlanta ad, *Seventeen,* December 1945, 27.
49. Carole King ad, *Seventeen,* June 1945, 46.
50. American Girl ad, *Seventeen,* May 1945, 124.
51. Flexnit ad, *Seventeen,* February 1945, 42.
52. Teen-Set Frocks, Landsburgh's Department Store ad, *Seventeen,* December 1944, 38.
53. Belt-Modes ad, *Seventeen,* February 1945, 21.
54. Saybrooke ad, *Seventeen,* August 1945, 50.
55. Connies ad, *Seventeen,* April 1945, 121.
56. Yearounder ad, *Seventeen,* January 1945, 16.
57. Joan Lord ad, *Seventeen,* December 1944, 25.
58. Jane Holly ad, *Seventeen,* February 1945, 56.
59. Thornton Hats ad, *Seventeen,* March 1945, 116.
60. Gail Berk ad, *Seventeen,* September 1945, 18.
61. See, for example, *Women's Wear Daily,* February 21, 1945, 31.

62. "Grooming and Beauty Guidance Found Need of Teen-Age Girls, but It Must Be Practical," *New York Times*, November 22, 1944, 16.
63. "Perfume a Man Trap? How Quaint! It's a Utility, Say Beauty Editors," *New York Times*, February 18, 1949, 20.
64. "Why snub 8 million customers?," *Cosmetics and Toiletries*, August 1949. Estelle Ellis Collection, Archives Center, National Museum of American History, Behring Center, Smithsonian Institution, Box 18, File 6.
65. Modess ad, *Seventeen*, August 1950, 238.
66. Tampax ad, *Seventeen*, May 1950, 114.
67. Kotex ad, *Seventeen*, July 1950, 31.
68. Kotex ad, *Seventeen*, September 1949, 171.
69. Kotex ad, *Seventeen*, September 1949, 171.
70. Kotex ad, *Seventeen*, September 1949, 171.
71. Kotex ad, *Seventeen*, December 1949, 51.
72. Kotex ad, *Seventeen*, July 1950, 31.
73. Kotex ad, *Seventeen*, January 1950, 86.
74. *Seventeen* articles: "First Orchid!" (October 1949, 4); "First School Beau!" (January 1950, 6); "First Fraternity Pin!" (November 1949, 6); "First Black Dress!" (February 1950, 4); "another radiant Camay bride" (September 1949, 4); "follow the lead of the lovely Camay brides" (October 1949, 4).
75. Bates ads, *Seventeen*, August 1945, 107.
76. See, for example, Verney ad, *Seventeen*, May 1945, 10.
77. Lunt ad, *Seventeen*, April 1949, 60.
78. Towle ad, *Seventeen*, February 1950, 33; Reed & Barton ad, *Seventeen*, June 1950, 25; Gorham ad, *Seventeen*, September 1950, inside front cover.
79. Gorham ad, *Seventeen*, December 1949, 9.
80. Rogers Sterling ad, *Seventeen*, October 1949, 27.
81. International Sterling ad, *Seventeen*, February 1950, 5.
82. Towle ad, *Seventeen*, February 1950, 33.
83. International Sterling ad, *Seventeen*, December 1949, 3.
84. International Sterling ad, *Seventeen*, April 1950, 5.
85. Gorham Sterling ad, *Seventeen*, April 1950, inside front cover.
86. International Sterling ad, *Seventeen*, March 1950, 5.
87. Lunt Sterling ad, *Seventeen*, September 1949, 58; also April 1950, 60.
88. Towle Sterling ad, *Seventeen*, October 1949, 37.
89. Gorham Sterling ad, *Seventeen*, December 1949, 9.
90. International Sterling ad, *Seventeen*, April 1950, 5.
91. Nobility Plate ad, *Seventeen*, November 1949, 27.
92. Towle Sterling ad, *Seventeen*, February 1950, 33.

93. Towle Sterling ad, *Seventeen,* November 1949, 33.
94. Reed & Barton ad, *Seventeen,* November 1949, 21.
95. Towle Sterling ad, *Seventeen,* September 1949, 25.
96. International Sterling ad, *Seventeen,* December 1949, 3.
97. Towle Sterling ad, *Seventeen,* September 1949, 25; also February 1950, 33; Lunt Sterling ad, *Seventeen,* September 1949, 58; International Sterling ad, *Seventeen,* December 1949, 3; also April 1950, 5.
98. Fine Arts Sterling ad, *Seventeen,* January 1950, back cover.
99. Towle Sterling ad, *Seventeen,* March 1950, 51; Gorham Sterling ad, *Seventeen,* April 1950, inside front cover.
100. Towle Sterling ad, *Seventeen,* September 1950, 51.
101. According to the Consumer Price Index calculator at http://www.minneapolisfed.org/index.cfm (accessed September 22, 2009).
102. Towle Sterling ad, *Seventeen,* March 1950, 51.
103. Towle Sterling ad, *Seventeen,* December 1949, 35.
104. Towle Sterling ad, *Seventeen,* April 1950, 33.
105. Towle Sterling ad, *Seventeen,* May 1950, 33.
106. International Sterling ad, *Seventeen,* October 1949, 7.
107. International Sterling ad, *Seventeen,* July 1950, 9.
108. International Sterling ad, *Seventeen,* August 1950, 5.
109. International Sterling ad, *Seventeen,* December 1949, 3.
110. Towle Sterling ad, *Seventeen,* May 1950, 33.
111. Nan Scott ad, *Seventeen,* March 1945, 30.

Chapter 5

1. See Gordon and Gordon 1987; Kaledin 2000; Sickels 2004.
2. Peterson 1964, 39.
3. "P.S.," *Business Week,* February 23, 1946, 90.
4. *Women's Wear Daily,* August 10, 1945, 13.
5. See Seebohm 1982. Snow's departure from *Vogue* ended her close friendships with publisher Nast and her former mentor Chase, both of whom considered her departure to rival Hearst publication *Harper's Bazaar* as an act tantamount to treason.
6. Peterson 1964, 220; see also "Teen-Age Magazine," *Life,* October 29, 1945, 77–80.
7. See Seebohm 1982. Richard Avedon, Francesco Scavullo's contemporary and fellow future icon, photographed many of its covers, while its art and design developed under the watchful eyes of Alexey Brodovitch and Lillian Bassman, industry peers of Cipe Pineles. After *Junior Bazaar*'s demise, Bassman switched careers to photography, and her photos accompanied an October 1949 *Seventeen* article entitled "Beauty Begins at Home." Her bio for "They Worked with Us This Month"

applauded her new pursuit, stating, "She is fast becoming a specialist in 'feminine photography.' Most of her pictures are of lingerie, women dressing, undressing, combing their hair" (*Seventeen,* October 1949, 50).

8. See Peterson 1964, 220.
9. Ogden 1999, 288.
10. Keresey 1984. See also Peirce 1995a. *Calling All Girls* underwent many name changes, reflecting readership shifts throughout its publication history: *Calling All Girls* (1941–1949), *Senior Prom* (1949–1951), *Polly Pigtails* (1953–1955), *Calling All Girls* (1955–1966), *Young Miss* (1966–1989), and *YM/Young and Modern* (1989–2004).
11. Personal correspondence between Helen Valentine and Walter Annenberg dated October 16, 1946, and October 18, 1946; copies in the author's possession, originals in the possession of Valentine Hertz Kass.
12. Estelle Ellis Collection, Archives Center, National Museum of American History, Behring Center, Smithsonian Institution, Box 17, File 12.
13. Estelle Ellis Collection, Archives Center, National Museum of American History, Behring Center, Smithsonian Institution, Box 17, File 13. For example, in the September 1946 supplement, home ec teachers, guidance instructors, and home ec club advisors were directed to an article in the September issue of *Seventeen* entitled "Home Life Is Their Business," which detailed the field of home economics as a career choice. The supplement then suggested lesson plans, activities, visual aids, key questions, field trips, and a bibliography that linked to the article and its topic. The issue offered similar help for "food and nutrition teachers" using the *Seventeen* articles on "King Peanut" (about "the importance of peanuts" as a farm product and inexpensive and healthful food choice, with recipes and party plan included) and "Eat It Up at Noon" (about preparing well-balanced lunches).
14. "It's Up to Youth" ad, *Seventeen,* November 1946, 298.
15. Faludi 1991; Honey 1984.
16. According to the government's own 1944 survey, nearly 80 percent of women in war production plants wanted to retain their jobs after reconversion. U.S. Department of Labor, Women's Bureau, *Women Workers in Ten War Production Areas and Their Postwar Employment Plans,* cited in Honey 1984, 224.
17. Honey 1984, 224.
18. "They Worked with Us This Month," *Seventeen,* December 1949, 38.
19. Bartky 1988; Bordo 1993; Brumberg 1997; Wolf 1991.
20. Joan Jacobs Brumberg, writing in *The Body Project,* describes the 1920s as a similar time period in which the "bob" became a symbol of "modern" life, as well as a way to distinguish young women from old. It was also associated with a slimmer physique—one that required "new internal constraints, one of which was controlling food intake." See Brumberg 1997, 102.
21. The largest issue during the entire period was the August 1946 issue (with back-to-school fashions), at 308 pages.

22. "Thank You for Your Letters," *Seventeen,* September 1950, 4.
23. Ogden 1999, 288.
24. *Seventeen,* September 1949, 96.
25. *Seventeen,* August 1950, 122.
26. See Scotford 1999 for more on Pineles's influence at the magazine generally, and on the fashion pages specifically.
27. "*Seventeen* Says Hello," *Seventeen,* September 1944, 33.
28. See Cohen 2003.
29. See Foner 1998.
30. "Those Little Touches," *Seventeen,* September 1949, 204.
31. Betty Gulesian, "Your First Piece of Real Jewelry," *Seventeen,* December 1949, 78.
32. "DAY Out…NIGHT Out," *Seventeen,* September 1950, 154.
33. "Boys Like Floaty Party Sheers," *Seventeen,* April 1950, 88.
34. "The Boys Speak Up," *Seventeen,* May 1950, 114.
35. Bartky 1998, 34. According to Bartky, "In contemporary patriarchal culture, a panoptical male connoisseur resides within the consciousness of most women: they stand perpetually before his gaze and under his judgment."
36. "A Better Figure for You," *Seventeen,* September 1950, 50.
37. "Get into Shape," *Seventeen,* January 1950, 26.
38. See Bartky 1988; Bordo 1993; Brumberg 1997; Wolf 1991.
39. "Scale That Figure Down," *Seventeen,* March 1950, 106, 107.
40. "Posture Perfect?," *Seventeen,* August 1950, 106.
41. "Figure on These," *Seventeen,* August 1950, 159.
42. Jean Campbell, "Pad That Frame," *Seventeen,* November 1949, 108.
43. "Proof… without Pudding," *Seventeen,* November 1949, 108.
44. "Thank You for Your Letters," *Seventeen,* January 1950, 4.
45. "Thank You for Your Letters," *Seventeen,* January 1950, 4.
46. Jean Campbell, "Who's a Dummy?," *Seventeen,* January 1950, 50.
47. Jean Campbell, "Who's a Dummy?," *Seventeen,* January 1950, 51.
48. "Make a Pretty Face," *Seventeen,* September 1949, 110.
49. Jean Campbell, "Beauty Begins at Home," *Seventeen,* October 1949, 102.
50. Jean Campbell, "On Your Toes," *Seventeen,* February 1950, 102.
51. "Up to Snuff," *Seventeen,* August 1950, 44. Sample quote: "You're not an ice-cream pop or a flower or a bird, you're a *girl.* It behooves you, therefore, to face each day as fresh and dewy and pretty-smelling as a water lily. And to stay that way. People expect it of you, that's why. You've got a reputation to keep up. And besides, if you don't, you'll feel miserable."
52. "What Makes a Pretty Girl," *Seventeen,* June 1950, 49; "Your Face . . . Its Care, Its Trimming," *Seventeen,* June 1950, 50; "Your Hair," *Seventeen,* June 1950, 52;

"Your Fragrance," *Seventeen,* June 1950, 53; "Your Hands," *Seventeen,* June 1950, 54; "Your Feet," *Seventeen,* June 1950, 55; "You Can't Be Almost Clean," *Seventeen,* June 1950, 56; "These Make a Pretty Girl," *Seventeen,* June 1950, 86. See Bartky 1998 for a Foucauldian analysis of the grooming process as discipline (see also Foucault 1995).

53. B. R. of Philadelphia, "Thank You For Your Letters," *Seventeen,* September 1950, 60.
54. "Thank You for Your Letters," *Seventeen,* September 1950, 60.
55. Covert 2002, 13. Covert found that advertisements in upper-class women's magazines published during World War II (*Harper's Bazaar* and *Vogue*) frequently asserted that the maintenance of beauty was the primary way these women could support the war effort. *Seventeen* used this phrasing in an ad for its June 1950 "Young Beauty" issue, stating: "Beauty is your duty. Do your very best to look your best. SEVENTEEN is ready to help, with the June 'Young Beauty' issue, on the newstands June 2" (*Seventeen,* May 1950, 207).
56. Margaret Mead, "Can Homemaking Really Be a Career?" *Seventeen,* November 1948, 116.
57. Eileen Murphy, "Wizardry in Four Walls," *Seventeen,* October 1949, 94.
58. Eileen Murphy, "Rising in Retailing," *Seventeen,* September 1949, 128.
59. Eileen Murphy, "Beauty is BIG BUSINESS," *Seventeen,* June 1950, 62.
60. Eileen Murphy, "On Minding Your KEYS and Cues," *Seventeen,* July 1950, 78.
61. Dickey Meyer, "You, Too, Can Work for Something," *Seventeen,* December 1949, 82.
62. Eileen Murphy, "Finance: Feminine Gender," *Seventeen,* April 1950, 92.
63. Eileen Murphy, "Labs and Lassies," *Seventeen,* February 1950, 90.
64. Eileen Murphy, "Labs and Lassies," *Seventeen,* February 1950, 165.
65. "If He Could Only Cook," *Seventeen,* April 1945, 76, 77, 108.
66. "Bake Him a Pie," *Seventeen,* April 1950, 112, 113.
67. "Jobs Have No Gender," April 1945, 18, 159.
68. Barbara Moench, "Who Does Your Laundry?" ("Why Don't Parents Grow Up? #57"), *Seventeen,* October 1949, 38.
69. Peter Leavy, "From a Boy's Point of View," *Seventeen,* April 1950, 81.
70. Peter Leavy, "Somebody Would Like to Meet You" ("From a Boy's Point of View"), *Seventeen,* June 1950, 16.
71. Peter Leavy, "Just the Way You Look Tonight" ("From a Boy's Point of View"), August 1950, 30.
72. Peter Leavy, "Just the Way You Look Tonight" ("From a Boy's Point of View"), August 1950, 30.
73. "Thank You for Your Letters," *Seventeen,* July 1950, 4.
74. "Editor's Note" ("From a Boy's Point of View"), *Seventeen,* August 1950, 91.
75. "Your Home and You," *Seventeen,* October 1949, 80 (picture), 81 (essay).
76. "To Market, To Market," *Seventeen,* October 1949, 56.

77. "At Home on the Range," *Seventeen,* September 1950, 92.
78. "Herbs and Spice Make 'Most Everything Nice," *Seventeen,* August 1950, 92
79. "Beginner at the Oven," *Seventeen,* May 1950, 68.
80. "Why Breakfast?," *Seventeen,* September 1950, 66.
81. "Bring It in a Basket," *Seventeen,* January 1950, 68.
82. "Practice on the Family," *Seventeen,* October 1949, 90.
83. "Family Favorites," *Seventeen,* November 1949, 100.
84. "Every Family Likes . . . Pancakes," *Seventeen,* November 1949, 116.
85. "Bake Him a Pie," *Seventeen,* April 1950, 112.
86. "A Box Social," *Seventeen,* August 1950, 178.
87. "Party Lifesavers," *Seventeen,* March 1950, 130.
88. "Simple But Super," *Seventeen,* April 1950, 64.
89. Beryl Walter, "Desserts on Ice," *Seventeen,* August 1950, 154.
90. Beryl Walter, "Rodeo Round-Up," *Seventeen,* September 1950, 168.
91. "Plan a Picnic," *Seventeen,* July 1950, 92.
92. Beryl Walter, "Open a Can," *Seventeen,* July 1950, 46.
93. Mimi Sheraton, "Your Room Comes of Age," *Seventeen,* September 1949, 118.
94. "Plan from a Picture," *Seventeen,* January 1950, 76.
95. Mimi Sheraton, "Small Rooms and How They GROW," *Seventeen,* March 1950, 122.
96. Mimi Sheraton, "Bird's-eye View of Two to a Room," *Seventeen,* August 1950, 180.
97. Mimi Sheraton, "Your OWN Living Room," *Seventeen,* October 1949, 108.
98. "1 Chest, 5 Finishes," *Seventeen,* July 1950, 44; "Make Your Own Lamp," *Seventeen,* August 1950, 194.
99. Mimi Sheraton, "A Good Night's Rest," *Seventeen,* February 1950, 106.
100. Described and analyzed in Chapter 3, "Teena Goes to Market."
101. "Does Your House Need These?," *Seventeen,* December 1949, 111.
102. "Your Treasure Chest," *Seventeen,* August 1949, 50.
103. "Your Treasure Chest," *Seventeen,* July 1950, 28.
104. Hagyard replaced Betty Betz after she (and her verse-writer) Anne Clark left *Seventeen* to write and illustrate a string of teen "how-to" books.
105. Betty Gulesian, "Shopping Takes More Than Money," *Seventeen,* March 1950, 167.
106. Detailed in Chapter 6, "Divorce in the Family."

Chapter 6

1. "The Editors Serenade You," *Seventeen,* September 1948, 108–9; see also Scotford 1999, 65.
2. Dickey Meyer, "They Do Unto Others," *Seventeen,* November 1946, 158–59, 215; "Swing Your Partner," 32–34; see also Scotford 1999, 58.

3. Personal correspondence from Helen Valentine to Walter Annenberg, dated October 16, 1946; copy in the author's possession, original in the possession of Valentine Hertz Kass.
4. Personal correspondence from Walter Annenberg to Helen Valentine, dated October 18, 1946; copy in the author's possession, original in the possession of Valentine Hertz Kass.
5. This version of the story is found in Ogden 1999. Estelle Ellis, however, remembers pressure from the business side of the magazine in this regard (personal email from Estelle Ellis dated July 11, 2006).
6. "Personnel," *New York Times*, April 28, 1949, 47.
7. "50 Girls and One Man," *Time*, May 16, 1949, 56–57.
8. "Seventeen Is Five," *Newsweek*, August 29, 1949,47–48.
9. Ellis, telephone interview, July 13, 2004.
10. Estelle Ellis at times intimates that this could have been more than a business relationship between Walter and Alice, but she never confirms it, saying instead: "Whether somebody screws somebody is not the point—whether they do it sexually. If they *screw* them ... professionally, it matters." Ellis, telephone interview, July 13, 2004.
11. Ellis, telephone interview, July 13, 2004
12. Helen Valentine, personal correspondence to Walter Annenberg dated February 15, 1950. A copy of this letter is in the author's possession; original in the possession of Valentine Hertz Kass.
13. "The Women," *Time*, March 6, 1950, 56–57. The "lone man" was entertainment editor Edwin Miller.
14. Eiseman, telephone interview, March 27, 2006.
15. "The Women," *Time*, March 6, 1950, 56–57.
16. Thompson hired Irene Kittle Kamp, her managing editor at *Glamour*, to replace Vilas as managing editor at *Seventeen*. Cipe Pineles's assistant, Joan Fenton, became art director. Rosemary McMurtry, formerly merchandise editor, became fashion editor. Interestingly, in light of earlier reports of Annenberg's desire to "get promotion, advertising and editorial departments working together to plug the magazine," the position of promotion director dropped from the masthead.
17. Sladkus, telephone interview, April 20, 2006.
18. Eiseman, telephone interview, March 27, 2006.
19. Sladkus, telephone interview, April 20, 2006.
20. Sladkus, telephone interview, April 20, 2006.
21. Sladkus, telephone interview, April 20, 2006.
22. Ellis, personal interview, June 19, 2003.
23. Alice Thompson, "Girls Is Funny People," *Seventeen*, April 1945, 118.
24. Reskin and Padavic 1994, 49–50.
25. Fox 1975; Honey 1984; Walker 2000.

26. Faludi 1991; Honey 1984.
27. On the September 28, 2006 edition of the *Today* show, psychologist Gail Saltz asserted that June Cleaver continues to be a fantasy feminine ideal for some contemporary men; http://www.msnbc.msn.com/id/15039140/ (accessed July 23, 2007). In addition, see chapter 2 of Coontz 1992 ("'Leave It to Beaver' and 'Ozzie and Harriet'") for more on 1950's sitcom homemakers.
28. Faludi 1991; Friedan 1963.
29. Wolf 1991, 14.
30. Friedan 1963. My use of the word "internalized" is conscious and considered. Although Friedan has been rather roundly criticized for describing the "feminine mystique" in terms of affluent middle-class women (women who could afford to follow its mandates, however unhappily), I would argue that as a pervasive cultural model, working women were subject to internalizing the feminine mystique as an ideal, potentially creating considerable cognitive dissonance. This seems to continue even today in the "mommy wars" debate (see, for example, Douglas and Michaels 2004).
31. Bagdikian 2000; Croteau and Hoynes 2001, 2003; Gamson, Croteau, Hoynes, and Sasson 1992; Gerbner 1998; hooks 1996; Kellner 1995a; Kilbourne 1995, 1999; McCracken 1993; Steeves 1993; Tuchman 1978.
32. Bagdikian 2000; Croteau and Hoynes 2003; Gamson, Croteau, Hoynes, and Sasson 1992; Steinem 1995.
33. Jhally 1995; Kilbourne 1999; Schor 1998.
34. *Life with Teena*. Conducted by Benson & Benson, Inc. in March, 1945. Published by Triangle Publications, 1945 and *Life with Teena: Volume II—Food.* Conducted by Opinion Research Corporation in June-August, 1946. Published by Triangle Publications, 1947. Estelle Ellis Collection, Archives Center, National Museum of American History, Behring Center, Smithsonian Institution, Box 18, Files 1–4.
35. See Benson & Benson, Inc. 1945, 82; and Opinion Research Corporation 1947, 91, 100, 102. Estelle Ellis Collection, Archives Center, National Museum of American History, Behring Center, Smithsonian Institution, Box 18, Files 1–4. The first survey gathered data from a sample of *Seventeen*'s readers in March 1945 and included the inquiry "What do you enjoy most about SEVENTEEN?" In answer, a majority of readers reported favoring the fashion articles (65 percent), followed by advice articles on appearance and beauty (11 percent). In comparison, only a tiny minority of the readership reported a preference for articles on "ideas in general" (3 percent).
36. Opinion Research Corporation 1947, 91, 100, 102. Estelle Ellis Collection, Archives Center, National Museum of American History, Behring Center, Smithsonian Institution, Box 18, Files 3–4.
37. *Life with Teena I* asked, "Do you think that you would like to work after you are married?," to which 66 percent of the respondents answered with a resounding "No" (15 percent answered "Yes," 19 percent, "Do not know"). *Life with Teena II* asked, "After you get married do you think you'll want to work or will you want to keep house?," a great majority (69 percent) reported wanting to keep house; only 13 percent wanted to work, and 14 percent wanted to do "both."

38. Estelle Ellis Collection, Archives Center, National Museum of American History, Behring Center, Smithsonian Institution, Box 26, File 3.
39. This letter is discussed in detail in Chapter 1, "The Birth of the Teen Magazine"; copy in possession of the author, original in the possession of Helen Valentine's granddaughter, Valentine Kass.
40. Marx 1906, 330.
41. Ellis, personal interview, New York City, June 19, 2003.
42. Ogden 1999, 288.
43. Raver 1992.
44. Murdoch sold *Seventeen* to K-111 Magazines in 1991, which became Primedia; in 2003, Primedia sold *Seventeen* to Hearst Magazines, its current owner.
45. Associated Press 2002.
46. Cornwell 2002.
47. Glueck 2002.
48. Nietzsche 1968; also Foucault 1980.
49. Ellis, personal interview, New York City, June 19, 2003.
50. Cooney 1982; Ogden 1999.
51. *Seventeen,* September 1984, 3.
52. *Seventeen,* October 1994, 22.
53. Sheppard 1967.
54. Personal correspondence from Nancy White to Helen Valentine, dated September 22, 1967. A copy of this letter is in the possession of the author; the original is in the possession of Valentine Hertz Kass.
55. Personal correspondence from Walter Annenberg to Helen Valentine, dated September 26, 1967. A copy of this letter is in the possession of the author; the original is in the possession of Valentine Hertz Kass.
56. Reichley 1970, 88–93.
57. Personal correspondence from William Rosen to Louis Banks, dated June 19, 1970. A copy of this letter is in the possession of the author; the original is in the possession of Valentine Hertz Kass.
58. Hall 1981, 227–40.
59. Carmody 1993, D6.
60. Valentine Oral History, 7. American Jewish Committee Archives.
61. Leman 1980, 77.

Epilogue

1. See Haupt quote in Chapter 6.
2. Peirce 1995b.
3. Carr 2003b, C1; Grantstein 2003, 45–46; Saltz 2004, 42–43.

4. Kelly 2006, 33.
5. Case 2007b.
6. *Seventeen* Myspace blog, http://blogs.myspace.com/index.cfm?fuseaction=blog.ListAll&friendId=43899896 (accessed September 5, 2009).
7. Case, 2007a, 30, 32.
8. Audit Bureau of Circulations 2008a.
9. Hearst Corporation website, http://www.hearst.com/magazines/seventeen.php.
10. Kelly 2006.
11. Magazine Publishers of America 2009. According to the U.S. Census Bureau (2002), of twelve- to nineteen-year-olds, 15 percent are Black, 15 percent are Hispanic/Latino, and 4 percent are Asian.
12. MRI Teenmark 2008 research, cited in *Seventeen*'s Media Kit, http://www.seventeenmediakit.com/r5/showkiosk.asp?listing_id=2986079&category_id=31773 (accessed September 5, 2009).
13. Hall's Magazine Reports, Jan.–Sept. 2008, cited in *Seventeen*'s Media Kit, http://www.seventeenmediakit.com/r5/home.asp (accessed September 5, 2009).
14. Carr 2003a, C1.
15. Hall's Magazine Reports, Jan.–Sept. 2008, cited in *Seventeen*'s Media Kit, http://www.seventeenmediakit.com/r5/home.asp (accessed September 5, 2009).
16. Audit Bureau of Circulations 2008b.
17. Case 2007b.
18. "Seventeen," *Brandweek*, September 4, 2000.
19. Case 2007b.
20. Ives 2007b, 8; Roberts and Eady 2007, 80.
21. Roberts and Eady 2007, 80.
22. Roberts and Eady 2007, 80.
23. Ives 2007a, 35–37.
24. The *Today* show, "E. L. Konigsburg interview," March 5, 2004.
25. Clifford 2008, 2; Flamm 2004, 19.
26. See, for example, the Magazine Publishers of America 2003 report, "Teen Market Research," http://www.magazine.org/marketprofiles (accessed September 7, 2009).
27. Ambroz 2008, 8–9.
28. Croteau and Hoynes 2003.
29. Actionista on MySpace, http://www.myspace.com/seventeen_actionistas (accessed September 5, 2009).
30. Actionista on YouTube, http://www.youtube.com/watch?v=dIFa3y3Ht-w&NR=1 (accessed September 1, 2009)
31. MRI Teenmark 2008 research, cited in *Seventeen*'s Media Kit, http://www.seventeenmediakit.com/r5/home.asp (accessed September 5, 2009).

32. MRI Teenmark 2008 research, cited in *Seventeen*'s Media Kit, http://www.seventeenmediakit.com/r5/home.asp (accessed September 5, 2009).
33. Harris Interactive, http://www.harrisinteractive.com/NEWS/allnewsbydate.asp?NewsID=667 (accessed September 6, 2009).
34. Grimm 2001, 58–9.
35. "Seventeen Magazine and Bank of America Partner," Reuters, http://www.reuters.com/article/pressRelease/idUS174535+06-Aug-2009+PRN20090806 (accessed September 6, 2009).
36. Bayott 2003, C8.
37. Sherman 2008.
38. Mediamark Research Inc. 2004, cited in Mallalieu and Palan 2006.
39. Magazine Publishers of America 2003 report, "Teen Market Research," www.magazine.org/marketprofiles (accessed September 7, 2009).
40. Magazine Publishers of America 2003 report, "Teen Market Research," www.magazine.org/marketprofiles (accessed September 7, 2009).
41. Magazine Publishers of America 2003 report, "Teen Market Research," www.magazine.org/marketprofiles (accessed September 7, 2009).
42. Slatalla, 2003, G4; Rohrlich 2003, F5.
43. Rohrlich 2003, F5.
44. Fickenscher 2005, 3.
45. Purdam 2000, WK1.
46. Armstrong 2008.
47. Armstrong 2008.
48. IMDb, "Top Grossing Movies for 2009 in the USA," http://www.imdb.com/Sections/2009/top-grossing (accessed April 15, 2010).
49. Ellis, telephone interview, July 13, 2004.
50. Ellis, telephone interview, July 26, 2003.
51. Valentine, unpublished essay, "What Are We Doing to Our Teenagers?" n.d. A copy is in the author's possession, original in the possession of Valentine Hertz Kass. I estimate the essay date around 1960 through two references made in it, the first to an article called "Teenagers Tell How to Be Popular," which ran in a 1958 issue of *Reader's Digest*, the second to a CBS television series entitled *Woman!*, which began in 1959.

REFERENCES

I. Books and Periodicals

Ambroz, Julian. 2008. "Marketing to Millennials." *Folio*, June, 8–9.

Armstrong, Jennifer. 2008. "Teen Nation: How the Kids Took over Pop Culture." EW.com, May 16, http://www.ew.com/ew/article/0,,20198638,00.html (accessed September 2, 2009).

Aronson, Amy Beth. 2002. *Taking Liberties: Early American Women's Magazines and Their Readers.* Westport, CT: Praeger Publishers.

Associated Press. 2000. "Billionaire Publisher and Philanthropist Walter Annenberg Dies at 94." October 1.

Audit Bureau of Circulations. 2008a. "Consumer Magazines, Teen." December 31, http://abcas3.accessabc.com/ecirc/magsrdssearch.asp (accessed July 20, 2009).

———. 2008b. "Consumer Magazines, Women's." December 31, http://abcas3.accessabc.com/ecirc/magsrdssearch.asp (accessed July 20, 2009).

Bagdikian, Ben. 2000. *The Media Monopoly.* Boston: Beacon Press.

Barthes, Roland. 1972. *Mythologies.* Trans. Annette Lavers. New York: Hill and Wang. (Orig. pub. 1957, Paris: Editions de Seuil.)

Bartky, Sandra. 1988. "Foucault, Femininity, and the Modernization of Patriarchal Power." In *Feminism and Foucault*, ed. Irene Diamond and Lee Quimby, 61–86. Boston: Northeastern University Press.

Bayott, Jennifer. 2003. "The Teenage Market: Young, Hip and Looking for a Bargain." *New York Times*, December 1, C8.

Bazzini, Doris G., William D. McIntosh, Stephen M. Smith, Sabrina Cook, and Caleigh Harris. 1997. "The Aging Woman in Popular Film: Underrepresented, Unattractive, Unfriendly, and Unintelligent." *Sex Roles* 36:531–43.

Bielby, Denise, and William Bielby. 1996. "Women and Men in Film: Gender Inequality among Writers in a Culture Industry." *Gender & Society* 10:248–70.

Beinhoff, Lisa, and Jon Bekken. 1995. "*Glamour*." In *Women's Periodicals in the United States*, ed. Kathleen L. Endres and Therese L. Lueck, 107–13. Westport, CT: Greenwood Press.

Blum, John Morton. 1976. *V Was for Victory: Politics and American Culture during World War II.* New York: Harcourt Brace Jovanovich.

Bordo, Susan. 1993. *Unbearable Weight: Feminism, Western Culture, and the Body.* Berkeley: University of California Press.

Brandweek. 2000. "*Seventeen.*" September 4.

Brumberg, Joan Jacobs. 1997. *The Body Project: An Intimate History of American Girls.* New York: Vintage Books.

Budgeon, Shelley, and Dawn H. Currie. 1995. "From Feminism to Postfeminism: Women's Liberation in Fashion Magazines." *Women's Studies International Forum* 18:173–86.

Business Week. 1944. "New Teen-Age Magazine." August 26, 94–95.

———. 1946a. "P.S." February 23, 90.

———. 1946b. "Teen-Age Market: It's Terrif.'" June 8, 72.

Carmody, Diedre. 1993. "Reaching Teenagers, without Using a Phone." *New York Times,* January 18, D6.

Carr, David. 2003a. "Coming Late, Fashionably, *Teen Vogue* Joins a Crowd." *New York Times,* January 13, C1.

———. 2003b. "Reinventing *Seventeen* with a View to Middle America." *New York Times,* November 24, C1.

Case, Tony. 2007a. "Trouble in Teen Land." *Mediaweek,* February 26, 30, 32.

———. 2007b. "Teen Mags Eye Web Expansion." *Mediaweek,* February 27, http://www.mediaweek.com/mw/esearch/article_display.jsp?vnu_content_id'1003549950 (accessed April 23, 2007).

Charmaz, Kathy. 2004. "Grounded Theory." In *Approaches to Qualitative Research: A Reader on Theory and Practice,* ed. Sharlene Hesse-Biber and Patricia Leavy, 497–516. New York: Oxford University.

Chernin, Kim. 1981. *The Obsession: Reflections on the Tyranny of Slenderness.* New York: Harper & Row.

Clifford, Stephanie. 2008. "Hearst to Close *CosmoGirl!,* But Its Web Site Survives." *New York Times,* October 11, B2.

Cohen, Lizabeth. 2003. *A Consumers' Republic: The Politics of Mass Consumption in Postwar America.* New York: Alfred A. Knopf.

Connell, R. W. 1987. *Gender and Power: Society, the Person, and Sexual Politics.* Berkeley: University of California Press.

Cook, Daniel Thomas. 2004. *The Commodification of Childhood: The Children's Clothing Industry and the Rise of the Child Consumer.* Durham, NC: Duke University Press.

Cooney, John. 1982. *The Annenbergs.* New York: Simon & Schuster.

Coontz, Stephanie. 1992. *The Way We Never Were: American Families and the Nostalgia Trap.* New York: Basic Books.

Cornwell, Rupert. 2002. "Obituary: Walter Annenberg." *The Independent* (UK), October 2.

Cortese, Anthony. 1999. *Provocateur: Images of Women and Minorities in Advertising.* Lanham, MD: Rowman & Littlefield.

Covert, Tawnya Adkins. 2002. "Beauty Is Your Duty: Defining the Role of Upper Class Women During World War II Through Advertising." Presented at the annual meeting of the Midwest Sociological Society, Milwaukee, WI.

———. 2003. "Consumption and Citizenship during the Second World War." *Journal of Consumer Culture* 3:315–42.

Crane, Diana. 1999. "Gender and Hegemony in Fashion Magazines: Women's Interpretations of Fashion Photographs." *Sociological Quarterly* 40: 541–63.

Croteau, David, and William Hoynes. 2001. *The Business of Media: Corporate Media and Public Interest.* Thousand Oaks, CA: Pine Forge Press.

———. 2003. *Media/Society: Industries, Images, and Audiences.* 3rd ed. Thousand Oaks, CA: Pine Forge Press.

Currie, Dawn H. 1997. "Decoding Femininity: Advertisements and Their Teenage Readers." *Gender & Society* 11:453–78.

———. 1999. *Girl Talk: Adolescent Magazines and Their Readers.* Toronto: University of Toronto Press.

Dellinger, Kirsten, and Christine L. Williams. 1997. "Makeup at Work: Negotiating Appearance Rules in the Workplace." *Gender & Society* 11:151–77.

Dinnerstein, Myra, and Rose Weitz. 1998. "Jane Fonda, Barbara Bush, and Other Aging Bodies: Femininity and the Limits of Resistance." In *The Politics of Women's Bodies: Sexuality, Appearance, and Behavior*, ed. Rose Weitz, 189–204. New York: Oxford University Press.

Douglas, Susan, and Meredith Michaels. 2004. *The Mommy Myth: The Idealization of Motherhood and How It Has Undermined Women.* New York: Free Press.

Duffy, Margaret, and J. Michael Gotcher. 1996. "Crucial Advice on How to Get the Guy: The Rhetorical Vision of Power and Seduction in the Teen Magazine *YM*." *Journal of Communication Inquiry* 20:32–48.

Durham, Meenakshi Gigi. 1996. "The Taming of the Shrew: Women's Magazines and the Regulation of Desire." *Journal of Communication Inquiry* 20:18–31.

———. 1998. "Dilemmas of Desire: Representations of Adolescent Sexuality in Two Teen Magazines." *Youth and Society* 29:369–89.

Evans, Ellis D., Judith Rutberg, Carmela Sather, and Charli Turner. 1991. "Content Analysis of Contemporary Teen Magazines for Adolescent Females." *Youth and Society* 23:99–120.

Faludi, Susan. 1991. *Backlash: The Undeclared War Against American Women.* New York: Anchor Books.

Featherstone, Mike. 2001. "The Body in Consumer Culture." In *The American Body in Context*, ed. Jessica R. Johnston, 79–102. Wilmington, DE: Scholarly Resources.

Fickenscher, Lisa. 2005. "Fulfilling Teen Dreams." *Crain's New York Business,* February 7, 3.

Flamm, Matthew. 2004. "Titles Face Teenage Wasteland." *Crain's New York Business*, August 23, 19.

Foner, Eric. 1998. *The Story of American Freedom*. New York: W.W. Norton & Co.

Foucault, Michel. 1980. *Power/Knowledge*. New York: Pantheon Books.

———. 1995. *Discipline and Punish: The Birth of the Prison*. New York: Vintage Books.

Fox, Frank. 1975. *Madison Avenue Goes to War: The Strange Military History of American Advertising, 1941–1945*. Provo, UT: Brigham Young University Press.

Friedan, Betty. 1963. *The Feminine Mystique*. Repr., NY: Dell Publishing, 1984.

Gaines, Jane. 1985. "War, Women and Lipstick: Fan Mags in the Forties." *Heresies* 18: 42–45.

Gamson, William A., David Croteau, William Hoynes, and Theodore Sasson. 1992. "Media Images and the Social Construction of Reality." *Annual Review of Sociology* 18:373–93.

Garner, David M., Paul E. Garfinkel, Donald Schwartz, and Michael Thompson. 1980. "Cultural Expectations of Thinness in Women." *Psychological Reports* 47:483–91.

Gerbner, George. 1998. "Cultivation Analysis: An Overview." *Mass Communication & Society* 1:175–94.

Gilligan, Carol. 1982. *In a Different Voice: Psychological Theory and Women's Development*. Repr., Cambridge, MA: Harvard University Press, 1993.

Gist, Marilyn E. 1993. "Through the Looking Glass: Diversity and Reflected Appraisals of the Self in Mass Media." In *Women in Mass Communication*, 2nd ed., ed. Pamela Creedon, 104–17. Newbury Park, CA: Sage Publications.

Glassner, Barry. 1992. *Bodies: Overcoming the Tyranny of Perfection*. Los Angeles: Lowell House.

Glueck, Grace. 2002. "Walter Annenberg, 94, Dies; Philanthropist and Publisher." *New York Times*, October 2, A1.

Goffman, Erving. 1979. *Gender Advertisements*. New York: Harper & Row.

Gordon, Lois, and Alan Gordon. 1987. *American Chronicle: Six Decades in American Life, 1920–1980*. New York: Atheneum.

Grantstein, Lisa. 2003. "Old-School Sophisticate." *Mediaweek*, October 20, 45–46.

Grimm, Matthew. 2001. "Content No Longer King." *American Demographics*, August, 58–59.

Gross, Michael. 1995. *Model*. New York: William Morrow & Co.

Hall, Stuart. 1981. "Notes on Deconstructing 'the Popular.'" In *People's History and Socialist Theory*, ed. R. Samuel, 227–40. London: Routledge.

Hamermesh, Daniel S., and Jeff E. Biddle. 1994. "Beauty and the Labor Market." *American Economic Review* 84:1174–94.

Hesse-Biber, Sharlene. 1989. "Eating Patterns and Disorders in a College Population: Are College Women's Eating Problems a New Phenomenon?" *Sex Roles* 20:71–89.

———. 1996. *Am I Thin Enough Yet? The Cult of Thinness and the Commercialization of Identity.* New York: Oxford University Press.

Honey, Maureen. 1984. *Creating Rosie the Riveter: Class, Gender and Propaganda during World War II.* Amherst: University of Massachusetts Press.

hooks, bell. 1996. *Reel to Real: Race, Sex and Class at the Movies.* New York: Routledge.

Horkheimer, Max, and Theodor Adorno. 1944. "The Culture Industry: Enlightenment as Mass Deception." In *Dialectic of Enlightenment.* Repr., New York: Continuum Publishing, 1975.

Isaacs, Susan. 1999. *Brave Dames and Wimpettes: What Women Are Really Doing on Page and Screen.* New York: Ballantine Publishing.

Ives, Nat. 2007a. "Where Have All of the Girls Gone?" *Advertising Age,* July 16, 35–37.

———. 2007b. "Magazines Teen Sites No Match for MySpace." *Advertising Age,* August 22, 8.

Jackson, Linda. 1992. *Physical Appearance and Gender: Sociobiological and Sociocultural Perspectives.* Albany: State University of New York Press.

Jameson, Fredric. 1979. "Reification and Utopia in Mass Culture." *Social Text* 1:130–48.

Jhally, Sut. 1995. "Image-Based Culture: Advertising and Popular Culture." In *Gender, Race, and Class in Media,* ed. Gail Dines and Jean Humez, 77–87. Thousand Oaks, CA: Sage Publications.

Joliffe, Lee, and Catlett, Terri. 1994. "Women Editors at the 'Seven Sisters' Magazines, 1965–1985: Did They Make a Difference?" *Journalism Quarterly* 71:800–8.

Johnson, Sammye. 1993. "Magazines: Women's Employment and Status in the Magazine Industry." In *Women in Mass Communication,* 2nd ed., ed. Pamela Creedon, 134–53. Newbury Park, CA: Sage Publications.

Johnson, Sammye, and Patricia Prijatel. 1999. *The Magazine from Cover to Cover: Inside a Dynamic Industry.* New York: NTC Publishing Group.

Kaledian, Eugenia. 2000. *Daily Life in the United States, 1940–1959: Shifting Worlds.* Westport, CT: Greenwood Press.

Kelly, Keith. 2006. "Seventeen Editor Quits to Start Her Own Projects." *New York Post,* November 7, 33.

Kellner, Douglas. 1995a. *Media Culture.* London and New York: Routledge.

———. 1995b. "Cultural Studies, Multiculturalism, and Media Culture." In *Gender, Race, and Class in Media,* ed. Gail Dines and Jean Humez, 5–17. Thousand Oaks, CA: Sage Publications.

Keresey, Gayle. 1984. "*Young Miss.*" In *Children's Periodicals of the United States,* ed. R. Gordan Kelly, 486–92. Westport, CT: Greenwood Press.

Kett, Joseph. 1977. *Rites of Passage: Adolescence in America, 1790 to the Present.* New York: Basic Books.

Kilbourne, Jean. 1995. "Beauty and the Beast of Advertising." In *Gender, Race, and Class in Media,* ed. Gail Dines and Jean Humez, pp. 121–25. Thousand Oaks, CA: Sage.

———. 1999. *Can't Buy My Love: How Advertising Changes the Way We Think and Feel.* New York: Touchstone.

Kramarae, Cheris. 1981. *Women and Men Speaking: Frameworks for Analysis.* Rowley, MA: Newbury House.

Lafky, Sue A. 1993. "The Progress of Women and People of Color in the U.S. Journalistic Workforce: A Long, Slow Journey." In *Women and Mass Communication,* ed. Pamela Creedon, 87–103. Newbury Park, CA: Sage Publications.

Laqueur, Thomas. 1990. *Making Sex: Body and Gender from the Greeks to Freud.* Cambridge, MA: Harvard University Press.

Leman, Joy. 1980. "'The Advice of a Real Friend': Codes of Intimacy and Oppression in Women's Magazines, 1937–1955." *Women's Studies International Quarterly* 3:63–78.

Life. 1945. "Teen-Age Magazine." October 29, 77–80.

Magazine Publishers of America. 2007. "Top 100 Audit Bureau Circulation Magazines," http://www.magazine.org/circulation/circulation_trends_and_magazine_handbook/22175.cfm (accessed on July 27, 2007).

———. 2009. "Teen Market Research," www.magazine.org/marketprofiles (accessed September 7, 2009).

Magazine War Guide. 1944–1945. Washington, DC: Office of War Information.

Malkin, Amy, Kimberlie Wornian, and Joan Chrisler. 1999. "Women and Weight: Gendered Messages on Magazine Covers." *Sex Roles* 40:647–55.

Mallalieu, Lynnea, and Kay Palan. 2006. "How Good a Shopper Am I?" *Academy of Marketing Sciences Review,* http://www.amsreview.org/articles/mallalieu05-2006.pdf (accessed September 1, 2009).

Mann, Jim. 1989. "Creating and Maintaining a Magazine's Tone of Voice." *Media Management Monograph* 17:1–16.

Mathieu, Aron M., and Ruth A. Jones, eds. 1943/44. *The Writer's Market.* New York: Writers Digest Magazine.

Marx, Karl. 1906. *Capital: A Critique of Political Economy.* New York: The Modern Library.

Marzolf, Marion. 1978. "American Studies—Ideas for Media Historians." *Journalism History* 5:13–16.

Massoni, Kelley. 2004. "Modeling Work: Occupational Messages in *Seventeen* Magazine." *Gender & Society* 19:47–65.

———. 2006. "'Teena Goes to Market': *Seventeen* Magazine and the Early Construction of the Teen Girl (as) Consumer." *Journal of American Culture* 29:31–42.

Mazur, Allan. 1986. "U.S. Trends in Feminine Beauty and Overadaption." *Journal of Sex Research* 22:281–303.

McCracken, Ellen. 1993. *Decoding Women's Magazines.* New York: St. Martin's Press.

Milkie, Melissa. 2002. "Contested Images of Femininity. An Analysis of Cultural Gatekeepers' Struggles with the 'Real Girl' Critique." *Gender & Society* 16:839–59.

Miller, Cristanne. 1987. "Who Talks Like a Woman's Magazine? Language and Gender in Popular Women's and Men's Magazines." *Journal of American Culture* 10:1–9.

Morgan, Kathryn Pauly. 1998. "Women and the Knife: Cosmetic Surgery and the Colonization of Women's Bodies." In *The Politics of Women's Bodies: Sexuality, Appearance, and Behavior*, ed. Rose Weitz, 147–66. New York: Oxford University Press.

Mulvey, Laura. 1975. "Visual Pleasure and Narrative Cinema." *Screen* 16: 6–18.

Newsweek. 1949a. "Bobby-Sock Forum." November 30, 89–90.

———. 1949b. "*Seventeen* Is Five." August 29, 47.

New York Times. 1942. "'Tricks' Bring Crowd to Buy War Stamps," October 18, 5.

———. 1944a. "Advertising News and Notes," May 15, 30.

———. 1944b. "Grooming and Beauty Guidance Found Need of Teen-Age Girls, But it Must Be Practical," November 22, 16.

———. 1945a. "Idea for Teen-Agers," April 21, 16.

———. 1945b. "600 Teen-Age Girls See Sewing Exhibition," April 22, 36.

———. 1949a. "Perfume a Man Trap? How Quaint! It's a Utility, Say Beauty Editors," February 18, 20.

———. 1949b. "Personnel." April 28, 47.

Nietzsche, Friedrich. 1968. *The Will to Power.* New York: Vintage.

Ogden, Christopher. 1999. *Legacy: A Biography of Moses and Walter Annenberg.* Boston: Little, Brown and Company.

Orenstein, Peggy. 1994. *School Girls: Young Women, Self-Esteem, and the Confidence Gap.* New York: Anchor Books.

Owen, Patricia, and Erika Laurel-Seller. 2000. "Weight and Shape Ideals: Thin Is Dangerously in." *Journal of Applied Social Psychology* 30:979–90.

Palladino, Grace. 1996. *Teenagers: An American History.* New York: Basic Books.

Peck, Diana. 1995. "*Mademoiselle.*" In *Women's Periodicals in the United States*, ed. Kathleen L. Endres and Therese L. Lueck, 197–204. Westport, CT: Greenwood Press.

Peirce, Kate. 1990. "A Feminist Theoretical Perspective on the Socialization of Teenage Girls through *Seventeen* Magazine." *Sex Roles* 23:491–500.

———. 1993. "Socialization of Teenage Girls through Teen-Magazine Fiction: The Making of a New Woman or an Old Lady?" *Sex Roles* 29:59–68.

———. 1995a. "*YM.*" In *Women's Periodicals in the United States*, ed. Kathleen L. Endres and Therese L. Lueck, 485–90. Westport, CT: Greenwood Press.

———. 1995b. "*Seventeen.*" In *Women's Periodicals in the United States*, ed. Kathleen L. Endres and Therese L. Lueck, 330–34. Westport, CT: Greenwood Press.

———. 1997. "Women's Magazine Fiction: A Content Analysis of the Roles, Attributes, and Occupations of Main Characters." *Sex Roles* 37:581–93.

Peterson, Theodore. 1964. *Magazines in the Twentieth Century.* Urbana: University of Illinois Press.

Pipher, Mary. 1994. *Reviving Ophelia: Saving the Selves of Adolescent Girls.* New York: Putnam.

Portelli, Alessandro. 1981. "The Peculiarities of Oral History." *History Workshop* 12:96–107.

Purdam, Todd. 2000. "Behind the Wheel and Driving the Nation's Culture." *New York Times,* September 17, WK1.

Raver, Anne. 1992. "And Mrs. Haupt, Seeing the Garden, Pronounced It Good." *New York Times,* April 12, 71.

Reichley, A. J. 1970. "Moe's Boy Walter at the Court of St. James." *Fortune,* June, 88–93.

Reskin, Barbara, and Irene Padavic. 1994. *Women and Men at Work.* Thousand Oaks, CA: Pine Forge Press.

Reuters. 2009. "*Seventeen* Magazine and Bank of America Partner," http://www.reuters.com/article/pressRelease/idUS174535+06-Aug-2009+PRN20090806 (accessed September 6, 2009).

Reynolds, Quentin. 1955. *The Fiction Factor.* New York: Random House.

Ritzer, George, Douglas Goodman, and Wendy Wiedenhoft. 2001. "Theories of Consumption." In *Handbook of Social Theory,* ed. George Ritzer and Barry Smart. London: Sage Publications.

Roberts, Johnnie, and Aisha Eady. 2007. "Ah, To Be Sweet Seventeen." *Newsweek,* August 27, 80.

Rohrlich, Marianne. 2003. "Now, Teenage Décor." *New York Times,* March 20, F5.

Rothblum, Esther D. 1994. "'I'll Die for the Revolution, But Don't Ask Me Not to Diet': Feminism and the Continuing Stigmatization of Obesity." In *Feminist Perspectives on Eating Disorders,* ed. Patricia Fallon, Melanie Katzman, and Susan Wooley. New York: Guilford Press.

Ruggiero, Josephine A., and Louise C. Weston. 1985. "Work Options for Women in Women's Magazines: The Medium and the Message." *Sex Roles* 12:535–48.

Saltz, Ina. 2004. "Blast from the Past." *Folio,* February, 42–43.

Scanlon, Jennifer. 1995. *Inarticulate Longings: The* Ladies' Home Journal, *Gender and the Promises of Consumer Culture.* New York: Routledge.

Scavullo, Francesco. 1984. *Scavullo: Francesco Scavullo, Photographs 1948–1984.* New York: Harper & Row.

Schor, Juliet. 1998. *The Overspent American.* New York: HarperPerennial.

Schrum, Kelly. 2004. *Some Wore Bobby Socks: The Emergence of Teenage Girls' Culture, 1920–1945.* New York: Palgrave MacMillan.

Scotford, Martha. 1999. *Cipe Pineles: A Life of Design.* New York: W. W. Norton and Co.

Seebohm, Caroline. 1982. *The Man Who Was* Vogue: *The Life and Times of Condé Nast.* New York: The Viking Press.

Seid, Roberta A. 1989. *Never Too Thin: Why Women Are at War with Their Bodies.* New York: Prentice Hall Press.

———. 1994. "Too 'Close to the Bone': The Historical Context for Women's Obsession with Slenderness." In *Feminist Perspectives on Eating Disorders*, ed. Patricia Fallon, Melanie Katzman, and Susan Wooley, 3–16. New York: Guilford Press.

Shafer, Jack. 2002. "Citizen Annenberg: So Long You Rotten Bastard." *Slate*, October 2, http://www.slate.com/id/2071870 (accessed August 15, 2009).

———. 2006. "Annenberg's Ticket Out of Hell." *Slate*, May 22, http://www.slate.com/id/2142154 (accessed August 15, 2009)

Shahar, Shulamith. 1994. "The Old Body in Medieval Culture." In *Framing Medieval Bodies*, ed. Sarah Kay and Miri Rubin, 160–64. Manchester, UK: Manchester University Press.

Sheppard, Eugenia. 1967. "Inside Fashion," *Women's Wear Daily*, September 18.

Sherman, Lauren. 2008. "Teen Retailers' Back-to-School Blues." *Forbes*, July 14, http://www.forbes.com/2008/07/14/retailers-teen-slump-forbeslife-cx_ls_0714style.html (accessed August 31, 2009).

Sickles, Robert. 2004. *The 1940's*. Westport, CT: Greenwood Press.

Signorielli, Nancy. 1997. "A Content Analysis: Reflections of Girls in the Media." *Kaiser Family Report*. Menlo Park, CA: Kaiser Family Foundation.

Silverstein, Brett, Lauren Perdue, Barbara Peterson, and Eileen Kelly. 1986. "The Role of the Mass Media in Promoting a Thin Standard of Bodily Attractiveness for Women." *Sex Roles* 14:519–32.

Silverstein, Brett, Barbara Peterson, and Lauren Perdue. 1986. "Some Correlates of the Thin Standard of Bodily Attractiveness for Women." *International Journal of Eating Disorders* 5:895–905.

Slatalla, Michelle. 2003. "Outfitting the Teenager's Dominion." *New York Times*, October 9, G4.

Smith, Dorothy. 1987. *The Everyday World as Problematic*. Boston: Northeastern University Press.

———. 1990. *Texts, Facts, and Femininity: Exploring the Relations of Ruling*. London: Routledge.

Steeves, H. Leslie. 1993. "Gender and Mass Communication in a Global Context." In *Women in Mass Communication*, 2nd ed., ed. Pamela Creedon, 32–60. Newbury Park: Sage Publications.

Steinem, Gloria. 1995. "Sex, Lies, and Advertising." In *Gender, Race, and Class in Media*, ed. Gail Dines and Jean Humez, 112–20. Thousand Oaks, CA: Sage Publications.

Striegel-Moore, Ruth H., Lisa R. Silberstein, and Judith Rodin. 1986. "Toward an Understanding of Risk Factors for Bulimia." *American Psychologist* 41:246–63.

Tiggemann, Marika, and Sarah Kenyon. 1998. "The Hairlessness Norm: The Removal of Bodily Hair in Women." *Sex Roles* 39:873–90.

Time. 1949. "50 Girls and One Man," May 16, 56–57.

———. 1950. "The Women," March 6, 56–57.

Tuchman, Gaye. 1978. "The Symbolic Annihilation of Women." In *Hearth and Home:*

Images of Women in the Mass Media, ed. Gaye Tuchman, Arlene Daniels, and James Benet, 3–38. New York: Oxford University Press.

Valentine, Helen. 1938. *Mary and Marie*. New York: Grosset and Dunlap.

Valentine, Helen, and Alice Thompson. 1938. *Better than Beauty: A Guide to Charm*. Repr., San Francisco, CA: Chronicle Books, 2002.

Walker, Nancy A. 2000. *Shaping Our Mothers' World: American Women's Magazines*. Jackson: University Press of Mississippi.

War Jobs for Women. 1942. Washington, DC: Office of War Information, Magazine Section.

Warren, Carol A. B. 1998. "Aging and Identity in Premodern Times." *Research on Aging* 20:11–35.

Who's Who of American Women. 1958–1959. "Alice Dickey Thompson." Willamette, IL: Marquis Who's Who.

Willemsen, Tineke M. 1998. "Widening the Gender Gap: Teenage Magazines for Girls and Boys." *Sex Roles* 38:851–62.

Wolf, Naomi. 1991. *The Beauty Myth: How Images of Beauty Are Used Against Women*. New York: Anchor Books.

Zuckerman, Mary Ellen. 1998. *A History of Popular Women's Magazines in the United States: 1792–1995*. Westport, CT: Greenwood Press.

Zukin, Sharon. 2004. *Point of Purchase: How Shopping Changed American Culture*. New York: Routledge.

Zukin, Sharon, and Jennifer Maguire. 2004. "Consumers and Consumption." *Annual Review of Sociology* 30:173–94.

II. Interviews, Oral Histories, Personal Correspondence, and Archival Sources

Annenberg, Walter. Personal correspondence to Helen Valentine, October 2, 1944. Original in the possession of Valentine Hertz Kass.

———. Personal correspondence to Helen Valentine, October 18, 1946. Original in the possession of Valentine Hertz Kass.

———. Personal correspondence to Helen Valentine, September 1967. Original in the possession of Valentine Hertz Kass.

Benson & Benson, Inc. 1945. *Life with Teena: A* Seventeen *Magazine Survey*. Princeton, NJ: Triangle Publications, Inc. Estelle Ellis Collection, Archives Center, National Museum of American History, Behring Center, Smithsonian Institution, Box 18, Files 1–2.

Cosmetics and Toiletries. "Why Snub 8 Million Customers?" August, 1949. Estelle Ellis Collection, Archives Center, National Museum of American History, Behring Center, Smithsonian Institution, Box 18, File 6.

Eiseman, Alberta. Telephone interview. March 27, 2006.

Ellis, Estelle. Oral History. September 10, 1990. American Jewish Committee Archives.

Ellis, Estelle. Personal email communication, July 11, 2006.

Ellis, Estelle. Personal interview in New York City, June 19, 2003.

Ellis, Estelle. Telephone interviews, June 26, 2003; July 13, 2004; July 6, 2004. Ellis (Estelle) Collection, Archives Center, National Museum of American History, Behring Center, Smithsonian Institution, Series 1 (Includes Box 17, File 11; Box 18, Files 1–4; Box 25, File 6; Box 26, File 1; Box 32, File 8; Box 38, File 5).

Ellis (Estelle) Personal Collection. "Who is Teena?" n.d.

Hertz, Barbara Valentine. Telephone interviews, February 18, 2006; February 27, 2006.

Opinion Research Corp. 1947. *Life with Teena: Volume II B food.* Princeton, NJ: Triangle Publications, Inc. Estelle Ellis Collection, Archives Center, National Museum of American History, Behring Center, Smithsonian Institution.

Rosen, Walter. Personal correspondence to Louis Banks, managing editor of *Fortune* Magazine, June 19, 1970. Original in the possession of Valentine Hertz Kass.

Sladkus, Ingrid Loewenstein. Telephone interview, April 20, 2006.

Tide, "*Seventeen*: A Unique Case Study," April 15, 1945. Estelle Ellis Collection, Archives Center, National Museum of American History, Behring Center, Smithsonian Institution, Box 18, File 5.

Valentine, Helen. Oral History. March 9, 1982. American Jewish Committee Archives.

Valentine, Helen. Personal correspondence to Walter Annenberg, October 16, 1946. Original copy in the possession of Valentine Hertz Kass.

Valentine, Helen. Personal correspondence to Walter Annenberg, February 15, 1950. Original copy in the possession of Valentine Hertz Kass.

Valentine, Helen. "What Are We Doing to Our Teenagers?" n.d. (unpublished essay).

White, Nancy. Personal correspondence to Helen Valentine, September 22, 1967. Original in the possession of Valentine Hertz Kass.

INDEX

Note: **Bold** page numbers refer to a figure or a table.

ABOUT THE AUTHOR

Kelley Massoni is a lecturer in sociology at the University of Kansas, where she teaches her students to become more critical media consumers. Her research on *Seventeen* magazine has been published in the *Journal of American Culture* and *Gender & Society*. She remembers very clearly the first time she opened a *Seventeen* magazine and beheld the "ideal" world within, including the flawless images of the teen girl models. In the pictures below, the author and her daughter Vanessa examine a *Seventeen* magazine in 1983.

Vincennes University Library